P9-DFI-479

Project Management for Healthcare

ESI International Project Management Series

Series Editor
J. LeRoy Ward, Executive Vice President
ESI International
Arlington, Virginia

Project Management for Heathcare
David Shirley
978-1-4398-1953-1

Managing Web Projects
Edward B. Farkas
978-1-4398-0495-7

Project Management Recipes for Success
Guy L. De Furia
978-1-4200-7824-4

Building a Project Work Breakdown Structure: Visualizing Objectives, Deliverables, Activities, and Schedules
Dennis P. Miller
978-1-4200-6969-3

A Standard for Enterprise Project Management
Michael S. Zambruski
978-1-4200-7245-7

Determining Project Requirements
Hans Jonasson
978-1-4200-4502-4

The Complete Project Management Office Handbook, Second Edition
Gerard M. Hill
978-1-4200-4680-9

Practical Guide to Project Planning
Ricardo Viana Vargas
978-1-4200-4504-8

Other ESI International Titles Available from Auerbach Publications, Taylor & Francis Group

PMP® Challenge! Fourth Edition
J. LeRoy Ward and Ginger Levin
ISBN: 978-1-8903-6740-4

PMP® Exam: Practice Test and Study Guide, Seventh Edition
J. LeRoy Ward
ISBN: 978-1-8903-6741-1

The Project Management Drill Book: A Self-Study Guide
Carl L. Pritchard
ISBN: 978-1-8903-6734-3

Project Management Terms: A Working Glossary, Second Edition
J. LeRoy Ward
ISBN: 978-1-8903-6725-1

Project Management Tools CD, Version 4.3
ESI International
ISBN: 978-1-8903-6736-7

Project Management for Healthcare

David Shirley

CRC Press is an imprint of the
Taylor & Francis Group, an **informa** business

CRC Press
Taylor & Francis Group
6000 Broken Sound Parkway NW, Suite 300
Boca Raton, FL 33487-2742

International Standard Book Number: 978-1-4398-1953-1 (Hardback)

Visit the Taylor & Francis Web site at
http://www.taylorandfrancis.com

and the CRC Press Web site at
http://www.crcpress.com

Contents

SECTION IV

SECTION V

SECTION VI

Preface

I was a healthcare professional. My first "real" job after graduating from college was as a licensed health inspector, then as a licensed health officer, and finally as a health administrator for a small town with a population of about 15,000 people. It was there that I became an accidental or incidental project manager. Until recently, project management was an "accidental profession." Few started out as project managers. They were usually something else and either were handed a project to undertake, or suggested an enhancement to an existing process, procedure, or product, and were told to "run with it." Either way, their primary job was doing something else.

As the health administrator, I was responsible for the animal control program in my town. Because I had a full-time animal control warden and an animal control van, the town suggested I offer those services to other local municipalities to generate income to be able to expand my program. Two of the abutting towns agreed and signed a contract with our Board of Health. Part of that agreement was to pick up stray dogs and cats. It immediately became clear that we needed a place to house the animals.

I drew on the variety of expertise of our board members, some who were in the building trades, to sketch out a design and a budget. It was then up to me to get the animal shelter built. It was also up to me to learn how to manage a project. That was 1970, and with a lot of pain and sleepless nights, I was able to manage the construction of the animal control shelter, on budget, on time, and within the quality specifications (or scope) that were required.

But that was not the only project I undertook while I was a health administrator. There were "Well Baby" clinics with doctors and nurses and indigent patients to coordinate, flu shot clinics to organize, and staff to manage. There was a food-borne illness outbreak to manage and an investigation to organize.

As I later became aware of the discipline called *Project Management* and the variety of tools and techniques available to me, I realized how much less anxiety I would have had to endure with my previous projects. There certainly is no guaranteed methodology to make every project a success. But there are tools and techniques to give project managers a much better chance for project success. Acceptance of the project management discipline has led to the acceptance of project management as a career, as a profession, and as a title. More and more organizations are hiring project management professionals, those trained and experienced in the discipline of project management.

The healthcare industry is no different. The same needs drive that industry—competition, budgets, schedules, and quality—as drive high tech or any other industry. More and more healthcare organizations are hiring project managers to manage the many projects they will undertake. Each industry, however, has its unique challenges and healthcare, again, is no different. One of the differences is that the human element looms much larger in the healthcare industry than in any other industry. Patient care is a major driver, and it has to be balanced with income received by the facility. Whether it is a profit-making entity or a non-profit-making entity, there is still a need to make money to continue to provide services. However, even with a for-profit healthcare facility, the welfare of the patient is still at the forefront and has to be properly managed within the framework of project management.

Affordable healthcare is an oxymoron. It is a matter of where you spend your money, because complete healthcare is nearly impossible to achieve without spending an inordinate amount of money. In some cases, food and housing take precedence over healthcare, out of necessity. Emergency rooms are being used more and more as primary care facilities for the under- or uninsured. It is a vicious cycle. The more uninsured there are, the more the insured have to pay to cover the extra cost of care for those who do not have it. The only way to improve the healthcare industry is to make it more efficient. One of the ways to make it more efficient is to closely manage and balance the competing demands of the time, cost, quality, risk, and human element of the projects that the industry undertakes. The best way to do that is to utilize the project management tools customized to the healthcare industry.

Like everything else, the healthcare industry is going high tech. That is the good news. The bad news is that now healthcare personnel will have to manage high tech projects, projects that will take project management tools tailored to help the healthcare professional easily plan, execute, and control their projects.

In the winter of 2004 I was watching one of the cable news shows. The interviewer was speaking with Dr. Robert Wachter who had just co-authored, with Dr. Kaveh Shojania, a book called *Internal Bleeding, The Truth Behind America's Terrifying Epidemic of Medical Mistakes* (Rugged Land, New York, February 2004, ISBN 159071016-9). I immediately ordered the book because I had a strong feeling that, while the book was in fact a close look at medical errors, it was also a book that defined future projects for the medical community. I was correct. The book did detail many medical errors, and in order to insure that the majority of those mistakes were not repeated, projects, whether new processes or procedures or updating equipment, needed to be undertaken. Those projects, in some way or another, affect the health and welfare of individuals, something that is unique to this industry.

NORTHWOODS COMMUNITY MEDICAL CENTER—A CASE STUDY

Note: Although inspired in part by true incidents, the following case study is fictional and does not depict any actual person, medical facility, or event.

For the purpose of this book I will use a fictitious medical facility to illustrate certain tools and techniques for managing a healthcare-based project. In order to put it in context, following is a brief description of the facility.

The Northwoods Community Medical Center (NCMC) is a 100-bed primary care facility located about 30 miles from a major city, where there are several medical facilities. However, to the west and northwest, it is the only facility within 150 miles. The areas to the northwest, southwest, and west are rural areas. To the southwest, it is the only facility within 75 miles. While NCMC has to compete for patients with the facilities in the metropolitan area, it primarily caters to the more rural population. While small, the hospital has expansion plans and hopes one day to become a complete tertiary care facility. At the present time NCMC provides most of the tertiary care, albeit on a limited, case-by-case basis.

The following are the key players of the medical center:

Chairman of the Board – William Worthy
CEO – Michelle Michaels
CFO – Elaine Dumont
Medical Director – Dr. Harold Chimers
Director of Security – Seth Baker
Director of IT – Maryann Lords
Director of Housekeeping – Daniel North

Let us take a closer look at the fictitious hospital Northwoods Community Medical Center (NCMC). NCMC offers a variety of services including surgical, obstetrics, mental health, educational, and emergency services. NCMC is a non-profit, acute care facility. The mission of NCMC is "to provide quality healthcare and healthcare education to the community."

Following are some of the projects that may be undertaken by Northern Medical Center. In order to attract more patients from the surrounding communities, the hospital administrators may undertake a lobby beautification project. The hospital is located in a city with a large population of foreign immigrants. The hospital may decide to design an outreach program specifically targeting that foreign population. NCMC may want to implement electronic medical records, or upgrade their computer facilities, or help prevent staff sharp injuries, or decide to have a helipad constructed, or implement a barcode system to protect patients against drug interactions, or hundreds of other projects. Additionally, there are regulatory and certification bodies that constantly affect the operation of NCMC. Sometimes, whether or not government funding flows to the institution depends on how quickly and efficiently new regulations (projects) are implemented. Another driving force behind effective and efficient project implementation is the Joint Commission on Accreditation of Healthcare (JCAHO). The commission is *the* accreditation body for healthcare facilities. JCAHO's mission is "to continuously improve the safety and quality of care provided to the public through the provision of healthcare accreditation and related services that support performance improvement in healthcare organizations" (www.jointcommission.org). In that effort there are continuous projects that need to be implemented in order to obtain and keep the certification status. The certification status is extremely important to NCMC because the certification is recognized nationwide as an indicator of high quality of service. As you can see, all of these are "projects" and can be aided by trained and disciplined project managers.

THE BOOK

This book will explore the discipline of project management from the perspective of the healthcare environment. The book is divided into six parts: defining a project, detailing a project, management skills required, and additional information. Together, we will dissect the project process and look at the management skills required to successfully manage a project, and some additional information to help the healthcare project manager understand related industries and program management. Defining a project will include the tools and techniques required to successfully plan a project, from identifying stakeholders and developing and gaining consensus on good requirements, to constructing a project plan. Detailing a project will include utilizing the project plan and executing on the budget, schedule, and quality objectives. It will also include managing project changes, milestones, and metrics. The final project phase, closure, will also include looking beyond the project's final deliverable and onto life cycle management. Section III, Management Skills, will review in detail the skills required to successfully manage the people and process of a project. At times, healthcare personnel may have to work with program management, or may even be part of program management and have to interact with pharmaceutical companies and medical device manufacturers. While not an in-depth look, this book will cover program management and how it relates to the healthcare industry and some of the project processes used by those companies involved in pharmaceuticals and manufacturers of medical devices. By giving the healthcare professional an inside look at the processes used, I hope to give an understanding of how those companies bring their products to market, and how healthcare professionals may adapt those processes for their own benefit.

It is inevitable that Information Technology (IT) will be part of the future of healthcare. The need to gain efficiencies through the use of IT will be important to the affordability of healthcare. While it is unlikely that the healthcare professional will be involved with the development of the software needed to drive the technological advances, there may be some customization needed to fully utilize the software in a particular healthcare environment. There have been volumes written on IT project management, so this book will not cover project management for the IT professional. However, it should be noted that the fundamental project management skills, defining and detailing a project, as well as the management skills required to successfully manage a project can be applied to IT professionals.

Managing healthcare projects using the discipline of project management is a skill that will help the healthcare professional better utilize limited resources, both human and monetary, and insure the highest possible quality of care to meet or exceed their stakeholders' expectations.

THE ENVIRONMENT OF HEALTHCARE

Each environment within the healthcare industry provides its own set of challenges and opportunities for the project manager. To further understand those opportunities and challenges, the following terms should have a common understanding: long-term care facilities, acute care facilities, medical practices, inpatient facilities, outpatient facilities, and the all-important tertiary care facility.

Long-Term Care Facilities

A long-term care facility is a facility that provides care for extended periods of time. It could be a nursing home or rest home (sometimes called skilled nursing facilities), assisted living facility, or convalescent home. The intent of these facilities is to provide care to individuals on a 24/7 basis, having nursing services available and on-call doctors, in case of situations when skilled nurses require the services of a doctor. It may also be called a chronic or hospice care facility. In some cases, long-term care facilities may accept patients with the intent of rehabilitating and then releasing them. The difference between that and an inpatient facility is primarily a matter of length of stay. It also differs from independent living facilities in the level of skilled nursing care. In an independent living facility, there may be a doctor or nurse on staff, but their purpose, for the most part, is to provide emergency care, not routine care, as in the long-term care facility.

Acute Care Facilities

An acute care facility is a facility that accepts patients on the basis of a relatively short stay. It could be a clinic, both for walk-in and emergency, or a facility that does surgery, diagnosis, or treatment. It may also be part of a larger, more comprehensive facility. While it is sometimes associated with the hospital emergency room, it is not intended to be that. Because of the lack of acute care facilities and the confusion around healthcare, people are turning more and more to hospital emergency rooms for their acute care, causing extreme overcrowding of ERs in some areas of the country, and unnecessary expense, as emergency treatment is very costly.

Medical Practices

A medical practice can be described as a facility that is usually run by a licensed physician who is primarily responsible for diagnosis, prescribing, and treatment. It may be a general practice (GP), sometimes known as primary care physician (PCP), or a specialty practice like orthopedics, internal medicine, or ophthalmology. The physician is usually associated with a hospital, particularly in the case of specialty practices. GPs may not be associated with any hospital, preferring to refer patients to specialty practices.

Inpatient Care Facility

An inpatient care facility can be another name for a hospital because inpatient care implies that the patient's condition requires admittance to a medical facility for treatment. The patient's condition for admittance also implies that there is a critical illness or severe trauma. Otherwise, the patient would be cared for on an outpatient basis.

Outpatient Care Facility

An outpatient facility is a facility dedicated to the treatment of individuals on a walk-in/walk-out basis. They may include public health clinics, places where general medical practitioners, occupational and physical therapists, chiropractors, dentists, and many other specialties treat patients. Some clinics may perform the duties of primary care. A clinic may also be associated with a large hospital facility and could be used to screen patients, similar to an emergency room. There are also very specialized clinics such as fertility and abortion clinics. Clinics may or may not have diagnostic equipment, such as x-ray machines.

SUMMARY

As you can see by these definitions, each one of the different types of medical facilities will have a set of project management processes and requirements. In most cases, there will be overlap of those processes and requirements. A good example would be the equipment requirements of a long-term care facility and a clinic that provide x-ray services. Both will need x-ray equipment. However, perhaps the criticality of the equipment needs may be different; therefore, the acute care facilities' equipment may have a higher quality requirement. That type of requirement must be included in the project manager's documentation.

Acknowledgments

This book is based on my nine years of teaching a graduate course in project management to healthcare professionals. I want to thank all of the students who provided welcome input that, combined with the course material, resulted in *Project Management for Healthcare.* I also want to acknowledge all of the people at Taylor & Francis–CRC Press, especially John Wyzalek, Senior Acquisitions Editor, Auerbach–CRC Press–Taylor & Francis; David Fausel, Project Coordinator; and Andrea Demby, Project Editor, who helped make this book possible. To Rich Maltzman, my friend and partner in EarthPM; Elizabeth Harrin (www.pm4girls.co.uk), all-around good person and "web" friend; Anna Heatley (http://www.virilion.com/) for her expertise in social media; and Alex and Sergey Korban, Aotea Studios (www.aoteastudios.com), poster providers extraordinaire, for their significant contributions to strengthen this book.

I would also like to thank my mother, father, and sister, who may be gone from the physical world, but who remain in my heart. You are my inspiration. To my dog Murphy, whose daily demand for a long walk, no matter what the season or weather, gives me some great thinking time as we walk the rocky beaches of Cape Neddick, Maine. And to my wife, Judi—without your unconditional love and support, I wouldn't be who I am.

About the Author

David Shirley has been an instructor and consultant, and has more than 30 years of experience in management and project management in the corporate, public, and small-business arenas.

As a member of the graduate faculty at New England College, Henniker, New Hampshire, he developed and teaches Managing Projects in Healthcare. As part of the Master's of Management (MoM) in Healthcare Administration and the MoM in Project Management and Organizational Leadership, he has taught project management at hospitals and businesses as well as online and on campus for the past seven years. He also developed, directed, and taught a project management certification program at Northern Essex Community College in Haverhill, Massachusetts.

David is a senior instructor and consultant for Action for Results and a senior instructor for ESI International, both leading project management education and training companies. He is also an adjunct professor for Southern New Hampshire University, teaching corporate social responsibility. As a distinguished member of technical staff with AT&T and Lucent Technologies Bell Laboratories, David was responsible for managing the first light-wave transmission products as well as several quality efforts. He was also AT&T's project manager for the first fiber-to-the-home effort in Connecticut, and was the Lucent Technologies program management director, managing several large telecommunications companies' equipment deployment. David has many years of experience in developing, leading, and managing teams.

David's educational background includes a BA degree in geology from Windham College, Putney, Vermont, and an honors MBA degree from Monmouth University in Long Branch, New Jersey. He also holds master's certificates in project management from the Stevens Institute of Technology, Hoboken, New Jersey, and American University in Washington, DC, and is certified as a Project Management Professional (PMP) by the Project Management Institute (PMI).*

* "PMP" is a certification mark of the Project Management Institute, Inc., which is registered in the United States and other nations. "PMI" is a service and trademark of the Project Management Institute, Inc., which is registered in the United States and other nations.

Section I

Definition

1

Defining a Project

WHAT IS A PROJECT?

To get started, one has to ask the basic question: What is a project? The short answer is everything. It can be as simple as a trip to the grocery store, painting a room in your house, or developing a new procedure to reduce sharp injuries in a clinic. It could be as complex as putting a man into earth orbit (the National Aeronautics and Space Administration [NASA] was one of the first organizations to embrace the discipline of project management) or instituting an electronic medical record (EMR) system for a hospital. So let us define the word *project* in project management terms. A project has several aspects:

- It is *something new* to undertake. If it were the same thing happening over and over again, it would be more of an ongoing activity. But even ongoing activities may have project aspects to them. Every 4 years there is a winter Olympics held somewhere in the world. You'd think by now that the assigned project manager would have all of the historical data from previous Olympics and could more or less rubber stamp all of the activities required to successfully complete the project. While it may be the case that the project manager has all of the data, and should have them, each Olympics will have its own set of new tasks to manage. The technology changes so quickly that in 4 years there may be an entirely new method to communicate with the rest of the world. Think about landlines and cables compared to wireless and satellites. Who knows where the future will take us, but the project manager has to be prepared.

- It has a *schedule*. In order to meet the definition of a project, a project has to have a starting point and an ending point. To state the obvious, in order for a project to be a project, it has to start. On the day, the hour, the minute a project begins, the "project clock" starts. As to when the project stops, that is the end point. During the project's definition, someone has a view on when the project should start and how long the project should take to accomplish the goal. We'll talk more about that process later in this chapter. For now, the starting point and ending point are two pieces of the definition.
- Projects *use limited organizational resources*. Let's face it: all project resources can be reduced to money, and organizations do not have unlimited funding. Whether you spend that money on human, infrastructure, equipment, or marketing resources, they will all require money, and that money is finite (limited).

Therefore, a project is something that is new, has a beginning and an end, and uses limited organizational resources. While the first two criteria are important, the "real" need for a project manager is to efficiently and effectively manage the limited organizational resources. That is a project manager's primary added value. By using the project management discipline outlined in this book, healthcare professionals can dramatically increase their efficiency and effectiveness in managing any project.

WHAT IS A PROJECT LIFE CYCLE?

A project life cycle (see Figure 1.1) is series of events a project undergoes from beginning to end. Some of the ways a project life cycle is portrayed are as follows:

1. Initiation, Planning, Execution, Closure
2. Startup, Planning, Execution, Close-Out
3. Identify Needs, Develop a Solution, Execute the Solution, Terminate the Project
4. Initiate, Design, Plan, Organize, Control, Close
5. Plan, Organize, Control
6. Plan, Implement, Control

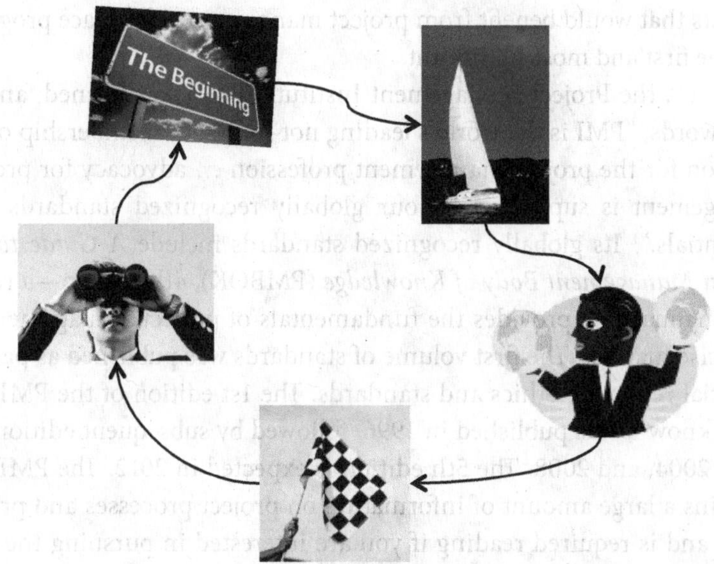

FIGURE 1.1
Project life cycle.

No matter how you define the life cycle of a project, it is the understanding that for a project there is a starting point, time to plan, implementing or executing, closing, and ongoing activities.

THE HISTORY OF PROJECT MANAGEMENT

Prior to embarking on a new subject, it is always good to have a little background or history. Today's project management doesn't have a long history. A primary driver for modern-day project management was the increasingly complex projects undertaken by the U.S. government and a need to somehow better manage and control those projects. I believe that the launch of the Soviets' Sputnik satellite in 1957 and the subsequent formation of NASA in 1958 were the two drivers of the discipline we know as project management. Those two events then led to the "space race," so that when President Kennedy in May of 1961 made the challenge before a joint session of Congress to "send a man to the moon by the end of the century," good project management became a critical skill. While there were other projects that would benefit from project management, the space program was the first and most significant.

In 1969, the Project Management Institute (PMI) was formed, and in their words, “PMI is the world’s leading not-for-profit membership organization for the project management profession ... advocacy for project management is supported by our globally recognized standards and credentials.”[1] Its globally recognized standards include *A Guide to the Project Management Body of Knowledge* (PMBOK), 4th edition—a reference manual that provides the fundamentals of project management in a concise manner. The first volume of standards was published as part of a special report on ethics and standards. The 1st edition of the PMBOK as we know it was published in 1996, followed by subsequent editions in 2000, 2004, and 2008. The 5th edition is expected in 2012. The PMBOK contains a large amount of information on project processes and procedures and is required reading if you are interested in pursuing the certification of the Project Management Institute, the Project Management Professional (PMP).

It wasn’t until the early 1990s that PMI really became a powerhouse behind the profession. In 1990, membership totaled approximately 8,500 members. However, in the 1990s companies like AT&T, where I was working, began to embrace the discipline and began using Project Manager as a legitimate title with a career path. AT&T also encouraged and paid for its project managers to join PMI. Thus began PMI’s growth spurt, and it now has almost 318,000 members in 140 countries.[2] For more information about the Project Management Institute and certification, go to their Web site at www.pmi.org.

ROLES AND RESPONSIBILITIES IN PROJECT MANAGEMENT

There are many roles within project management:

- Project Director – high-level management, may manage a group of project managers
- Project Manager
    - Sets communications
    - Develops processes and procedures

    - Plans and estimates (time/cost)
    - Provides status and tracking
- Project Leader (sub-role to the project manager) – may lead certain aspects of the project, i.e., scheduling, project tracking

PROJECT MANAGEMENT AND THE HEALTHCARE ENVIRONMENT

Project management in the healthcare environment is unique from project management in other industries in several ways. The first reason, and a compelling one, is a difference in the skill set of the practitioners. Rather than a difference of technology or methodology, it is that healthcare professionals already have the people skills required to be good project managers. In contrast, while Information Technologists may have a good grasp of project management and the technical issues of their projects, they may need to hone their "people skills." While I know that there may be disagreement because of some differences in "bedside manner," in general, healthcare professionals are in the "people" business. As with most businesses, healthcare success is based on the results of customer satisfaction surveys. Rather than focusing on how a product works, healthcare professionals focus on how the customer feels and how the experience feels to the customer.

During my last 8 years of teaching, I had my students take a personality test available online. I kept a record of the results—by personality type, not by student. I compiled those results into an informal study of my students' personalities. The results are much different for my students in the healthcare industry as opposed to those on campus or at various business locations. While not surprising to me, and probably not to you, those results tend to support the uniqueness of healthcare workers. Most of the workers fall into the category of guardian. A guardian personality tends to be more protective of those with whom they interact. They are family oriented, and I don't necessarily mean immediate family, but they are adoptive of those around them to form a family. They are serious and concerned—traits that are critical to their jobs. Additionally, guardians are very procedure oriented and follow processes—another great trait for healthcare workers.

There are projects themselves within the healthcare environment that make healthcare unique. While one can argue that other industries have life and death situations, there is no doubt that the healthcare industry has them. Therefore, some, and I'll go out on a limb and say probably most projects initiated in the healthcare environment have some aspect of life and death involved. Some examples that I have seen over the years are as follows:

- A template to gain approval to land and deploy a helicopter at a medical facility

  The team leader for an air ambulance service was "reinventing" an approval process every time there was a request from a medical facility to take advantage of the service. Because the requirements were standard—distance from the buildings, size of the landing area, approach procedures, etc.—it was logical to undertake a project to build a template that only needed to be tweaked for a medical facility's request. Developing the template reduced the approval times, thus potentially saving lives.
- A "safe room" in a psychiatric facility

  A need was determined that there weren't ample facilities to accommodate agitated psychiatric patients. A project was undertaken to design, plan, and implement a safe room, with padded walls and flooring to accommodate a patient who may become agitated in a particular situation and needs a safe place to recover. The padded walls and floors allowed patients to thrash without danger of injuring themselves against an unforgiving floor and walls. While the primary purpose was to insure the safety of the agitated patient, it also protected the staff by allowing them to take the patient somewhere safe, away from the general population and potential weapons like chairs, tables, and lamps.
- A project to reduce sharp injuries in the operating room

  Sharp injuries are better characterized as a prick by a dirty needle. The potential of injury by exposure to human immunodeficiency virus (HIV), hepatitis B virus, or hepatitis C virus are real risks to hospital staff, especially nurses. According to some studies done by the International Healthcare Worker Safety Center, University of Virginia, and their Global Initiative for Healthcare Worker Safety and Occupational Exposure, "Needle sticks and sharp injuries are the most common cause of occupational infections among healthcare workers, responsible for an estimated 1,000 HIV, 66,000 hepatitis B and 16,000 hepatitis C cases annually to health workers around the globe (World Health Organization 2003)."[3] One of the hospitals I worked with wanted to further reduce their sharp injuries. A project was developed to identify the potential areas of most exposure and to reduce that exposure by developing better hypodermic needle handling and disposal.

- A project to develop a new hospital gown
  This project was of particular interest to me because existing hospital gowns can be very uncomfortable and confusing as to which way to put them on. There was an obstetrician/gynecologist (OB/GYN) in one of my classes, and we talked about my confusion with the hospital gowns. His advice was to put it on whichever way you want to because it really doesn't matter to him or other doctors. They would get to where they need to go no matter which way the gown is donned. However, while not being a life and death situation, patient comfort is a concern. Projects will be undertaken for that reason.
- Another non-life-threatening situation, but a justifiable project, is a beautification or gentrification effort. Hospitals and medical facilities are not immune from competition. One way to try to entice patients to a facility is to give the facility more "curb appeal." New, luxurious entrances, fountains in lobbies, piano players in waiting rooms, coffee shops, and gourmet dining are all projects aimed at differentiating one medical facility from another.

These are but a few of the many projects that are initiated every day by medical facilities all over the world. Make no mistake; they are projects, and whether large or small, they need to be properly managed to get as much as possible out of the limited resources available.

ESTABLISHING RELATIONSHIPS IN HEALTHCARE

Projects are all about relationships, between you and your stakeholder, your team, your customers, your management, even your vendors or suppliers. To help properly establish a relationship I have created a set of questions. In the beginning phase of establishing a relationship the following questions should be addressed:

- Why do we need this relationship?
- What is in it for them?
- What is in it for me?
- Did we consider any other partnering options?
- What process did we use to consider the other options?

The second phase of the process occurs just prior to commitment. The following questions can be asked:

- Why did we choose this partner?
- What risks is this partner taking?
- What risks are we taking?
- What is the fundamental goal of this relationship?
- How was this funded?

The third phase is the actual commitment. These questions are similar to those you ask during the beginning phase above:

- Do we have the buy-in from management for this partnering arrangement?
- Was there a management representative?

The fourth phase is the actual project phase, and again these questions should come to mind:

- How were the joint plans developed?
- Is there an escalation process? (See Chapter 8.)
- Was the fundamental goal of the partnership realized?

And finally, some general questions to consider are as follows:

- What worked?
- What didn't work?
- How were decisions made?
- What was the level of trust with the partners throughout the project?
- What, if any, incentives were used?
- Had the partnering teams done a project together before this one?

No matter whom you partner with, and you will partner, answering these few questions can make the relationship healthier (excuse the pun).

DIFFERENCES IN MANAGEMENT

There are four major types of management (see Table 1.1) within an organization: *strategic*, *operations*, *crisis*, and *project management*. It is important to understand the differences between these different types in order to appreciate where the project manager fits and his or her added value.

Strategic Management

What I consider the highest level of management, but not necessarily the most important level, because all levels of management will contribute equally to the success of an organization, is *strategic management*. Strategic managers, or those on the strategic management team, make the high-level decisions that can affect what projects are undertaken and what projects are not. Strategic management is the visionary management of an organization. Strategic thinking must include the vision/mission as an input. And it follows that an organization must have a vision/mission by which to coordinate all the organization's activities. It is incumbent on the project manager to understand that vision/mission and to be able to communicate it to the project team. I equate the lack of a vision/mission as being lost in the woods on a dark night without a flashlight, compass, or GPS. One may eventually find one's way home, but it is highly unlikely that it will be a pleasant experience.

Strategic thinking is the visionary aspect of the organization. It involves managing to the 5-year or 3-year plan, for instance. It provides the long-term direction for the organization. Strategic thinking allows for the dovetailing of the organization's direction, with new projects to support that direction. It is *proactive* by nature. If strategic management becomes reactive, it is called "micromanagement" and this is not a good thing.

Operations Management

Another type of necessary management within an organization is *operations management*. Operations management is the management of the

TABLE 1.1

Major Types of Organizational Management

	Strategic Management	Operations Management	Crisis Management	Project Management
Proactive vs. reactive	Proactive – visionary in nature	Proactive – managing day-to-day operations	Reactive – the very nature of crisis management	Both – proactive in planning, organizing, and controlling the project; reactive when issues occur
Temporary vs. ongoing	Ongoing – the big picture, looking for the next best thing	Ongoing – managing the day-to-day operations	Temporary – hopefully crisis can be quickly handled	Temporary – projects are temporary per definition
Preventative vs. corrective	Preventative – when visionaries become corrective it is called "micromanagement"	Preventative – keeps the "machinery" oiled	Corrective	Both – preventative due to the planning aspect; corrective when dealing with issues—the difference between crisis management and project management is that, for the most part, crisis managers Band-Aid and project managers correct via process change

day-to-day operations of an organization. It may include the management of the organization's physical facilities, for instance, those people involved with making sure that computer access is available and that the lights and heat/air conditioning work. Operations management is also a *proactive* type of management, managing the *ongoing* operations of an organization. It is *preventative* in nature. I'll use the analogy of a lube, oil, and filter change in a car. It is part of a regular maintenance procedure in order to keep the car in good shape.

Crisis Management

This is definitely a reactive type of management. It is *temporary* in nature, at least we hope. Crisis management is there for those unusual circumstances that require an immediate *corrective* action. The corrective action may take the form of a Band-Aid™ to "stop the bleeding." An instance where crisis management may be applied would be in the situation of a major hacking event into an organization's computers. Immediate, decisive action must be taken to insure the security of the computer system. The activity will probably be of the type that does not correct the root cause of the problem, but rather blocks the attempt. It may be that all outside connections are temporarily suspended. It is not the ideal situation, but impedes the immediate threat. A *project* will need to be undertaken to properly address the root cause of the situation. This brings us to the final form of management within an organization: *project management.*

Project Management

This is a management type that spans the ongoing versus temporary and the corrective versus preventative nature of the other management types. Project management is an ongoing activity; however, there are times when a project manager needs to become a crisis manager. The difference between what a crisis manager does and what a project manager does is that once the crisis has passed, the project manager begins the process of developing a long-term, process-oriented, and permanent solution. In general, crisis managers are too involved in solving "crises" to develop permanent solutions. However, the project manager will use input from crisis management, as well as operations and strategic management at times, to address the permanent solution. Connecting with operations and strategic management will enable a solution that can be operationally managed and can fit within the strategic direction, making the solution much more effective.

SUMMARY

Understanding project management within the healthcare environment starts with a definition of a project, the multiple forms a project life cycle can take, what types of projects are undertaken in the healthcare environment, and how project management fits in the overall scheme of organizational management. These are the basic building blocks to prepare the healthcare professional for a more detailed look at the discipline. Think about what has to be done in a project and use the following guidelines for reference:

- Define the project
- Develop the work breakdown structure
- Estimate time and budget
- Develop the schedule
- Monitor the project's progress
- Control the project
- Close it out

KEY REVIEW QUESTIONS

1. Define *a project.*
2. Define *project life cycle.*
3. What is the most compelling reason that the healthcare environment is different from that of other industries?
4. What are the four major types of management within an organization, and how do they differ from each other?
5. Define *project management.*

ENDNOTES

1. Project Management Institute Web site, About Us, http://www.pmi.org/AboutUs/Pages/Default.aspx
2. PMI Today, *PMI Fact File*, Project Management Institute, Newtown Square, PA, July 2010.
3. International Healthcare Worker Safety Center, University of Virginia, *Protecting healthcare workers worldwide from occupational exposure to bloodborne pathogens.* http://www.healthsystem.virginia.edu/internet/safetycenter/internetsafetycenter-webpages/DefiningtheProblem.cfm

2

Planning for a Project

WHY ARE PROJECTS CHOSEN?

Personal

Not to give the wrong impression, but when I use the term "personal" in choosing a project, I mean that there is some personal interest or personal investment in the project, usually by an organizational leader, and sometimes by the chief executive. In a medical facility it may be the Chief Executive Officer, Director of Information Technology, Chief of Surgery, Board of Directors, or others in the power structure of the organization. The choice may even fit into one of the other categories, competitive or financial, but often it does not, at least from an initial analytical view. It could also be that the reasoning behind the decision to choose one project over another is not readily justified by conventional means. The decision may be based on "gut," for instance. The decision may also be based on factors only known to the initiator. Sometimes executives may have information that they do not want to share for a variety of reasons. Intellectual property issues may be one of those concerns. Sometimes there is an altruistic issue that is close to the heart of an executive involving a project that may in fact be detrimental to the bottom line. But because of the strength of feeling by the executive, the project is undertaken anyway. Not all projects are undertaken because of profitability. We'll see more specifics about this in the sections on the "competitive" and "financial" reasons that projects are chosen.

Financial

The most obvious reason that projects are chosen is for financial reasons. There is no doubt about it; companies need to stay in business, bailouts notwithstanding. Companies need due diligence to investigate and analyze the financial aspects of undertaking a project. A fundamental reason to undertake a new project is to add to the bottom line. There are two ways to increase an organization's bottom line: increase revenues or reduce expenses. What types of projects would an organization undertake to increase revenues?

- A project designed to improve the efficiency of healthcare delivery is one example. Electronic medical record (EMR) implementation is a large-scale project designed to improve those efficiencies. Preprinted forms, keyed data entry (rather than illegible handwriting), and immediate retrieval of a patient's medical records can improve efficiency by reducing or eliminating medical errors associated with inaccurate or unavailable records.
- Increasing patient processing is another way to increase revenues. Increasing patient through put should allow for additional billing, thus additional revenues.
- One area that seems to be a big problem in medical centers is long patient wait times. In a hospital, for instance, the emergency department (ED) can be a bottleneck to patient flow. According to a recent article by Chelsey Ledue,[1] "Emergency departments at many hospitals have been overwhelmed in the past year, as more patients without health insurance use the ED as a primary care solution." That is not a surprise to those who follow what is happening with healthcare in this country. Because the ED is the area where patients wait to enter other facilities within the hospital, undertaking projects like improving the accuracy and efficiency of the triage in the ED can help to get patients to the right place more quickly. According to the same article, "… one ED director says simple fixes such as shuffling around a surgery schedule can help a hospital improve time management in the ED."

  Another way to improve throughput in an ED is to have more accurate and efficient triage procedures, perhaps including updated questionnaires, specific education for triage personnel, and more complete patient education. Any reduction in patient wait time is multiplied by the number of patients per year, which can result in a huge savings of hospital resources. A secondary, but nonetheless critical, benefit of getting patients to the right place in a timely and accurate manner will be an increase in patient and staff satisfaction.
- Undertaking projects to purchase and deploy the latest equipment, although there is an initial cost associated, will increase the bottom

line in the long run by enabling quicker processing of patients. For example, adding a new magnetic resonance imaging (MRI) machine, while adding $1–3 million to expenses, could increase revenues by $2½ million per year based on 2,500 additional MRIs per year at $1,000 average per MRI. A computerized axial tomography (CAT/CT) scanner can cost upwards of $3.8 million and generate $2 million in revenue based on 2,000 CAT scans per year at $1,000 average per CAT scan. Other equipment, such as ultrasound, x-ray, laparoscopic, etc., should also be considered.

However, when considering equipment purchases, all costs should be considered including physical space requirements, financing costs, and personnel needs (technologists/doctors).

Competitive

Competition is not the first thing you think about when you think "healthcare." We look at all of the advertisements for automobiles, breakfast cereals, and retailers, and we can see that competition for limited dollars is stiff. There are limited healthcare dollars, too. I am certainly not saying that competition is not good for the industry, because it is. It fosters efforts to contain costs, improve quality, and encourage ways to "stretch" those limited resources. And it is that interest in stretching the limited resources where project management can be very beneficial. So what projects can be undertaken to increase a healthcare provider's competitiveness?

Beautification of facilities is a common project. Both interior and exterior beautification projects are undertaken by healthcare facilities to attract patients and thus patient dollars. Perception goes a long way for people's confidence. An attractive front entrance, newly painted waiting rooms with comfortable chairs, and inviting treatment rooms are all projects that healthcare facilities complete to try to differentiate themselves from others in the area.

Specialization is another way that healthcare facilities try to differentiate themselves from others. Some will emphasize orthopedics, cardiology, pulmonology, thoracic surgery, pediatrics, or another specialty, hoping that the specialty will attract new patients. Patients who take advantage of those specialties may have a tendency, if it was a good experience, to stay with the facility for all of their medical services. There is an interesting specialization that goes to the heart, excuse the pun, of the healthcare crisis, and that is a specialization in obesity—not treating, but rather accommodating obese patients. Projects would include wider, more comfortable waiting room chairs, increased wheelchair availability, substantial beds, etc. According to the Centers for Disease Control and Prevention, almost one-third of Americans are obese, so while being a bit controversial, this type of specialization makes sense.

Safety

Another reason that projects in healthcare are proposed is for safety reasons. Safety can affect the general public, patients, and employees. For instance, a project to improve the safety procedures of handling biohazard materials will protect the health and welfare of those in all three categories—the public, patients, and employees. Sharp injuries occur more frequently in patient rooms and in the operating theater. A project to reduce sharp injuries would probably be targeted to a limited population of medical facility employees. An overhang to protect the entrance of a medical facility and a heated walkway in areas of potential icing problems are examples of exterior projects designed for the safety of all users of a medical facility. One thing to remember, however, is that safety is related to finances in that if safety initiatives are not considered, there could be a negative effect on insurance premiums as well as the potential liability that could occur should there not be the necessary emphasis on safety.

Regulatory

Anyone associated with the healthcare industry is familiar with the maze of regulations and regulatory agencies. For the federal government the agencies include

- Health Insurance Portability and Accountability Act (HIPAA) – privacy protection
- Department of Health and Human Services – human research regulation
- Agency for Healthcare Research and Quality – information technology and electronic medical record regulation
- Health Resources and Services Administration – healthcare training
- National Institute of Health – biomedical research
- Environmental Protection Agency
- U.S. Department of Agriculture – food safety

- Office of Civil Rights – nondiscrimination
- Food and Drug Administration
- Office of Inspector General – fraud
- Centers for Disease Control and Prevention
- Centers for Medicare and Medicaid Services

State agencies include the following:

- Departments of Health
- Medical Boards
- Departments of Insurance

Then there are the local regulators and also private organizations like the Federation of State Medical Boards and the Joint Commission on Accreditation of Healthcare Organizations (JCAHO). It is a wonder that most projects in the healthcare industry aren't focused on regulations.

Summary

Projects in healthcare are undertaken for a variety of reasons. Projects can be for personal, financial, competitive, safety, and regulatory reasons. It is important to understand the reasoning behind project choice, because it is easier to get buy-in from stakeholders (and we'll look closely at stakeholders in Chapter 3) when the reasoning is understood and explained. It is only human nature to want to know the reasons.

DECISION-MAKING TOOLS FOR CHOOSING A PROJECT

There are a variety of tools available for the decision makers to use when choosing a project. It is important for the project manager to understand that a variety of tools are available so that they can help the organization's decision makers choose the best way to use their limited resources.

Root Cause Analysis

It is not by accident that I am defining root cause analysis first. I believe that this is probably the most important tool a project manager can recommend to an organization to determine project selection. Granted, it implies that there is an issue(s) that needs to be addressed. And I believe that the driver for a large number of projects being considered in an organization is issue related, particularly with quality improvement. Think of it as an equation. One side of the equation is the effect; the other side of the equation contains a list of potential causes. The object is to find the cause or causes that will balance the equation. I find it easier to research one effect at a time, and *always* keep in mind that for any one effect, there could be multiple causes. Just because you have identified one cause doesn't mean that your job is done.

Take a fishbone or Ishikawa diagram as an example. Developed by Kaoru Ishikawa in the 1960s as a tool to identify quality issues, the fishbone is an effective method to identify all of the potential causes for any specific effect. As you can see from the example in Figure 2.1, it is important to first determine the major influencers. I try to fit these standard categories to my issue: people, machinery, environment, methods, measurements, and materials, but all issues may not have all of these influencers. Within each of the major influencer categories, think about what could influence those factors. For instance, factors that could influence your human resources potential could be training, competence, and over-stressing. While you

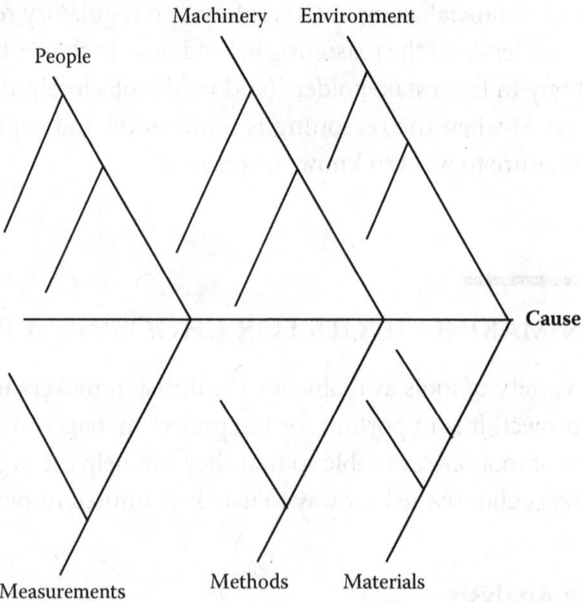

FIGURE 2.1
Fishbone diagram example.

may find that the resources you are using do not have the training they need, just fixing that may not fix the issue. The issue also may be affected by the maintenance of the equipment. If you had ended your analysis after you found the lack of training of your resources, you would not have resolved your issue. Once you go through the exercise to identify all of the potential *causes* for your *effect*, follow through with the analysis.

An emergency meeting has been called by the Northwoods Community Medical Center CEO, Michelle Michaels. In attendance are Chairman of the Board William Worthy, CFO Elaine Dumont, Medical Director Dr. Harold Chimers, and Director of IT Mary Ann Lords. A recent survey has shown that there are some troublesome trends beginning to appear. Specifically, revenues are down, as is customer and employee satisfaction. It is up to this group of individuals to determine a course of action that will stem the negative tide. They decide to construct a fishbone diagram to determine the root cause of the decrease in both revenue and patient satisfaction (see Figure 2.2).

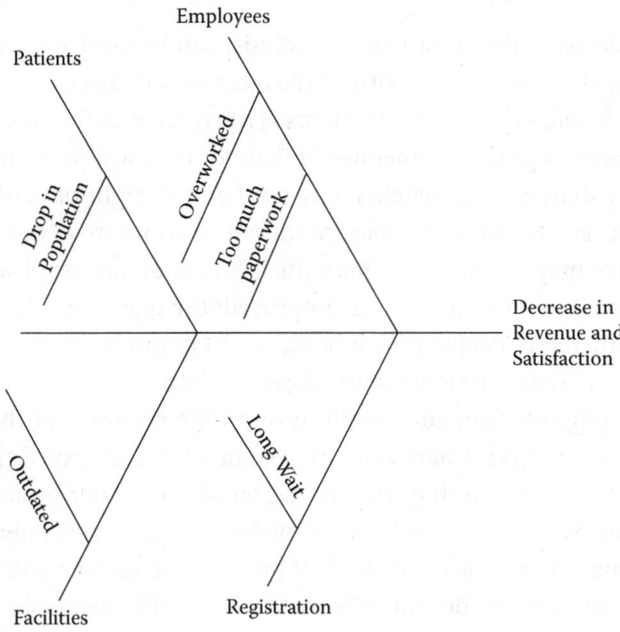

FIGURE 2.2
Fishbone diagram NCMC.

After reviewing the brief fishbone diagram, it was determined that the combination of long wait time in registration and the excessive amount of paperwork that the employees had to deal with were the cause of employee and patient dissatisfaction, and as a result of the patient dissatisfaction, fewer patients were using the medical facilities, resulting in reduced revenues. It was also determined that the excessive paperwork was causing inefficient uses of human resources within the facility and more costs. The question now is, what can be done to reduce wait times and decrease paperwork to make the resources more efficient and bring back patients, thus increasing the bottom line (revenues-costs)?

Since the NCMC uses manual patient data entry, Mary Ann proposes that NCMC consider going to an electronic medical record (EMR) system. Elaine, being the CFO, wonders what the benefits will be versus the cost of the system. The group, however, agrees that this proposal should be considered seriously as a potential project and suggests that the next step of cost-benefit analysis be taken.

Cost-Benefit Analysis

Another decision tool, cost-benefit analysis, can be used alone or in conjunction with other tools, as with all the tools we will discuss. Cost-benefit analysis contrasts the potential benefits of a project with the potential costs of the project. A point to remember is that, for the most part, costs can be objectively determined. Benefits may not be as straightforward or easily quantified. For instance, a project undertaken to improve the quality of patient care may not be easily quantified. It is not a matter of whether or not the quality of patient care has improved; the question is how to measure that increase. People have a tendency to ignore surveys unless they are unhappy. That can significantly skew the data.

Expert judgment can add significantly to the accuracy of the benefits and costs of a project. Chances are that someone has executed the type of project you are considering. Depending on whether your project is leading edge or trailing edge will determine how much expert judgment can assist in making a project decision. If projects are leading edge, chances are that little cost or benefit information is readily available. Consider the project of NCMC, however. EMRs have been and are being deployed throughout the world. Therefore, information on costs and benefits is readily available.

As a cost-benefit analysis of the EMR Project for Northwoods Community Health Center showed, based on current cost data and historical benefit data, the project would positively affect NCMC's bottom line in addition to significantly improving employee and patient satisfaction. Since this project is in large part focused on new information technology, the executives for NCMC decided that the EMR Project should be the responsibility of the IT Department.

One of my personal favorites is the *force field analysis.* The basis of force field analysis is making a determination of one choice over another by looking at the forces that are in favor of the decision and the forces against the decision. One of the advantages of force field is that the "forces" can be weighted based on the importance of certain forces. As you can see in Figure 2.3, using the weighting factors determined by NCMC, the decision is 14 points for and 12 points against. One caution when using a force field analysis is that the weighting factors should be considered very carefully. They are really the subjective part of the exercise and will significantly influence the decision. Using expert judgment and any objective standards available to help determine those weighting factors will aid in making the correct decision for the organization.

One of the simplest decision-making tools is the plus/minus/implications method. The implication piece of this tool also uses weighting to

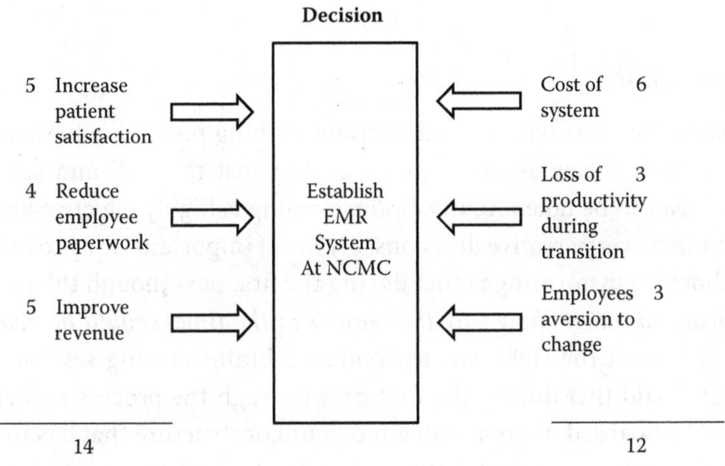

FIGURE 2.3
Force field analysis (EMR).

Plus	Minus	Implications
Increase in quality of life (3)	Fewer cultural events (−3)	More fresh air and outdoor activities (2)
Cost of living is less (4)	Have to leave friends (−3)	Need to make new friends (−2)
Company will pay for relocation (4)	Have limited time to sell house (−2)	Be able to buy bigger house (2)
11	−8	2

FIGURE 2.4
Plus/minus/implications. The decision is whether to apply for a new job that would require a transfer. The salary is the same, but the setting is more rural and the cost of living is less.

help with the decision-making process. The same caution applies any time you use weighting, and again, collecting as much data as possible on a plus or a minus will increase the accuracy of the decision. Because it is so simple to use, it doesn't take a lot of resources. Figure 2.4 is an example of a plus/minus/implications method. As you can see by the example, the pluses outweigh the minuses, so the best decision is to take the transfer. Of course this is a simple example and the tool can be expanded to include many more decision points with pluses, minuses, and the implications. The tool should be expanded significantly when making business decisions.

Brainstorming

Probably the most widely used decision-making method is brainstorming, or "let's throw as much as we can against the wall and see what sticks." Not to be taken lightly, brainstorming is highly effective and can lead to some very creative decisions. The most important thing to remember about brainstorming is that during the first pass though the process, *all ideas, no matter how silly they sound at the time, should be boarded.* So let's look at the right way to conduct a brainstorming session. Even though I said that during the first pass through the process everything should be boarded, there is still a modicum of structure that has to be in place. It is very easy to get distracted, so the facilitator needs to keep the group focused on the issue. Brainstorming sessions usually begin with an opportunity. For example, an opportunity for NCMC is that it could be the first in the area to offer a new technology, like GE's new Vscan® handheld ultrasound.

That brings us to the second most important point when conducting a brainstorming session, which is to *get the right people in the room.* This may not be as easy as you might think. People are busy and a brainstorming exercise may not seem like the best way to spend their time. You do need the decision makers in the room, and besides, because of their position in the organization, they are probably creative managers and strategists—just what you need for an effective session. Once the right people are in the room it is time to start the process. *Make sure that there are plenty of places to capture ideas*—whiteboards are less effective than the large Post-It® easel pads. Not only can you tear the paper off of the easel and post it on the wall, but you can also take all of the pages back to your office to have a permanent record of the session. So, now that you have enough places to record information, and the right people are in the room, you can start the actual exercise.

The first pass through the process is a "controlled free-for-all." The ideas will be coming fast and furious, so you may want to have several recorders. That's why it is important to have plenty of easels. The second pass through the process is to *get clarification* on the first-pass information. Because the information was coming fast and furious, some of it may have been written incorrectly, or even incoherently, which is fine because now is the chance to clarify. Also, while getting the clarification, now is the time to *remove duplicate ideas* from the easels and start to group ideas together. Once that part of the exercise is over, you should have plenty of ideas that are clarified and grouped by similarity. Now the hard work begins, and this is why the right people have to be in the room. There will be financial and strategic decisions to be made, and having those decision makers in the room will expedite the process of the final decision. And when you think about it, it is much more efficient for the participants, too. By doing it on the spot, they won't be required to spend additional time on it.

The final pass in the process is to *get the decisions made*, in our case, whether or not it makes sense for NCMC to pursue Vscan® hand-held ultrasound technology. When we get to Chapter 3 on the Work Breakdown Structure, we'll talk about a special kind of brainstorming session called "cards-on-the wall."

Of course there are many other decision-making tools that can be used. We will look at some that have a cross function use when we look at the quality aspects of managing projects in healthcare, and detail another tool when we look at developing a work breakdown structure.

Consensus Building

A decision that is made by consensus by definition is not a unanimous decision in most cases. It is also not a decision that is made by "majority rule." Majority rule implies that some have been outvoted. What it is, however, is a decision that has been made in a collaborative environment. A collaborative environment consists of people listening to each other, a free flow of ideas, and generates a decision by which everyone can agree to abide. There may be strong disagreements during the process that may cause project managers to heavily rely on their facilitation, conflict management, and negotiation skills. But the effort is worth it because a good, solid decision that everyone has bought into will be the result.

Organizational Structure Influences on Project Choices

The way an organization is structured can have an influence on the way projects are chosen. In order to better understand the influences, we'll look at the way organizations are structured. The structure not only has an influence on the way projects are chosen, but also, as we will see in later chapters, how projects are implemented.

Functional Organization

A functional organization is probably the most difficult structure for a project manager. It is characterized by a hierarchy that is organized by discipline. Each discipline has a definitive chain of command. The information, therefore, is compartmentalized with only the "function managers" potentially having the "big picture." Because of that chain of command, the communication process tends to be vertical. The difficulty with managing a project with vertical communication is that the information is filtered. Rather than getting information directly from the source, all information comes through the function manager, like the children's game "telephone" or "whisper down the lane." The more people who "filter" the information the more scrambled it is likely to become. An additional problem for the project manager is that the "power" within an organization resides with the functional manager. There is a tendency to control rather than share that

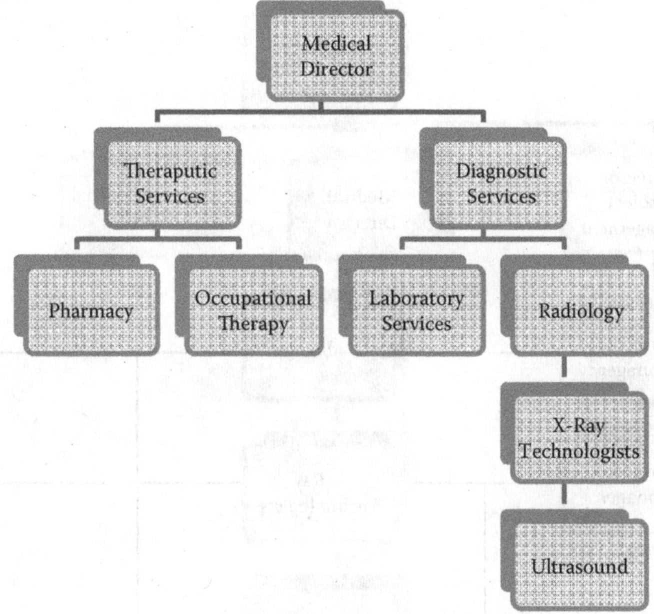

FIGURE 2.5
Functional organization.

power. Because the project manager holds no currency in an organization like that, there is no impetus for team members, who are directly influenced by the function manager, to set a project as a priority. Their priority is to the function manager who, more than likely, controls their performance appraisal and compensation. Interestingly, a disadvantage of a functional structure is one of the advantages for some: a clear chain of command. There is no doubt about who you have to get on board to get something done. See Figure 2.5 for a representation of a functional organization.

Matrixed Organization

There are different types of matrices, but basically, a matrixed organization allows for much more committed cross-functional participation. There is a project manager assigned to the project, and the additional resources (project team members) are then "loaned" to the project manager on a full-time basis for either the duration of the project or the duration of the function needed for the project. The distinction is that some project team members need to be assigned to the project for the duration, and we'll discuss who needs to be assigned through the project

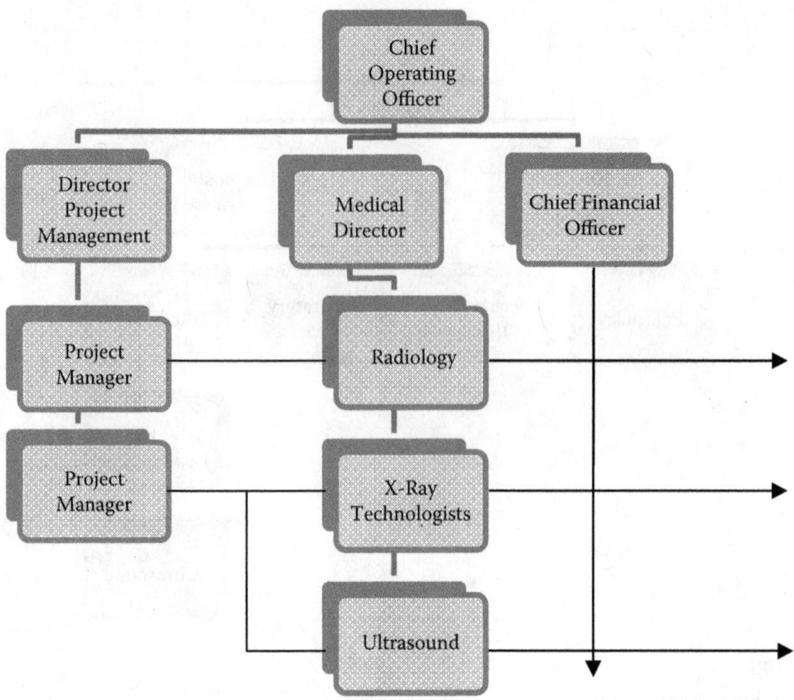

FIGURE 2.6
Matrixed organization.

and who can be assigned temporarily. A modified matrixed structure makes a lot of sense in the healthcare field. Although the team members assigned may not agree, it is the best way to manage projects in healthcare. Specifically, the structure is modified so that part-time team members are assigned. That way, the regular scheduled work can be accomplished as well as the project work. The disadvantage is that at times it almost feels like two full-time jobs, and that is a real concern. The reality is, however, that healthcare workers should be concerned with projects in the organization because they will have a direct effect on the present as well as future delivery of healthcare. See Figure 2.6 for a representation of a matrixed organization.

Project-Focused Organization

While a functional organization structure may be the most difficult for the project manager, a project-focused organization is the easiest for the project manager. A project-oriented organization is just that, organized

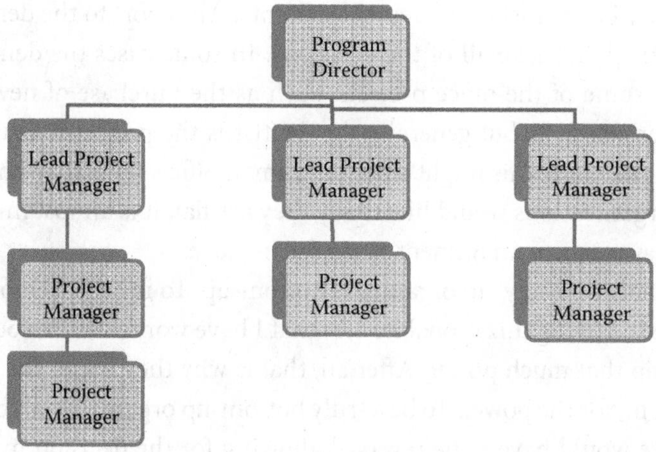

FIGURE 2.7
Project-focused organization.

by project. The project manager reports directly to an upper manager, sometimes even the chief executive of the company. Product manufacturing organizations are much more likely to structure their organization by project (product). The project manager will have dedicated staff assigned on a per-project basis. Because of dedicated teams for each project, it is relatively expensive. It is much more difficult to justify a project-focused organization in a healthcare setting, but a project-focused organization is included here for completeness. Because of the uniqueness of the functions provided by healthcare providers, doctors, nurses, and technologists, it would be very difficult for a project manager to be familiar with all of healthcare's nuances. Also, the focus of a healthcare organization is much broader, and is less likely to be consistently project focused. See Figure 2.7 for a representation of a project-focused organization.

There are several "new" ways of slicing up the "organizational pie." One of these new structures is the "flat" structure. In a nutshell, a flat organization has no intervening organization structure between the worker level and upper-management level. Some organizations will designate "lead" workers on projects, but all workers are basically on a peer level. A slight modification to this structure may be that, instead of reporting to the CEO, for instance, there may be an executive council to which all other employees report. It can be an effective way for smaller healthcare facilities to organize. Most private, single physicians' offices are organized that way. In a dentist's office with one principal dentist, there is probably office help, dental hygienists, and dental assistants. All report to the dentist and the dentist will make all of the decisions. In some cases the dentist may delegate some of the office projects, such as the purchase of new equipment, for example, but generally the dentist is the project manager. You can see that while this might work for a small office, no matter how much larger organizations would like to say they are flat, it is almost impossible not to have some management structure in place.

The final "new way" to organize is bottom-up. To me this is mostly hollow words. No organizational leaders that I have worked with would want to give up that much power. After all, that is why they are in the position they are in, for the power. To be a truly bottom-up organization, the power structure would have to be reversed allowing for the decision making to come from the bottom of the organization. One of the major difficulties with a bottom-up decision-making organization is that the top of the organization usually owns the big picture, the overall view, and the strategy. Unless there is meticulous communication between the levels, the projects probably won't connect with the mission or goal of the organization, making the project ineffective.

When choosing a project, the various structures will have a significant impact on the types of projects chosen. If the organization is functional, the decision makers will be the functional managers. Except for a few organizations, like the military, for instance, this type of organization is outmoded. With limited resources, and doing more with less, it is unlikely that an organization will stay functionally organized. It was the way medical facilities were structured, where department heads (functional managers) had a lot of power. As mentioned, resources (money) became scarcer, and cross-training and cross-functionality became more and more desirable. Decision making therefore moved from individuals to teams.

Matrix organizations allow for more consensus building, which is a critical tool for project teams. The decision-making process in project-oriented organizations is fairly clear-cut and easy. Projects are chosen that have a direct impact on the organization's ultimate goal. It just happens to be a very expensive structure. Most organizations have or are moving toward a type of matrix organization to efficiently utilize resources, more easily connect with the goal and mission of the organization, and make better project decisions.

Other Considerations for Project Choice

One of the areas that should be carefully considered is the area of regulations and standards. This area is often overlooked in the early stages of project planning and can have significant impact on whether or not to choose a particular project. Once the project is chosen, however, regulations and standards will play a large role in defining the project's success or failure. Unfortunately, having to deal with them in a later stage of the project planning process, or in some cases, during the implementation phase of a project, can have a costly effect on project resources, leading to extending the project's timeline and budget.

Regulatory and Industry/Organization Standards

Information that is critical to a project is the relevant data from standards and regulatory agencies, industry best practices, and the organization's own policies, procedures, and standards.

- Joint Commission on Accreditation of Healthcare Organizations (JCAHO) – a not-for-profit organization that provides accreditation programs for its subscriber medical facilities. Though not a "regulatory" agency, accreditation carries a lot of weight in the industry. http://www.jointcommission.org/
- Various state regulatory agencies
- Agency for Healthcare Research and Quality (AHRQ) – part of the U.S. Department of Health and Human Services (HHS), AHRQ provides information about patient quality and safety, clinical practice guidelines, data, and survey information. http://www.ahrq.gov/
- Centers for Medicare and Medicaid Services (CMS) – part of the U.S. Department of Health and Human Services, CMS provides regulation and guidance relative to Medicaid and Medicare, as well as information on COBRA and the Health Insurance Portability and Accountability Act (HIPAA), enforced by HHS. http://www.cms.hhs.gov/
- Centers for Disease Control and Prevention (CDC) – another agency within the U.S. Department of Health and Human Services, the CDC can provide a myriad of information on disease prevention and treatment, with too many "centers, institutes, and offices" to mention here. The CDC can be an important source of information to the project manager, especially in determining levels of

risk associated with particular projects. Identifying the potential risk areas and addressing them in the project's scope can affect the needed resources. http://www.cdc.gov/

- National Institute for Health and Clinical Excellence (NICE) – for information about patient safety and quality for the United Kingdom. http://www.nice.org.uk/
- World Health Organization (WHO) – according to their Web site, "WHO is the directing and coordinating authority for health within the United Nations system. It is responsible for providing leadership on global health matters, shaping the health research agenda, setting norms and standards, articulating evidence-based policy options, providing technical support to countries and monitoring and assessing health trends." http://www.who.int/en/

Industry best practices, as well as lessons learned is information that can affect the scope of a project. Becoming aware of those best practices can lead to a more efficient use of project resources, while an awareness of lessons learned can show which practices should be avoided and make the project as efficient as possible.

An organization's policies must be considered in the scope statement in order to ensure that the project's description will not be in conflict with the organization's quality policy, for example.

KEY REVIEW QUESTIONS

1. What are four reasons why projects are initiated in healthcare?
2. What are the two most common ways to organize a healthcare enterprise?
3. How can expert judgment help in decision making?
4. What is the difference between brainstorming and consensus building?

ENDNOTE

1. Ledue, Chelsey, Associate Editor, Healthcare Finance News. *Small changes can reduce patient wait times in ED*, July 30, 2009, http://www.healthcarefinancenews.com/news/small-changes-can-reduce-patient-wait-times-ed

3

Getting Started

PROJECT SPONSOR

Now that the project decision-making process is complete, what are the next steps?

From Chapter 2, we learned that once projects are chosen, they have to be planned, implemented, and controlled. It is now time to begin the preliminary project planning by *identifying the project sponsor*, because, without exception, to have a successful project, you must have a sponsor. You're probably asking what a project sponsor is, what the project sponsor's role is, and why it is so important to have a project sponsor.

A project sponsor is the person (and in rare cases, persons) who has the accountability to ensure that the overall project meets the criteria set forth. We'll discuss the criteria, or the assumptions and constraints on a project, a little later in this chapter. For now, suffice it to say that there are criteria that must be met. The sponsor has the authority to commit the necessary resources for a project to begin and continue. The sponsor provides a support structure for the project manager. If these are not enough reasons for the sponsor to be considered important, there is one more. Most critical to the project is that, by nature, *projects always prompt change.* With rare exceptions, people do not like change, especially in the healthcare field. There are good reasons for reluctance to change, like tried and true methods and procedures. However, going forward in healthcare it will be all about efficiency. I'm not saying to sacrifice quality of care for efficiency; I am saying that in order to move forward and keep the standard of care we will have to find ways to do things more cost-effectively, and that is efficiency. Because of the resistance to change, there is going to have to be a champion who is high enough in the pecking order so people listen. It is a matter of walking the walk. That is the most important "job" of the project sponsor. Not only does it show the rank and file that it is important enough to be supported by upper management, it also grants certain authority to the project manager to be able to successfully execute the job. Think about it. What kind of credence would you give a project that has no visible support from management? The signal is that the project is not important enough for them to be involved. *One of the primary reasons projects fail is for a lack of a sponsor.*

After the decision to go forward with the EMR Project, Dr. Chimers volunteered to be the executive sponsor for the project. Since the IT Department will be leading the project effort, it was determined that another executive should be designated as the sponsor. The majority of changes will directly affect the medical staff; the medical director is the logical choice.

PROJECT CHARTER

Now that the project decision has been made and a sponsor chosen, the next item that has to be done is to put together a *project charter.* While the project's sponsor will have the accountability to put together the charter, input will need to be gathered from the other organization leaders. So what is a project charter, and what does it entail?

A project charter is the initial defining document of the project. There should be an "information block" that contains the name of the organization, the name of the project, the date the charter was written (as well as a place for version numbers), and a place for signatures of the project authorizers. Instead of the version number being in the information block, it may be included on the last page of the document. Wherever it is displayed, it *must* be there. Too many times there is confusion around the latest version of the charter.

The "meat" of the project charter will contain five key pieces of information (see Figure 3.1): (1) An overview of the project, (2) the project's authority, (3) high-level milestones, (4) project organization, and (5) key project escalation contacts.

I. Describe your Project, Include:
    a. Name of organization
    b. Name of the project
    c. Overview
        i. Issue or opportunity project addresses
        ii. Project goal and objectives
        iii. Project scope
        iv. Assumptions and/or constraints
        v. Stakeholders
        vi. Success criteria
    d. High level milestones

II. Authority (under whose authority will the project be undertaken)

III. Milestones
    a. High level
    b. Detailed (if known)

IV. Organization and Key Contacts
    a. Describe in detail, including an organizational chart, how the project is organized (matrix, functional, project)
    b. Key contacts
        i. Project resources
            1. Project team members
        ii. Escalation and jeopardy owners (see Chapter 12)
        iii. Additional authorizers
            1. Funders
            2. Resource providers

FIGURE 3.1
Template for a project charter.

- Overview – The overview of the project will include information about the issue or opportunity that the project is addressing. It will include a brief description of the project itself, the goal and objectives, the project scope, any assumptions and constraints, project stakeholders, and the success criteria.
- Authority – The project's authority will include a statement from organizational leaders relative to the importance of the project and the fact that resources will be committed (human and financial).
- Milestones – Prior to undertaking any project, the organization's leaders must have an idea of the timeframe within which they expect project completion. This is captured here.

- Organization/Key Contacts – Not all projects are organized the same. Just as there are different ways to organize (functional, matrixed, etc.), there are also different ways to organize for project management. A description of how this particular project is organized will allow participants to understand future processes to be defined, like escalation and jeopardy.

GOALS AND OBJECTIVES

Let's break down the information further. What is a *goal* and what is an *objective*? A goal is a high-level, sometimes abstract state that a project strives to achieve. As examples, some goals in the healthcare environment may be to increase the safety of patients and staff, make the medical facility more appealing, or be more efficient. As you can see, these are more abstract, with no concreteness. That is what a goal should be, because after the goal is defined, the next step is to define the objectives required to meet the goal. Objectives are the "direction" needed to reach the goal. They need to be very specific in order to provide that direction to keep the project focused. They should be *SMARTER*.[1]

You may have heard about SMART objectives. SMART as an acronym that has been around for many years. SMARTER, however, adds an important dimension.

*S*pecific – The objective should be very specific. One objective for the new EMR system for NCMC is that the system will be designed for integration into all of the medical offices associated with NCMC.

*M*easurable – The objective will have a measurability component to be able to access whether the objective has been met. The project manager will test every office within the NCMC "family" to assure that there is integration with the EMR system.

*A*ttainable – The objective will be reasonable and have a possibility of being achieved. If the financial assessment of the deployment of an EMR system in an organization similar to NCMC is approximately $1.5 million, the expectation is that NCMC will allocate some similar amount of money. Should the objective be set at $500,000, the objective would be considered unattainable, and therefore unrealistic.

*R*elated to the Goal – The objective should in some way map back to the project's goal. Too many times, objectives are added to a project later that do not relate to the goal. This can only cause confusion within the project team and lead to "scope creep," which we will consider later in this chapter. *The goal of the EMR system for NCMC is to address patient satisfaction and increase the bottom line.* All objectives identified should be related to those goals. In most cases it is recommended that there is only one goal. But, there are exceptions to that rule. In the case of NCMC, it was determined that the EMR project could directly affect both of these goals.

*T*imely – Having a timeframe for an objective is necessary; otherwise, the objective will have little meaning. If we allow an objective to be stated without a timeframe, it will eventually fall to the bottom of the priority list because it has no urgency. It is like adding a project objective without a measure. How will we know whether or not it has been achieved as stated?

*E*nvironmentally *R*esponsible – It is increasingly important for environmental responsibility to be included when defining project objectives. As central to an objective as timeliness and specificity, the adherence to environmental responsibility can determine whether or not a project is successful. More and more consumers and employees are looking to companies who demonstrate environmental responsibility. When looking at environmental responsibility, project managers should consider not only the product of their project, but also the process surrounding the project. Environmental responsibility for the product of the project answers question like the following:

1. Are we doing any harm to the environment in the design or production of this product?
2. Have we considered the most environmentally friendly raw materials for this product?
3. Have we considered cradle-to-cradle life cycle management for this product? In other words, have we considered the waste that this product will produce at the end of its life cycle, and is there a way that the product can be a zero waste producer like what happens in nature?

Environmental responsibility for the process of the project answers questions like the following:

1. Have we considered all the green methods we can employ during the planning, organizing, and implementing of our project?

a. Do we turn out lights when we don't need them?
b. Do we reuse water bottles rather than plastic, recyclable ones?
c. Are we traveling rather than using teleconferences?
d. When we do have to travel, are we purchasing carbon offsets?
e. Are our electronic needs—personal computers, printer, copies—as energy efficient as they can be?

I have just scratched the surface for environmental responsibility considerations when managing projects. If you are interested in reading more on this subject see *Green Project Management* (CRC Press, 2010), co-authored by Richard Maltzman and me.

PROJECT PLAYERS

Often called project stakeholders, in order to properly plan a project the project manager needs to identify project players *and their influence*. This is a critical building block that will help establish other processes, especially future communications. Project players are defined as anyone who has an interest in the project. They may be internal: CEO, CFO, project manager, project team members, development team members, and others within the organization. They may be external to the organization: customers, abutters, and environmentalists. They may have interests in the project and, more importantly, they may be opposed to the effort. The process to determine the project's players is a perfect time to use the brainstorming technique. The wider the range of people involved in the exercise, the more diverse and complete the list. It is extremely important to capture the variety of stakeholders, because imbedded within that list will be your key players or key stakeholders, and you certainly don't want to miss a key stakeholder. *Another reason projects fail is that a key stakeholder was not informed because he or she was not identified.*

So how do you separate the key players from the other players? While not hard and fast rules, I do use guidelines I've developed over the years. First and foremost, who funds the project? After all, the chief resource of any project is money. Your funder could be one person or a board/committee. Obviously, with a board/committee, the stakeholder process becomes more complicated. The more members you have to deal with, the more complicated it can become. Each member usually has his or her own reasons (or agenda) for supporting or not supporting a particular project. The project manager must now identify the key stakeholders within that board/committee. There will be stakeholders who are the most influential. When meeting with that group of individuals it is important to *observe* more that participate. There will be subtle and not-so-subtle hints as to who is in charge. Believe me, no committee is perfectly balanced. There will be people who have more influence than others. Once the influencers are identified, you will have to determine what type of communications are necessary for the group and for those influencers. It may be different. We will look at communications in detail within a project.

The next "rule" is to look to those who have the most to gain and the most to lose should the project be implemented (see Table 3.1). For instance, in the case of NCMC's project to implement an EMR system, the person who has the most to gain is Mary Ann Lords, Director of IT, and perhaps one of the people who has the most to lose is the salesperson who is supplying

TABLE 3.1

Identifying Influencers and Influence

Step 1 – Identify Influencers

Using a brainstorming technique (see Chapter 2), determine the stakeholders for your project. This list will be very large at this point.

Step 2 – Determining High-Level Influence

Using that list begin to narrow it down by determining whether each influence will negatively or positively affect the project.

Step 3 – Determining Detailed Level of Influence

Look first at the list of influencers who may positively affect the project and determine, to the best of your judgment, on a scale of 1 to 10, how much influence they will have on the project. Do the same for the negative influencers.

Step 4 – Influencers with Influence

The influencers with a 7 or higher score are in the major influencer category. Those with scores of 5 and 6 are in the important category, and those below 5 are in the minor influencer category.

Step 5 – Determine Level of Communications

The level of communications will depend on the score of the influencer and the stage of the project. For instance, high-level financial people may be involved in the initial planning. Once the budget has been approved, they may not need a high level of communication, but will still remain in the high influencer category.

the present system of paper documentation. They are both stakeholders and may have influence over the project.

At this point in the project you have two important tools: the project charter and the definition of the project stakeholders with their influence levels. Those will be considered as inputs to the next stage of the project process, *developing a project plan.*

PROJECT PLAN

Simply put, the project plan answers the following questions to complete the project:

- What are the tasks involved?
- When do we need to complete each task?
- In what sequence will the tasks be?
- Who and what resources will we need?
- Are there any projects that will be compromised by doing these tasks?
- What measurements will be used to determine if we are on track?

The Project Charter

Just to reiterate, the project charter contains the overall view of the project. It includes information relative to the

- Project sponsor/key contacts
- Project purpose and objectives
- Project manager
- Project completion date (or timeframe)
- Overall project budget

Scope Statement

It is here that my view differs somewhat from the traditional view of project management. The term "statement of work" (SOW) has been used for years to describe a document within the project plan. I prefer to use "scope statement" (SS) instead of "statement of work." The SS contains similar information, but

I wanted to include a reference to the SOW so that when you see it in other project management (PM) literature you will know what it is.

Requirements and Expectations

The real work for the project manager begins with the development of the scope statement. It is a document that will detail the work that needs to be done in the project. It should reference the detailed requirements that will need to be met in order to successfully complete the project. This is a good point to have a brief discussion about requirements versus expectations. Is there a difference between a requirement and an expectation? If so, which is more important to the success of a project? Let me start with a little example.

For the past few months, NCMC has been implementing a new project to reduce the sharp injuries in the operating room (OR). The requirements focused on the handling of suture needles. Attached to the statement of work was a requirement that an area of the OR be set aside for accessibility by the surgeon to suturing needles. Hand-to-hand passing of these needles was eliminated. The expectation was that the surgeon would be able to request a "3-0 silk" and the suture needle with the proper thread would be easily available for the surgeon to acquire and use, but without being handed the needle. However, the requirement was only for the area to be set aside. In fact, the needle with the 3/0 thread was readily available to the surgeon, but it was still in the sterile packaging. The surgeon had to pick up the package and open the needle before it was ready to use.

In this case, the requirement of setting aside an area was met; however, the surgeon's expectation was not.

A requirement can be defined in several ways. It can be a necessary objective of the project or a written specification. Requirements or specifications can be easier to define than expectations. For instance, a requirement is that the lighting in the OR must be of 125,000 lux (the international standard measurement for lighting). The lights provided must be 220 V AC with a range of 1,200 meters for a 9-foot high ceiling. Whether or not the requirement has been met is measurable. I always think of requirements and specifications as easily measurable.

Expectations, on the other hand, are much more insubstantial. A doctor would expect to have enough light in the OR to see to operate. For some doctors, meeting the above noted specifications may not provide them with the light they had expected. Therefore, you can meet all of the requirements yet miss expectations. You can meet every requirement of the project yet have very unhappy customers in the end.

So, how do we deal with the potential discrepancies between requirements and expectations? Simple, we align them. *Not aligning requirements and expectations is another cause of project failures.* This is a major reason why you define project stakeholders, particularly the key stakeholders. One success criteria in the project must be meeting or exceeding the key stakeholders' expectations. The first step to reach that goal is to fully understand the key stakeholders' expectations. Now that you have identified those stakeholders, a continuing dialogue is the only way to assure that the expectations are understood.

- Rephrasing the expectations is one way to help clarify their true meaning. Restating what you believe to be the expectations and then asking the question, "Is that what you are expecting?" is an effective way to do that. Sometimes there needs to be several conversations in order to get to the basic expectations. Don't be afraid to ask again until you, as project manager, completely understand the intent of the expectations.
- Getting it signed is another way to help clarify expectations. After asking the question, "Is that what you are expecting?" the next step would be to document it and have the key stakeholder sign the document stating what is expected. Of course, there are no assurances as to whether the expectations and requirements are aligned, but this is a major step toward that end. At this point it is arguable whether or not this now becomes a project requirement because it is in writing. Whether or not it is considered a requirement does not matter. What matters is that the expectations for the key stakeholders and the requirements of the project are not in conflict.

Bringing the surgeons in to look at a prototype or mock-up of the 125,000 lux lighting and getting their approval would go a long way to aligning the project's requirements and expectations.

A word of caution here—different key stakeholders will probably have different expectations and different interpretations of the requirements. It is imperative that all key stakeholders agree with the requirements and expectations for a project to be successful. A requirements/expectations document signed by the key stakeholders is a necessity when there are conflicting expectations.

Detailed Project Description

The scope statement includes a detailed description of what the project is expected to provide, and, very important for clarity, what the project is *not* expected to provide. The SS should include a reference to all requirement/specification documents that are added as attachments. It is the "what" of the project; however, it will not be in as much detail as the work breakdown structure (WBS), discussed later in this chapter, as the project's scope is one of the inputs to the WBS. The scope of the project is based on the project's charter and the project's expectations as well as those requirement/specification documents. The SS should also contain information such as the location of the work to be done.

NCMC will include the main facility in the EMR Project and several satellite locations, but will not include other satellite locations. The addresses and contact information including accessibility will be detailed in the SS, as will the locations not included.

Milestones and Deliverables

Specific milestones and deliverables known in this stage of the planning effort will be included in the SS. A milestone is a point in time that requires no resources and has a duration of zero (there is no time associated with it). Microsoft Project, a popular scheduling tool, uses a diamond shape to represent a milestone. It is used to measure the progress of a project.

A milestone for the NCMC Project would be the point in time when all of the hardware used for EMR is on site.

The deliverable in this case is the hardware. It is that tangible part of the project that is required. A deliverable in most cases has a timeframe associated with a start date and a complete date. If the deliverable is significant, it may have a milestone attached. A deliverable is an important concept in project management and we will be talking about that concept throughout the book.

Acceptance/Success Criteria

While different, I put both acceptance and success criteria in the same category because of their relationship. Both criteria relate to meeting and exceeding the stakeholder expectations. The major difference in the two can be the project team's view of the success criteria and the customer's acceptance criteria. It is not necessarily a bad thing to differ if the difference is directionally correct. What I mean by that is that the project team should have more aggressive goals for the success criteria than the customer has for its acceptance criteria. Acceptance criteria are the customer's minimum requirement to "accept" the product, process, or procedure. The target for the project team should always be to exceed that minimum requirement. Aiming for the more aggressive target doesn't guarantee project success, but if the team should fall short of that goal, chances are better to meet the customer's expectations. If, however, the aim is at the target and there is a shortfall, chances are slim that customer expectations will be met; therefore, the customer will be reluctant to accept the product, process, or procedure. Whatever the case, the customer's acceptance criteria *must* be clearly articulated and agreed upon by the team and the customer, and a formal acceptance document and signoff has to occur when the project is complete. More about project closure in Chapter 10.

CONTRACTUAL SPECIFICATIONS

Finally, and related to the customer expectations and acceptance, are any contractual specifications. We'll look at contractual issues in project closure more closely in Chapter 10 and in contracting and buying, Chapter 9, in the body of the contract as well as in any clauses. Suffice it to say that the identification and management of these issues will be of paramount importance to the success of the project, and in the case of producing a product, it could determine whether or not payment is made.

Remember, the scope statement is a critical part of your overall project plan and a building block for further project documentation.

THE WORK BREAKDOWN STRUCTURE

Undoubtedly the most important document the project manager will create is the work breakdown structure (WBS). It is the project's roadmap. Without an accurate and complete WBS, the project is lost. I can't emphasize enough how important the WBS is, and I have seen projects undertaken without one have disastrous results. In some cases, salvaging them was extremely costly in time and money, and some could not be salvaged after hundreds of thousands of dollars had been spent on the project and on efforts to revive it. So what is it and why is it so important?

The Project Management Institute™ defines the WBS as "a deliverable-oriented hierarchical decomposition of the work to be executed by the project team to accomplish the project objectives and create the required deliverable. It organizes and defines the total scope of the project."[2] Let's "decompose" the definition. The WBS will be organized in a top-down manner, with a high-level category for each major deliverable. Each major deliverable will be broken down into finer and finer detail. The WBS will contain all of the tasks required to deliver the project. A type of brainstorming is the best technique I have found for creating the WBS, and it works for huge projects with multiple layers, as well as simpler projects. That technique is called "cards-on-the-wall" (COTW). The technique has been around a long time and is rather low tech, which is perhaps the reason it is often neglected. How would I apply this technique to NCMC's EMR Project?

- Supplies needed: Post-It® notes, pens, transparent tape, black yarn, and laptop or other device for end-of-session recording.
- Bring all the key players to an off-site location. It should be off site because I do not want the interruptions from day-to-day activities to interfere with the sessions. Have one contact number for emergencies. Otherwise, cell phones off. This is a big project for

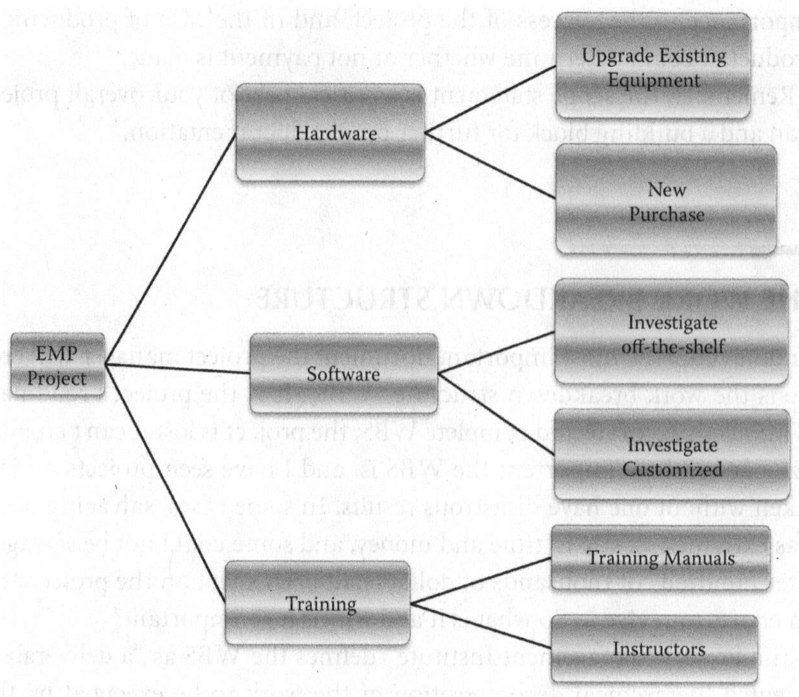

FIGURE 3.2
Cards-on-the-wall.

NCMC, in that it will be both costly and time-consuming. The effort to get the upfront planning right is critical.

- Divide the key players into groups representing project deliverables.
- Supply each group with packs of 3″ × 5″ Post-It® notes, pens, and transparent tape.
- Direct each person to write a single task that he or she has to complete on a Post-It® note and stick it up on the wall.
- Once all the tasks have been identified by each person, for each deliverable begin to put the tasks in order as they need to be, for instance, which tasks need to be completed before the next task begins.
- Take some black yarn and begin to tie tasks together. See Figure 3.2 for a partial result of the COTW exercise for NCMC.

The purpose of the WBS, therefore, is to capture all of the tasks required to successfully complete the project. It is the scope of the project in excruciating detail. Exercises like cards-on-the-wall can make developing the WBS more fun, but it is a lot of work that will pay off. It is those defined tasks that are the instructions for both the core and the extended project teams.

DEALING WITH THE CREEPS

There are four project creeps for which a project manager needs to be on the lookout: scope, hope, effort, and feature creep.

- Scope Creep – This refers to additional requirements that may be added on after the project scope has been documented and agreed upon. It could happen when a stakeholder's expectations are not aligned with the project's expectations. There may have been ambiguity in the project requirements, for example. There are two ways to deal with scope creep: one is proactive and one is reactive. The proactive approach is to make sure that the project requirements are properly documented and understood by all. The second, the reactive approach, is to use the change control system (see Chapter 8) to manage scope change requests.
- Hope Creep – This is one of those tongue-in-cheek creeps. Hope creep occurs when a team member gets behind on his or her deliverables but *hopes* to catch up. When creating your project environment, the environment has to be safe enough for an individual, if he or she does get behind, to be able to come forward with issues while there is time to correct them. A team member may be overwhelmed by his or her task or simply have the wrong skill set to accomplish the task. There are times when, due to budgetary or personnel constraints, the best people or the right people are not on a project. Communication and the ability to raise issues are most important in those instances.
- Effort Creep – Another tongue-in-cheek creep, effort creep involves some of the same issues and resolutions as hope creep. Effort creep happens when a team member is working very hard at a task, but not having any traction, falls behind. It is different than hope creep because the team member has no hope of catching up, because the team member is already working as hard as he or she can. Once again, it is important to have the proper project environment so that

the team member can raise the issues prior to them becoming an obstruction to the entire project.

- Feature Creep – Feature creep happens more often that you think. It occurs when a team member decides that there is an additional feature, in the case of software development, or some additional "nicety" that the customer would like, without any consideration for the project's change control system, or how the change may affect the project as a whole. This can also be called "gold plating," giving the customer more than they asked for at no cost to them, and usually with a cost to the provider. If all project members are educated in the change control process, especially the reasons it is in place, then feature creep usually isn't a problem.

KEY REVIEW QUESTIONS

1. What is a primary reason for projects to fail?
2. What is the function of a project charter?
3. What can be done to minimize scope creep?
4. What is the most important document the project manager can produce?

ENDNOTES

1. Maltzman, Richard, and Shirley, David, *Green Project Management,* CRC Press, Boca Raton, FL, 2010, pp. 35–36.
2. *A Guide to the Project Management Book of Knowledge*, 4th edition, Project Management Institute–Global Standard, Newtown Square, PA, 2008, p. 445.

Section II

The Details

4

Managing Time

In order to manage a project's time element, you need to develop a schedule. Developing a schedule requires the definition of four things: (1) what needs to be done, (2) who will accomplish those tasks, (3) how much time each of those defined tasks will need, and (4) the sequence of those tasks, including which need to be done first (dependencies) and which can be done in parallel. We defined what needed to be done when we established the project's work breakdown structure. Most everything we do with both time and cost will be dependent on that WBS.

ESTIMATING TIME

One of the more difficult exercises for anyone is to be able to estimate how much time it will take to do a task that is unfamiliar, meaning a task that they have not performed themselves. Even when you perform the task yourself, do you really know how much time it took? You do if time is imperative. In projects, time is imperative. *The project manager's mantra is on time, within budget, and of the quality expected* (in other words, meeting or exceeding customer expectations). Here's the dilemma. Having an accurate schedule is a necessary project element. Managing to that accurate schedule will be a component for overall project success. A project manager cannot have every experience necessary to accurately estimate each and every task of each and every project. Therefore, to overcome the dilemma the project manager must have tools and techniques in his or her arsenal.

Historical Information

One of the best ways to estimate a task is to have some data relative to the task or a similar task. That data comes from documentation prepared for previous projects.

Lessons Learned

Lessons learned is specific project documentation. It can take the form of an *action item register.* An action item register is a formal mechanism for recording issues that arise during project execution. Information contained in an action item register can provide insight into how long specific tasks were delayed because of issues. However, it may not have been that the item was delayed, but rather that the item was underestimated in the first place. Lessons learned may also be *contained in the project's schedule* in the form of changes because of underestimating, overestimating, or just because of efficiencies realized. In the case of efficiencies realized, the project manager needs to decide whether or not the current project has the potential to realize those efficiencies or not. If the decision is that the current project will realize efficiencies, the project manager may then decide to be more aggressive in the schedule. Or, the project manager may elect to keep that information and not build those efficiencies into the schedule, but rather monitor the situation to see if it can be pulled in at a later date, saving project resources.

Finally, lessons learned may be contained in *informal project documentation.* Informal project documentation is saved project correspondence like e-mails, phone logs, the project manager's notebook, computer files, etc. There may be valuable information about project task accomplishment contained in those informal papers. *Always keep your project files, no matter how mundane the information may seem.*

Expert Judgment

The least expensive method for estimating the time to perform a function is to find someone who has performed the function before. The next best method is to find someone who has performed a similar function. Obviously, the first-hand experience will be the best and most accurate estimate of time. *Expert judgment should always be the first thing you think about, no matter what the project task.*

3 Point Estimating Technique

$$\frac{\text{Optimistic Estimate (OE)} + \text{Most Likely Estimate (MLE)} + \text{Pessimistic Estimate (PE)}}{3}$$

$$\frac{\text{6 hours} + \text{8 hours} + \text{12 hours}}{3} = \text{8.67 hours}$$

6 Point Estimating Technique

$$\frac{\text{OE} + (4)\ \text{MLE} + \text{PE}}{6}$$

$$\frac{\text{6 Hours} + (4)\ \text{8 Hours} + \text{12 Hours}}{6} = \text{8.33 hours}$$

FIGURE 4.1
Comparison of 3 Point and 6 Point estimating techniques.

3 and 6 Point Estimates

The 6 Point Estimate used to be the most popular of this type of estimate. Lately, the 3 Point Estimate has been gaining favor, particularly with the Project Management Institute™. The major difference I see is that with the 6-point technique, a project manager can "weight" the "most likely" scenario by a factor of 4. Both techniques are averages. I'll use the following numbers for the scenarios. My best estimate of performing the function is 6 hours. My worst estimate of performing the function is 12 hours. The most likely estimate is just that—given your best judgment, how much time do you think the task will take? The most likely estimate may take some online or hard-copy research, questioning people who have done similar tasks, etc. (see Figure 4.1). In this instance, the most likely would be 8 hours. Which do you think is more accurate? My personal opinion is that the weighted 6 Point Estimate is more accurate if the research was done. However, if the research hasn't been done or there isn't any other information available, then the 3 Point Estimate is probably sufficient. Either one is more accurate than guesstimating, because at the least some thought was given to the three scenarios: best, worst, or most likely estimate.

Getting Estimates

In some cases, project managers will not have to provide estimates for all of the project tasks, but rather will have to get some estimates from the core and extended project team members. It will then be a matter of determining whether or not to "trust" the data given or push back.

Trusting the Data

Unfortunately, whether nature or nurture, I'm a skeptic. I don't think I was born a skeptic, but you can be sure that as a long-time project manager, it has certainly been nurtured. So I am very reluctant to trust someone else's data without a second source to confirm it. One of the reasons that I don't trust people's estimates of time and costs is because of a little thing called the "fudge factor." There is a tendency for people to "add" in some extra to insure that there is enough time to accomplish the task. The more familiar the task is, the less fudge factor is needed. A little fudge never hurt anything, right? Wrong. Think of the WBS and all the tasks that need to be accomplished. Start at the bottom and work your way up. We'll look at this phenomenon more closely when we look at cost estimating. But for now, think about a 10-level WBS. At each level, the person responsible for the task adds 10% "just in case." By the time the estimate gets to the top level, the estimate has been inflated by 100%.

Another reason to be skeptical of the data is the evaluation of the data provider. If you do not trust the data provider, the data will also be suspect. Suspicion of the source is also a barrier to communications that we will look at in more detail in Chapter 11. So how might you minimize the potential of getting faulty information from a suspect source? Multiple estimates or a "shotgun" approach might help. Then compare the estimates and average them, if appropriate. The issue, however, is that you must be discrete about your requests or there will be resentment from the parties involved.

Pushing Back

Whether to push back or not is an easy decision. Pushing back, if not done with sensitivity, can give the impression that you suspect the data, and conversely suspect the source. Again, as a project manager, suspicion (skepticism) is one of my best friends. I try my best not to be accusatory when I am questioning data or data sources, but rather that I need the source's help to ensure that I have the right information to convey to customers, whether it is an external customer or upper management. Pushing back is part of your job to ensure that the information you are using to develop the schedule, the schedule that has to be managed for the life of the project, is the best information you have.

If you trust the data, and think that it is accurate, it may still be a time for a tough decision. Should I add my own "fudge factor"? The short answer is yes. The reason is that there are project risks, both opportunities and threats, that will affect the project. We'll talk more about project risk in Chapter 9. You want to have some contingency time built into the project to mitigate the threats and be able to take advantage of the opportunities. If you get to the end of the project and have some time left, it is better to be able to give some back than to have to ask for additional time because you didn't add it in the beginning.

Who Will Do the Tasks?

Why is it important to determine who will do the various project tasks prior to defining the time needed to do the tasks? The answer is, because while you may have the greatest project schedule put together, if you can't get the people to perform the tasks on your schedule, then the schedule won't be accurate. Who you need for the project can also affect the schedule. For instance, if the task requires a person with a particular skill set, and that skill set is not readily available, there are alternatives: (1) Wait for the resources to become available, (2) provide training to an individual for that specific need, or (3) pay a premium for the resources. All of the alternatives could cost additional resources, either extra time in the case of the first two or extra cost in the third. Isn't it better to know what you are dealing with before putting the schedule together than after?

UNDERSTANDING SCHEDULING TOOLS

There are many software tools on the market that can be used once the project's activities are defined and sequenced, and the durations are estimated. The most popular basis for these tools is the Precedence Diagramming Method (PDM). It is a visual representation of the events that occur on a project and the sequence in which they occur, including the task successors and predecessors. It incorporates and expands on the work breakdown structure.

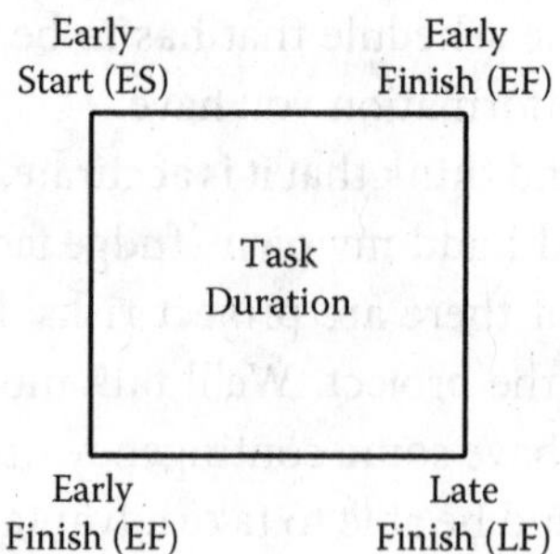

FIGURE 4.2
Network diagram.

Network Diagram

Figure 4.2 is a fundamental representation of a PDM also known as a diagram with the *activities on the node* or a *project network diagram.* As you can see in Figure 4.3, there are activities and pathways between those activities. There is a start (S) and a finish (F). In between there are durations for each task. By adding those durations together the project's duration can be determined … with some "thought." First, the paths through the project need to be calculated. By looking at the diagram it is easy to see that there are three paths through the project, from start through activities: A-B-C-G to finish, A-D-G to finish, and A-E-F-G to finish. As you can see, all paths go through A and through G. Adding the tasks on each path, ABCG takes 13 weeks, ADG takes 8 weeks, and AEFG takes 11 weeks. The critical path through the project is defined as the path that determines the earliest completion date of the project that includes *all* of the necessary tasks. If one of the tasks designated on the critical path is delayed, the end data of the project will also be delayed. Tasks that are not on the critical path may

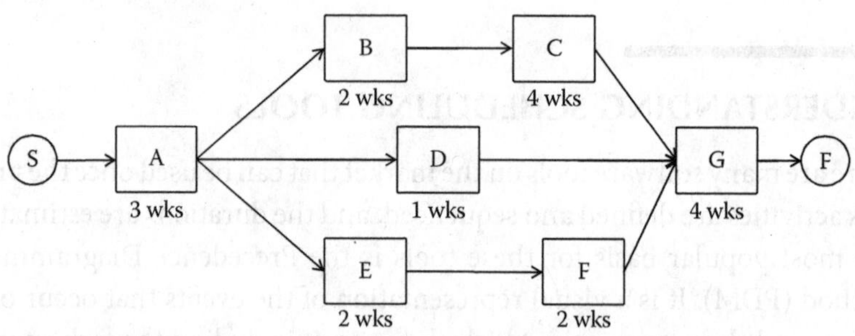

FIGURE 4.3
Example of Simple Network Diagram.

have float, which is the amount of time that a task may be delayed without affecting the end date of the project.

A closer look at Figure 4.3 reveals the critical path as ABGC. Therefore, the project as defined will take 13 weeks to complete. It is the earliest date that all of the project elements, A-B-C-D-E-F-G, can be completed. If, for instance, task G is delayed by 1 week, the end date will be affected (delayed) by 1 week, meeting another criteria of the definition of critical path. However, if we delay task D 1 to 5 weeks, the project's end date will not be affected. However, if task D is delayed 5 weeks (task D has 5 weeks of float), it now becomes a task that cannot be delayed any further without affecting the project's end date. At that point, task D would be placed on the critical path, and there would be multiple critical paths (perfectly acceptable) for this project.

There is more information that can be gleaned from Figure 4.3. Looking at path A-E-F-G, we can see that tasks E and F can be delayed 1 week or task E may be delayed 2 weeks or task F may be delayed 2 weeks. Therefore, tasks E and F each have 2 weeks of float. But *here is the caution*: path A-E-F-G has a total of 2 weeks of float. There is a tendency to add the task floats together. It you did that, you would mistakenly think that there is 4 weeks of float on the project, not the 2 weeks that would not affect the project end date. As you can see, the network diagram is a very powerful tool for visually communicating the project's schedule, identifying activities that may have been missed or may be on the wrong path, and seeing the dependent tasks. This is the same information that is used in a Gantt chart, but just a different visual representation.

Start–End–Float

The automated project scheduling tools calculate the critical path for you, but how do they do it? Let's use the information in Figure 4.1. We'll add the following information to each task: early start date, early finish date, late start date, and late finish date, using Figure 4.2. To determine the early-start dates and early-finish dates we will do a *forward pass* through the project. As mentioned, software-scheduling tools available on the market will do this automatically. But I feel it is important to understand how the software does it, so that we can better understand the interpretation and ensure that we are getting the output expected from the input values.

The early start date for a task is the *earliest* day (or whatever timeframe you are using for your project—for instance, some short-term projects may be completed in a day; therefore, the timeframe could be hourly), in this instance, that the task can start considering the task's predecessors. Figure 4.4 shows the beginning of calculating a forward pass. Task A starts on day 1 and takes 3 days to complete; therefore, it will be worked on day 1 and day 2, and will end at the close of business on day 3. Figure 4.5 shows the completed forward pass. The project will end at the close of business on day 14. Therefore, the project takes 14 days. As noted in Figure 4.5, *always carry the latest Early Finish date forward.*

Once the *backward pass* has been completed, the "float" for each task can then be calculated. Figure 4.6 shows the backward pass through the project. As noted in Figure 4.7, when carrying Early Finish dates backward through the project, *always carry the earliest Late Start day.*

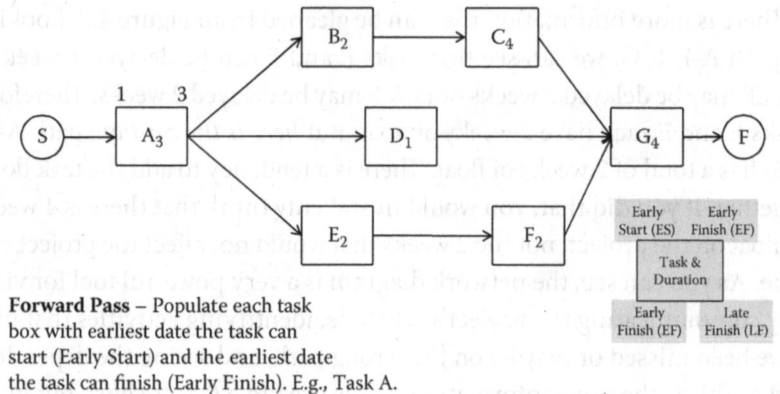

FIGURE 4.4

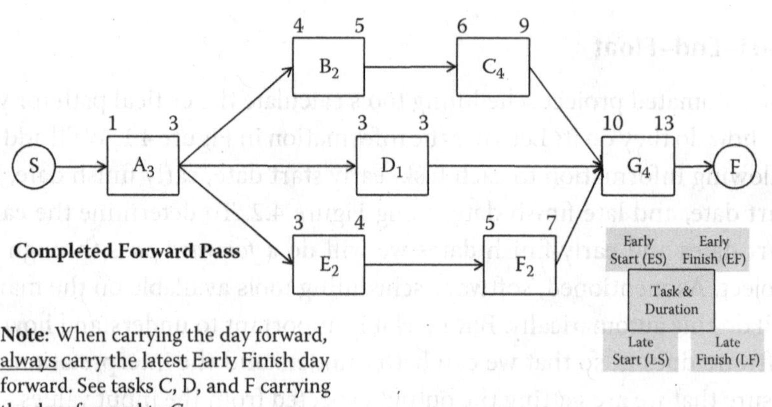

FIGURE 4.5

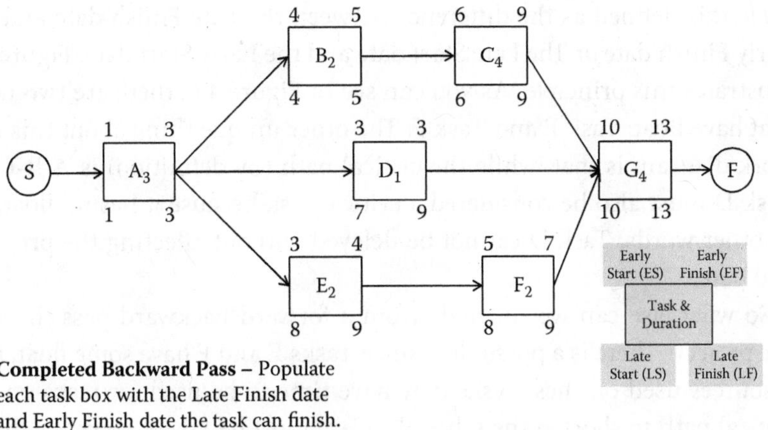

Completed Backward Pass – Populate each task box with the Late Finish date and Early Finish date the task can finish. Always carry the earliest "Late Start" date backward. See Tasks, E, D & B to Task A.

FIGURE 4.6

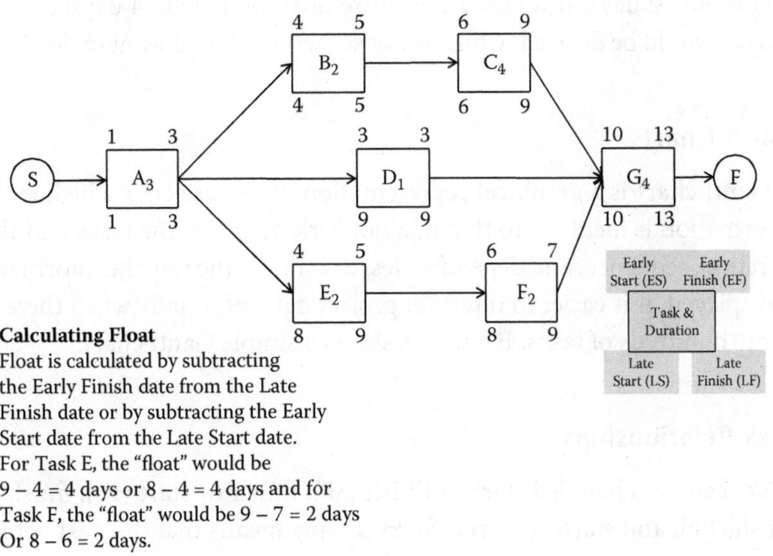

Calculating Float
Float is calculated by subtracting the Early Finish date from the Late Finish date or by subtracting the Early Start date from the Late Start date. For Task E, the "float" would be 9 – 4 = 4 days or 8 – 4 = 4 days and for Task F, the "float" would be 9 – 7 = 2 days Or 8 – 6 = 2 days.

FIGURE 4.7

Float is defined as the difference between the Late Finish date and the Early Finish date *or* The Late Start date and the Early Start date. Figure 4.6 illustrates this principle. As you can see in Figure 4.6, there are two tasks that have float: Task E and Task F. The other unique thing about this network diagram is that, while the critical path (by definition) is A-B-C-G, Task D must also be considered a critical task because it has no float, or, in other words, Task D cannot be delayed without affecting the project's end date.

So what else can we conclude from a forward/backward pass through the project? There is a possibility, since Tasks E and F have some float, that resources used on these tasks may have time to be used for tasks on the critical path to shorten the schedule. Care must be taken, however, that if this is the case, a recalculation of the critical path would need to be done to ensure that tasks that were not on the critical path of the project do not suddenly end up on the critical path. Another decision that could be made is to delay the start of Task E and/or Task F because Tasks E and F have some float. This brings me to the final point: be careful about calculating total float on a project. *It is not cumulative and can be tricky!* In other words, if I delay the start of Task E for 2 days, because Task E is a predecessor to Task F, the start of Task F will also be delayed 2 days. Therefore, Task F will now start on day 8 and conclude on day 10, therefore losing its float. In effect, even though Task E has 4 days of float, the cumulative float for path A-E-F-G is only 2 days. If we used the entire float for Task E, 4 days, the total project would be delayed, which is not something you'd want to do.

Gantt Chart

A Gantt chart is a graphical representation of the project's schedule. The information is identical to that of a network diagram: the tasks and their duration, sequence, and dependencies. Because of the way the information is displayed, it is easier to interpret project data, especially when there are many hundreds of tasks. Figure 4.8 shows a simple Gantt chart.

Task Relationships

Tasks can be scheduled start-to-finish (SF), finish-to-start (FS), finish-to-finish (FF), and start-to-start (SS). SF simply means that the next activity cannot begin until the previous task (or predecessor task) is completed. FS is a more complex relationship. A good example would be an operating

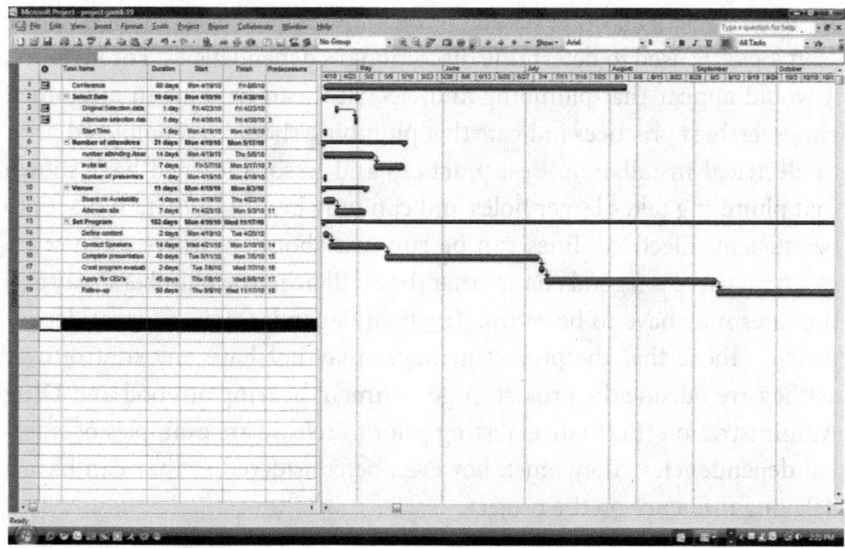

FIGURE 4.8
Gantt chart example.

room that needs uninterrupted power. A storm knocks out the power and the generator starts to keep the operating theater lighted and the necessary equipment functioning. The generator will not shut off (or finish its operation) until the main power is restored (started). An example of FF would be if you had multiple pieces of equipment being installed, and there is a task called "installation inspections complete," which means that as the equipment is being installed, inspections can be done. However, the "installation inspections complete" task will not be considered finished until the installation of the last piece of equipment is finished. If you have two tasks, one of which is to pour concrete for the foundation of the addition to a hospital and the other is to level the concrete, leveling can start simultaneously to the pouring, which is an SS relationship.

Other Dependency Considerations

There are three types of dependencies to be considered: mandatory, discretionary, and external. Mandatory dependencies are, as the name suggests, those dependencies that are inherent in the work. They may be physical limits imposed on the task. The relationship of a mandatory task is a finish-to-start relationship. In order to renovate a room, demolition of the room must take place. Discretionary dependencies are those tasks that are to be done in an order based on the knowledge of best practices. More "soft logic" is used to determine discretionary dependencies. For instance, it would appear that plumbing and electrical can be done in any order. However, best practices indicate that plumbing should be completed prior to electrical installation. Best practices and lessons learned have shown that plumbing takes larger holes and can only be run in certain places to be efficient. Electrical lines can be run just about anywhere. If they are run first, there is a good chance that they will be in the plumbers' way and the lines may have to be rerun. The final dependency is external dependencies, those that the project manager may not have any control over as they are outside the project. A government hearing or Food and Drug Administration (FDA) drug testing prior to release are examples of external dependencies. They must, however, be considered as they can have a delaying influence on the project.

Leads and Lags

Leads and lags can and should be considered when constructing the project schedule. Most project management tools, like Microsoft Project, for instance, allow for leads and lags. Lead time is used to overlap two tasks. For instance, for a beautification project, you should select the furnishings when the renovation is 50% complete. Lead times are entered into the schedule as negative (–) time. If the renovation will take 10 weeks, then the task of selecting furniture would be entered in the schedule as 10d–5d. The selection project would then begin 5 days into the renovation.

Lag time is delay or wait time. If you needed to pour a concrete slab prior to building a new addition, then the concrete will need some time to cure. Lag time is positive (+) time. For instance, if the task for pouring the foundation takes 2 days and the concrete takes 4 days to cure, then the task would be entered as 2d+4d so that the next finish-to-start task would not start until day 7. It is more accurate to enter the task as 2d+4d because entering 6d would indicate that pouring the concrete would take 6 days when in fact it only takes 2 days.

Calendars and Updating

There are two other considerations when putting together your schedule: (1) what your calendar will be and (2) how often the schedule needs to be updated. You calendar is the time that will be spent on the project. For instance, do you work four 10-hour days, or five 8-hour days, or something different? Will you be working holidays, or are there some holidays that need to be considered during the project's "life"? The software tools that you may be using to schedule your project will allow for these modifications to your schedule. If you are not using a tool, then make sure you consider the project's calendar.

When to update the project's schedule is an important consideration. The schedule is likely to change throughout the life of the project and may also be dependent on stakeholders' expectations. As the project progresses from planning to implementation, some tasks that were planned may take longer than anticipated due to equipment or resource availability, for instance, and the schedule will need to be modified, and maybe some other tasks further along in the schedule will need to be modified as well in order to keep the project's schedule. Additionally, requests may need to be made to project stakeholders to delay the project due to some risks that were identified but could not be mitigated. We'll talk more about risks in Chapter 13.

Sequencing Tasks

Prior to putting the final project schedule together, there is something else that needs to be determined: the order in which tasks have to be completed for the project to be successful. Sequencing tasks is a difficult undertaking. Many factors are required to properly sequence tasks:

- What are the tasks that need to be accomplished?
- Who is needed to accomplish the tasks?
- Who is available to accomplish the tasks?
- What tasks are first (predecessors)?
- What tasks have to follow (successors)?
- What are the dependencies or relationships between tasks and between people?
- If there are external products needed, when can those be obtained?
- What are the project milestones that must be met?
- Are there any assumptions or constraints that could affect the sequence of tasks?
- Is there anything else unique to this project that needs to be considered?

SCHEDULE DEVELOPMENT

Now that all project activities have been defined and sequenced, including the establishment of predecessor/successor relationships, and you've analyzed those sequences, durations, and resource requirements, the project schedule results. If all of the issues have been accurately addressed, the schedule should almost "fall out" of the exercise. It will be a matter of transferring the information to a project-scheduling tool or, in the case of a very small project, using a spreadsheet program.

SCHEDULE CONTROL

While we will talk about overall change control in Chapter 8, it is important to understand that some of the project management functions, particularly scheduling and cost, may need their own change control process. One of the necessary evils of a project is controlling the schedule in the event of a delay in the project. Two measures that may be employed in a project to help mitigate risk (see Chapter 9) are *crashing* and *fast tracking. An important thing to remember is that only tasks that can be crashed or fast tracked will benefit from these methods.* To fully understand the meaning of this statement, we'll look at crashing and fast tracking in some depth, because they are important tools in schedule risk mitigation. Both methods are used when a task or tasks on the critical path become delayed with the potential to affect the final project delivery date, or even putting interim milestone dates in jeopardy.

Crashing

Crashing a schedule means adding more resources to the task or tasks that have been delayed. Crashing a schedule will most likely add costs to the project. The other caution about crashing is that a particular task may not be able to be crashed. I use the example of a plumber under a sink. As much as you might like to get your plumbing problem completed sooner, there is only room for one plumber under the sink, so even if you hired a second plumber to help, it would not help the schedule. However, perhaps the plumber under the sink is willing to work more than the normal

8-hour day to help the project schedule (a schedule based on 5 days a week, 8 hours per day—see Calendars and Updating section). You will have to pay overtime, but at least the project can be crashed without trying to squeeze two plumbers under the sink.

Fast Tracking

Fast tracking is a little more involved than crashing. You will be changing the sequence in which the task or tasks you will be fast tracking are done in order to accomplish those tasks quicker. Fast tracking usually involves parallel effort. Tasks that had been scheduled in sequence may now be scheduled in parallel. The concern is that if Task B is waiting for Task A to complete because of some input needed, then if Task B were to be started without that input, when Task A completes in parallel, the outcome of Task A may be different than expected. That difference would not have as much impact on Task B had the input been given prior to the start of Task B, because of adjustments that could have been made to Task B, but may have a significant impact requiring rework or even scrapping of the effort for Task B.

A second method, and one with less risk, is breaking the task into smaller pieces and adding resources to the smaller tasks in an effort to speed up those tasks. For instance, continuing with the plumber example, perhaps the task involved requires the plumber to install the faucet and then make the connections under the sink. By breaking the project into cold water and hot water installation, one plumber can be installing the hot-water faucet while another plumber is making the cold-water connections.

Finally, perhaps the project needs to be evaluated for some options (see Chapter 8) to determine whether or not the project needs to change direction. Sometimes a task can neither be crashed nor fast tracked, and a more drastic approach may be necessary.

Managing project time is one of the major tasks that a project manager must undertake. On time is one of the keys to project success.

KEY REVIEW QUESTIONS

1. What are three of the forms that lessons learned can take?
2. What is the precedent diagramming method?

3. Why is project float not cumulative?
4. What is the difference between fast tracking and crashing?

5

Managing Project Costs

Managing costs, along with managing the project's time and scope are the keys to running a successful project. Remember the project manager's mantra from the previous chapter: "on time, within budget, and of the quality expected." Just like successfully managing a project's time, managing the cost depends on good groundwork.

Never ask of money spent
Where the spender thinks it went.
Nobody was ever meant
To remember or invent
What he did with every cent.

—Robert Frost

You may be able to get away with that sentiment when you are a famous poet, but as a project manager you need to account to your project sponsor (and stakeholders) for every dollar (or every cent) spent on the project.

ESTIMATING COST

Estimating costs requires the careful consideration of project resources—the people, materials, and equipment that are needed to successfully complete the project. It will involve choices and trade-offs, and requires the complete project definition. Where do you find that definition? You find that definition in the work breakdown structure (WBS). That is why a complete and accurate WBS of the project is so important. However, never consider the WBS "frozen." Like most project documents, these documents "live" until the end of the project. Changes to the documents may be necessary as conditions surrounding the project change. If you remember from our previous discussions, projects operate in a dynamic social, cultural, economic, and environmental climate.

To begin the process you need to answer the following questions:

- Who and what are needed?
- Who and what can do the work?
- Who and what are available?
- What level and competence is required?
- How will those resources be used?
- How will they affect the project's costs (and schedules)?

Some of the questions may seem to be similar, but those subtle differences can make the difference between project failure or project success. When we ask the question, "Who and what are needed?" it is asking for the best-case scenario, as if we are in a "perfect world." We already know from our real-world experiences that we rarely get everything we ask for. Once we have the answer to the first question, we need to ask the second one. "Who and what can do the work?" is asking what the minimum requirements are to do the project. Who are the individuals, and what functions will have to be performed? The next question focuses even more on the availability of the project's resources. "What level and competence is required?" is specifically asking about the human resources needed for the project. Do we need high-level managers in order to accomplish the tasks, or can we use lower-level, and therefore less expensive, managers to perform the tasks? The second part of the question deals with the competence of either the higher- or lower-level staff.

Even though we'll talk about project risks in more detail in Chapter 8, this is a good time to discuss the risk of, "How will those resources be used?" and, "How will they affect the project's costs (and schedule)?" These are both risks to the project. Will we need to use them full time or part time, and if we use them full time could it be full time plus overtime (which may affect costs and time)? The next short vignette further addresses potential effects on the project.

The EMR system requires that for the first year NCMC have a full-time first-shift administrator to manage the system and provide technical support. It also requires that there be a standby person on second and third shifts in case of any problems. Mary Ann Lords, IT Director, suggests that there are three IT personnel who will be furloughed because of recent funding cuts, and that the budget cost analysis consider those people in the equation. The advantage of the internal personnel is that they are already integrated into the organizational culture. They have also had internal leadership, safety, and project training required by the organization. New hires will have to attend training and it will take time to be integrated into the culture. That adds to the cost of bringing in someone from the outside. The disadvantage is that the internal people do not have all of the expertise required in the support role, and expenditures will have to be made to educate them. NCMC needs to consider the time required to train the individuals and if that will delay the project's complete date, as well as the time to educate and to integrate the new hires.

Cost Categories

When considering costing and budgeting, there are some specific cost categories to consider: direct costs and non-direct costs.

Direct Costs

Direct costs are costs that are directly attributable to the project. Let's take the example of the electronic medical records system (EMR) for NCMC. Basically, an EMR system is software loaded onto a hardware platform that provides a menu of functions including evaluation and management coding, laboratory interfacing, prescription information, scheduling, billing, custom forms if needed, history and physical exam information, patient chart information (subjective, objective, assessment, plan—SOAP), Health Level 7 interfaces if needed, for example. The software, training manuals, and trainers are examples of direct costs to the project. Those costs can be directly attributable to the project.

Variable Costs

Variable costs are costs that change directly in proportion to the level of production. If the company is producing the software for NCMC's EMR system, they also are producing software for other healthcare facilities. The disk used to hold the software will vary in number depending on the number of orders the company has for the software, as will the packaging used for each disk.

Indirect Costs

Indirect costs, therefore, are costs that are not directly attributable to the project. They may also be called *fixed* costs. They would be costs that are not easily assignable to specific functions, but may be used cross-functionally. For instance, the computer hardware on which the EMR system resides has multiple software applications, like the project management software used to schedule and manage the EMR project. Again, projects are undertaken in a dynamic environment, and project managers need to be dynamic in their approach. Fixed/indirect costs may also be the security guard assigned to the building; the receptionist; the general lighting, heating, and air conditioning for the building; the CEO's salary; or any other cost that is incurred on a project that cannot be specifically attributed to the project or product of the project. *Overhead* and *burden* are other terms that may be used for indirect costs.

Special Case Costs

Standard costs are costs that I consider "estimated costs." They are usually assigned to tasks that have been done over and over again, so that they have certain predictability. For instance, the costs of loading software onto NCMC's servers have been done over and over by the IT staff of NCMC. Therefore, once the effort of loading the software has been defined in the WBS, the hourly rate (or standard rate) can be applied to the effort. It doesn't need to be calculated again. However, one consideration that should be made with standard costs is that they are based on procedures that have been done many times. What they may not consider, as mentioned previously, is the dynamic environment and the definition of a project, particularly the word "uniqueness." It is likely to be an average, with the "actual costs" being higher or lower than they should be.

Sunk costs are costs that are *unrecoverable*. No matter what future circumstances occur on the project, these particular costs will not be recovered. This can cause a serious dilemma between the project manager and the project's stakeholders. Sometimes sunk costs are used to justify continuing a project. Large amounts of money (time can also be translated into money) have been spent on the project. In the face of, "We've already spent millions on this project; therefore, we need to continue it," the project manager must view the project from this point in time going forward, *not* this point in time looking backward and forward. If the project, according to the project team, financially doesn't make sense going forward, then the project doesn't make sense going forward, no matter how much time and effort was spent on the project. Pressure may be exerted to continue a project that does not make any sense to the project manager to continue; therefore, the project manager must carefully document the reasons for discontinuing a project for cause.

Capital Costs

Capital costs are costs for assets that have a useful life, usually defined as a year or more. Some projects will not have capital costs. Consider NCMC's EMR project. If computer hardware is considered part of the project, then the hardware having a useful life of more than 1 year would be a capital expenditure. The expenditure will have to be included in the project budget; the fact that it is a capital expenditure will be an accounting consideration, usually not part of the project information.

ASSESSING COSTS

Types of Estimates

See Table 5.1.

Order of Magnitude

An *order of magnitude* budget estimate is the type of estimate that you give your boss when you are caught in the elevator and asked, "I have an idea for a project to do X and Y; how much do you think that will

TABLE 5.1

Types of Estimating

Type of Estimate	Accuracy Range
Order of magnitude	–25% to +75%
Budget	–10% to +25%
Definitive	–5% to +10%

cost?" That estimate will be a "seat of your pants" estimate with very little thought or preparation. Prior to giving that estimate it should be clear that the estimate is very rough and has a very limited scope of accuracy. Some numbers that have been put on the accuracy of an order of magnitude estimate are –25% to +75% accuracy. In other words, there is a 100% swing in the accuracy.

Budget Estimate

A *budget estimate* is an estimate with a much better accuracy level, and therefore it requires some research in order to meet that accuracy level. It is not the type of estimate that a project manager can give off the top of his or her head, unless, of course, there is some historical data that the project manager possesses. The accuracy of a budget estimate is between –10% and +25%, with only a potential swing of 35%. As you can see, some thought and information will have to go into a budget estimate.

Definitive Estimate

The most accurate estimate that a project manager will have to give is a *definitive estimate.* That estimate has a –5% to +10% level of accuracy. When can the project manager honestly give a definitive estimate? The answer to that question is when and only when the work breakdown structure is complete and tested for accuracy. Giving a definitive estimate prior to that point in the project planning is a scenario for project failure. Time, cost, and quality management is the key to the successful management of a project, and cost is one of those criteria.

Pro Forma Assessments

Pro forma directly translated from Latin means "for form." A pro forma is an initial profile of project costs. Pro forma estimates tend to be refined until there is a particular level of comfort. Pro forma estimates can be order of magnitude, budget, or definitive estimates.

Other Estimating Considerations

There are additional costs and cost categories that should be considered, especially when making definitive estimates. For instance, there are costs incurred during the end of the implementation and the beginning of revenue-producing operations. The costs could be training, testing, travel, temporary labor, and added monitoring, for example. *Contingency allowances* and *management reserves*, although considered in risk response planning, should also be part of project budget estimating. A contingency allowance is usually used to allow for unplanned events, especially for projects that are leading edge, or information on similar past projects indicates the potential to overrun costs. It is a lump sum amount, controlled by either the project sponsor or the project manager, in some cases. Management reserves are specific accounts set aside for the contingency allowance. For projects that are undertaken in volatile environments, like a recession or period of rapid economic growth, an inflation or escalation allowance should be considered.

Estimating profit—if making a profit on the project is part of the project planning, then an estimate of profit should be included. The basic formula for estimating profit is as follows:

$$\text{Profit} = \text{Revenues} - \text{Costs}$$

For example,

1. Organization's return on investment (ROI) = 7%
2. Investment = $100,000
3. Working Capital = $10,000
4. Project Life = 2 years

Solving for the Average Yearly Profit (AYP):

$$0.07 = \text{AYP}/\$110{,}000 \text{ (Investment + Working Capital)}$$

$$\text{AYP} = \$7{,}700 * 2 \text{ Years} = \text{Total Profit of } \$15{,}400$$

Evaluating the results of the profit-estimating example we can see that the total profit for the project after 2 years is $15,400. The organization needs to determine if the 7% ROI will be sufficient for the $110,000 investment in the project. This project would likely be compared to any other anticipated projects and also to passive investments to determine the best use of the organization's resources. Always remember, however, that ROI is not the only reason to use an organization's resources.

Cost Estimating Tools

There are a couple of cost estimating techniques to help estimate project budgets: analogous, parametric, bottom up, 3/6 point estimating, and computerized tools.

Analogous Estimating

Probably one of the least expensive techniques to use to estimate costs is analogous estimating. Just as the word implies, analogous uses previous projects' similar tasks to estimate current project task costs. There are a couple of sources for this information: expert judgment and proper project close-out documentation. I'll talk more about proper project close-out in Chapter 10. For now, project close-out documentation should contain not only the estimated project costs, but also the actual costs. By manipulating the data using present-day costs of money, for instance, and depending on how closely related the tasks are, the cost estimates could be extremely accurate using analogous estimating.

Parametric Estimating

The National Aeronautics and Space Administration (NASA) defines parametric estimating as "one that uses Cost Estimating Relationships (CERs) and associated mathematical algorithms (or logic) to establish cost estimates. For example, detailed cost estimates for manufacturing and test of an end item (for instance, a hardware assembly) can be developed using very precise Industrial Engineering standards and analysis. Performed in this manner, the cost estimating process is laborious and time consuming. However, if history has demonstrated that test (as the dependent variable) has normally been valued at about 25% of the manufacturing value (the independent variable), then a detailed test estimate need not be performed and can simply be computed at the 25% (CER) level. It is important, though, that any CERs used be carefully tested for validity using standard statistical approaches."[1] For those who are interested in more detail about parametric estimating, NASA provides a detailed *Parametric Cost Estimating Handbook*, available at http://cost.jsc.nasa.gov/PCEHHTML/pceh.htm. A point to remember is that there needs to be a Cost Estimating Relationship like cost per square foot to be most effective. For instance, if the average cost to remodel a hospital room is $500/sq ft, then the estimate of the cost to remodel 10 rooms at approximately 300 square feet each is $1,500,000.

Bottom-Up Estimating

The most accurate and also the most time-consuming, and therefore the most expensive, cost estimating technique is bottom-up cost estimating. It uses the work breakdown structure as a basis to estimate costs. Each task is estimated and then the tasks are added together as you reverse the decomposition. The major deliverable costs are then added together to get the total cost of the entire project. When I said that this may be the most accurate of the methods, if it is done correctly, that statement is true. However, there is a tendency for people to "pad" their task estimates. This is really a response to the risk of underestimating a project task. However, if there is too much padding added to an estimate, the project's total budget may exceed the organization's budget guidelines, effectively killing the project.

Once all of the cost estimating exercises are complete and costs have been determined for all project tasks, a budget is then put together. The budget may then go through several cycles to revise estimates, update costs, or remove any items that have been determined to be nonessential or not be directly related to the project. After the final budget has been approved by the sponsor, the project manager then begins the process of allocating those costs as the project unfolds.

ALLOCATING BUDGETED COSTS

Once project costs have been budgeted it is just a matter of spending the money on the resources that have been identified, right? Not so fast. Budgeting the project costs is a matter of efficiently allocating the project budget that has been based on the project's task estimates. Since, by definition, projects consume limited resources, and money is one of the most limited resources, efficiently allocating that limited resource will contribute to the success of the project. So the question is how do project managers and their project teams determine the most effective use of the project budget? In other words, are the financial resources allocated based on how they were budgeted? The answer is not necessarily. The object of disciplined project management is to look for ways to conserve resources because both time and costs are estimates; therefore, there will probably be overestimations and underestimations. It is almost as if you are trying to establish a contingency in real time.

What are some of the tools that can help you allocate costs? The tools used to allocate costs are the same tools that were used for estimating costs:

- Analogous – uses similar project data to allocate funds
- Parametric – uses cost estimating relationships and mathematical algorithms
- Bottom up – allocating costs based on the WBS
- Computerized tools – populating spreadsheets with data and formulas and then manipulating the costs to see how the bottom line is affected

Managing project costs, along with managing project time, quality, and expectations are the four most important functions the project manager can perform in order for a project to be successful.

KEY REVIEW QUESTIONS

1. What are key questions that need to be asked prior to estimating project costs?
2. Give an example of each of the following: direct cost, variable cost, and indirect cost.
3. What are the three types of estimating and their accuracy ranges?

ENDNOTE

1. *Parametric Cost Estimating Handbook,* Introduction, p. 1, http://cost.jsc.nasa.gov/pcehhtml/pceh.htm

6

Managing Project Quality

Believe it or not, quality initiatives and the focus on quality as we know it today is a relatively new endeavor. There are two considerations when managing project quality: (1) the quality of the product of the project, whatever that may be, and (2) the quality of the process for managing the project. Both of those issues will be considered. However, before we get into the considerations, let's first take a look at the history of quality from a general domestic view, an international view, and finally a specific healthcare environment view.

HISTORY OF QUALITY IN THE UNITED STATES

Traditionally, when manufacturing was in its infancy and major production houses were more like "sweat" shops, inspection was the quality management of choice. Most everything was handmade until Henry Ford put in the first moving assembly line in 1913. Even after that invention, manufacturers continued to use inspection. That was a perfectly plausible approach as long as we had a captive audience for our products. We could afford the scrap involved with inspecting quality in rather than building quality in. The costs of scrapping could be absorbed by increasing the product costs. Even when the first quality efforts were undertaken in the thirteenth century by various guild members, again, that was on a one-to-one basis and the cost of the products reflected the amount of the quality effort. There were actually committees formed to "inspect" goods for flaws. This is still an example of quality by inspection.

It wasn't until early in the twentieth century that "quality gurus" began to surface, studying manufacturing processes and connecting the dots between the quality of the product of the manufacturing process and the process of manufacturing the product. Interestingly, but not so unusual after I explain, AT&T was used as a testing ground for not only quality efforts, but also motivational efforts, as detailed in Chapter 7. Western Electric, the manufacturing arm of AT&T, had a facility know as the Hawthorne Works in Cicero, Illinois, from 1905 until it closed in 1983. Early telephone equipment, the "high tech" electronics at the time, was manufactured there. For the first time, goods were being manufactured requiring skilled labor that needed to deal with tight manufacturing tolerances and high quality. No longer could a manufacturer rely on inspection to insure quality. Walter Shewhart, a Bell Laboratories (AT&T's research and development arm) engineer, first realized that in order to manage quality, data was needed. Shewhart was also known as the "father of statistical process control." Using the Hawthorne Works as a testing ground, Shewhart developed Statistical Process Control methods to address data collection and the Shewhart Cycle Learning and Improvement Cycle, "combining both creative management thinking with statistical analysis. This cycle contains four continuous steps: Plan, Do, Study and Act. These steps (commonly referred to as the PDSA cycle)"[1] are the precursor to continuous improvement.

Around the late 1930s, W. Edwards Deming, working as a mathematical physicist for the U.S. Department of Agriculture (USDA), invited Shewhart to lecture on statistics. I believe that this is when Deming was bitten by the "quality bug." He was always statistically focused, but now he was combining an extensive knowledge of statistics and mathematics to the new field of quality improvement. While working at the Bureau of the Census in the early 1940s, Deming was asked his opinion on ways to aid the war effort. His advice was to present a short course on Shewhart's methods. The advice was accepted, and courses were held often with Deming as instructor. The influence of these courses formed the basis of the statistical quality control movement. Because of his earlier work with the USDA, Deming was sent to Japan to help the war-torn country with repairing its agricultural production. On a later trip, Deming made contact with Japanese statisticians and developed a great relationship with them and other Japanese. Some of the people Deming made contact with were engineers and scientists involved with the reconstruction of Japan's manufacturing industry. Deming began teaching and consulting statistical process control to the Japanese, who embraced the study and began to apply it to their quality problems. What Deming gave the Japanese was the confidence to pursue quality excellence, and the rest is history.

TABLE 6.1

Quality Trilogy

Quality planning	• Identify the customers. • Determine the needs of those customers. • Translate those needs into our language. • Develop a product that can respond to those needs. • Optimize the product features so as to meet our needs and customer needs.
Quality improvement	• Develop a process that is able to produce the product. • Optimize the process.
Quality control	• Prove that the process can produce the product under operating conditions with minimal inspection. • Transfer the process to Operations.

In the meantime, his quality efforts in the United States fell on relatively deaf ears. As a matter of fact, it took nearly 30 years of getting beaten by Japanese automotive quality for Ford Motor Company to "invite" Deming and his ideas into their automotive manufacturing. As a result of instituting Deming's quality initiatives, Ford became a quality leader capturing the SUV market with its Ford Explorer during the 1990s.

Another quality "guru" of the time was Joseph Juran, who also helped Japanese quality efforts and has ties to Shewhart, Deming, and AT&T's Hawthorne Works. In 1926 Juran worked in the new Inspection Statistical Department at the Hawthorne Works, a department championed by Walter Shewhart. Juran worked in the quality management field for more than 70 years. His *Quality Control Handbook*, first released in 1951, is still used as a reference. "Dr. Juran was the first to incorporate the human aspect of quality management which is referred to as Total Quality Management (TQM)."[2] A second book, *Quality Is Free*, written in 1979, is a seminal work that points out the fact that the expense of quality is outweighed by the benefits of quality efforts, yielding a zero sum. Table 6.1[3] outlines the major points of Dr. Juran's quality management ideas.

PROJECT QUALITY MANAGEMENT

The Project Management Institute[4] provides the following fundamentals for Project Quality Management: project planning, quality assurance, and quality control.

Project Planning

The project planning process includes identifying the relevant project standards—industry, organizational, stakeholder—and how to satisfy those project standards. Industry standards include best practices and regulatory requirements. The organization will likely have its own quality policy, while stakeholders may have more obtuse standards that have to be investigated, including those that drive purchasing decisions. A leading philosophical tenet is that quality must be planned in, not inspected. This is the philosophy that was adopted by those early quality gurus, as opposed to the original quality efforts of allowing quality to be inspected in. Within the planning process certain factors must be considered: cost-benefit analysis including project constraints (cost, schedule, *quality*, and scope), benchmarking from other similar projects, and the use of other quality tools to be discussed later in this chapter.

Quality Management Tools

I'd like to briefly cover some of the more relevant quality tools that may be used or at least understood by the project manager: flow charts, cause and effect diagrams, checklists, Pareto diagrams, histograms, control or run charts, and scatter plots.

Flow Charts

Probably one of the most widely used tools for quality management is the flow chart. It is a great visual representation of a process from beginning to end. It also allows the user to manipulate the tasks within the process flow for optimization. The most effective way to use flow-charting is to first gather all the information relative to the process flow, experiential data, and lessons learned. The best method is then to capture the flow using the standard flow chart shapes: rectangles for processes, diamonds for decision points, and so on. Once the flow is captured then it is best to try to find someone who is familiar with the process to double check the flow. Once that is done, you can try different scenarios in the flow chart until you feel that it captures the best flow. Trial that flow against the current process. If the new one is more effective than the present one, standardize the new one.

Cause-and-Effect Diagrams

One of my favorite quality tools is the cause and effect diagram, also called a fishbone or Ishikawa. (It is also used in project planning [see Figures 2.1 and 2.2]). First introduced in by Kaoru Ishikawa in the 1960s, the cause and effect diagram is a graphical representation used to group ideas into usable and actionable categories. When done properly, it is an easily understandable view of the potential causes of an issue to be investigated, hopefully leading to a successful issue resolution. From my experience with cause and effect diagrams, it is usual to work your way through the causes and find an issue resolution among the choices and stop the investigation. It is important, however, to consider the rest of the choices because underlying the effect could be multiple causes.

Check Sheets

The most common of all quality tools, and one you may not even think of as a quality tool, is the check sheet, or as known in some circles, the checklist. It is as simple as a shopping list or to-do list, but can be a critical piece of a project manager's toolbox. In the "heat of battle," details can be overlooked, unless those details are captured on your checklist. By having those details captured and ready at hand, the project manager can easily check to make sure that those details are being addressed.

Pareto Charts

Another important quality tool is the Pareto chart (see Figure 6.1). These charts are particularly effective when looking for the frequency of events as compared to each other. The purpose of a Pareto chart is to graphically represent the different events to see which of the events occur the most and order them from left to right from the most to the least occurring event. Because of the arrangement by frequency it is easy to determine the event to be considered first by looking to the left columns. Some of the issues to consider for determining or reviewing a Pareto chart are what categories to use to group the issues, what measurements to use, what time period to cover, and how to determine the appropriate scale.

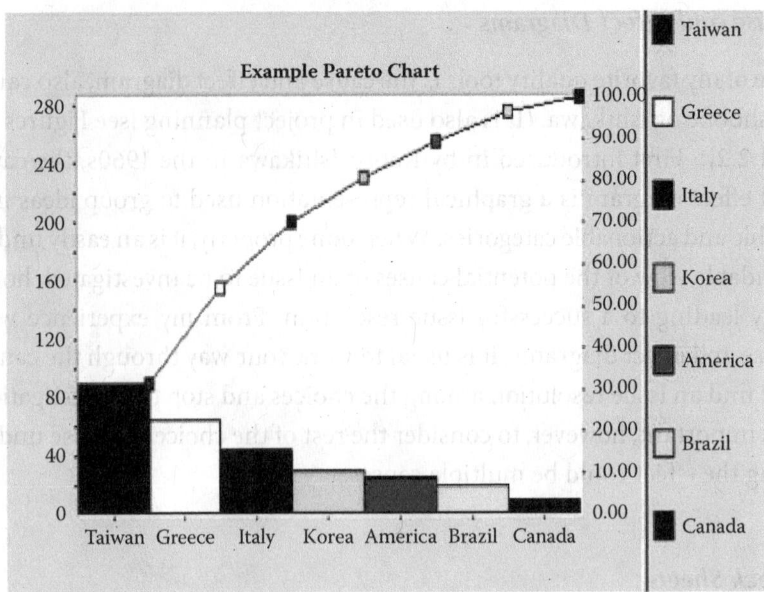

FIGURE 6.1
Pareto chart example.

Histograms

Histograms are also "frequency" charts (see Figure 6.2). They differ from Pareto charts in that histograms represent data ranges rather than individual data points. A histogram is constructed from a frequency table. The frequency intervals are shown on the x-axis and the number of data points are collected on the y-axis.

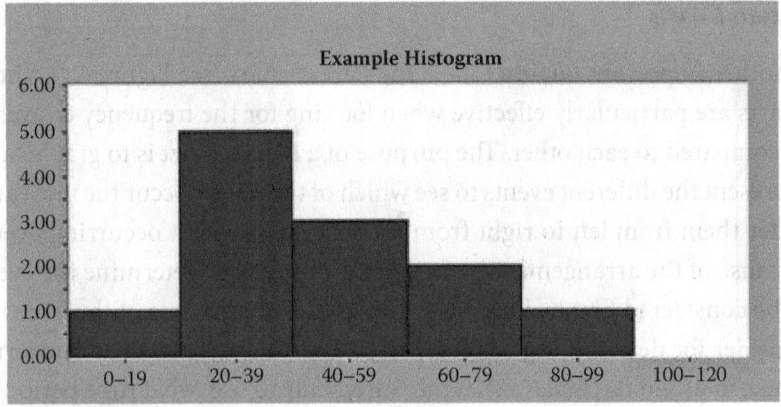

FIGURE 6.2
Histogram example.

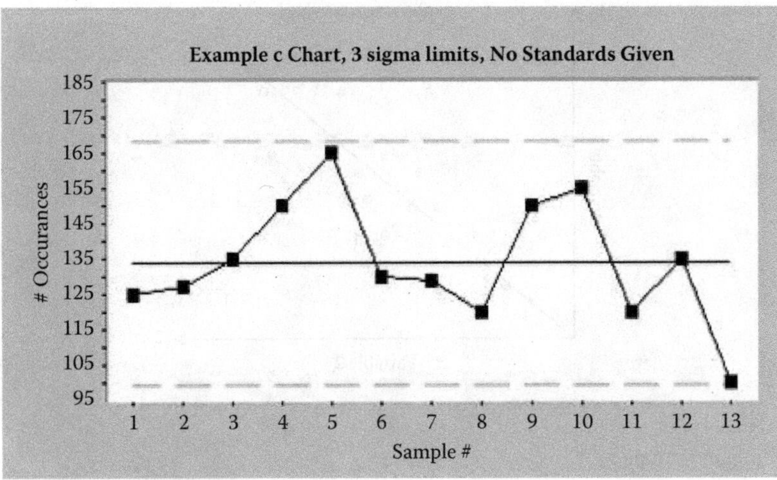

FIGURE 6.3
Control chart example.

Control Charts

Most healthcare professionals are familiar with control charts, also known as run charts (see Figure 6.3). They are usually used for process control and are represented by using an average or mean and an upper and lower control limit to the process. The process is charted against its mean to see how much deviation there is in the process. The upper and lower limits are sometimes defined using different sigma or standard deviations from the mean. If the process exceeds the upper control limit or goes below the lower control limit, the process is judged to be out of limits and may need corrective action.

Scatter Plot

The final quality tool of interest is the scatter plot (see Figure 6.4). A scatter plot is used to map the relationship between two variables. The stronger the correlation between the variables, the straighter the line in the scatter plot. Scatter plots can handle a large amount of data points. They can also be used to determine trends by plotting the data points.

Project Quality Control

Quality control (QC) may be thought of as the first line of quality defense. It is both a function within an organization and a methodology. As a function, the QC department looks at the details of the *product and the*

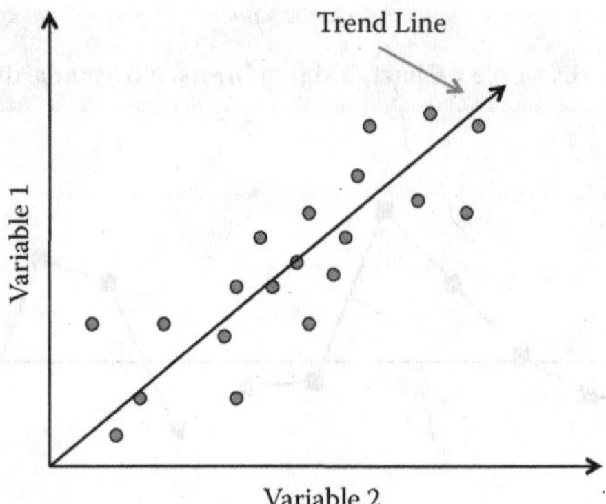

FIGURE 6.4
Scatter plot example.

processes. In a manufacturing environment, QC may take random samples from the production line to ensure that the quality specifications of that product are within acceptable limits. When looking at processes, QC uses tools like control charts (discussed in detail later in this chapter) to ensure that the processes are within the specified control limits. Those are examples of methods to monitor the project's *product* and *processes*. However, for the project manager, controlling the quality of the project management process, is the first order of business, although the output (or product) of the project and its related processes are critical to the overall success. Examples of project management processes are the communications plan, overall quality plan, and the jeopardy process.

Project Quality Assurance

Quality assurance (QA) is both a function (and department) within an organization and the methodology involved in assuring quality within a product or process. The QA department within an organization is the department that ends up "checking the checker." It is the sampling organization that samples the samples. In other words, QA will sample the samples that have been taken by QC to ensure that the QC department is following the organization's quality control policy and that the quality assurance initiatives are effective. Quality assurance looks at the "big picture." It looks at the elements of the project in totality. Once again, QA also looks at the processes involved as well as the product of the project, assuring that those processes are adequately controlled by QC.

What Is Quality?

In order to appreciate quality efforts, quality should be defined. There are many different views as to what quality means, and all are relevant to the project manager. It is imperative that the project manager understand the viewpoint of those who are the stakeholders in the project. Additionally, in any project, the variety of stakeholders can provide a variety of different understandings of what quality means.

A Transcendent Approach

Transcendent quality is a more philosophical than real approach to quality, although those who view quality as transcendent may not even know that they view it that way and feel that their view is very real. This is the nature of a transcendent approach. There is an innate quality of excellence that is potentially indefinable. "Quality is neither mind nor matter, but a third entity independent of the two … even though Quality cannot be defined, you know what it is."[5] This is also the nature of transcendent quality: "You know it when you see it." When transcendent quality is a focus of a stakeholder, it can be very difficult, not only to identify the quality driver, but to also know how to satisfy that driver.

Product-Based Approach

The product-based approach is much easier to manage because it is "real." In other words, the nature of a product-based approach is that there is some ingredient or attribute that gives it a suitable or desirable quality. There is some measurable attribute that is more desirable if present and less desirable if not. If that attribute is present, the stakeholder is willing to pay more. "Differences in quality amount to differences in the quality of some desired ingredient or attribute."[6] In healthcare, patient survey results can give insight into the attributes that can improve the quality of an organization based on a product-based approach.

User-Based Approach

User-based quality "lies in the eye of the beholder." It is a personal view, although different from the transcendent approach. This quality approach uses the marketplace as a balance. It is more of a universally acceptable quality approach based on many, many users having the same "fitness for use" and personal view of the particular quality of a product. It is a shared "personal view" based on market demand for a certain quality feature. "In the final analysis of the marketplace, the quality of a product depends on how well it fits patterns of consumer preferences."[7] Again, a patient survey can contribute to the understanding of a user-based approach to improving quality. One of the scores that may be of interest is the "bedside manner" of the doctors and nurses.

Manufacturing-Based Approach

The most straightforward and easily understandable quality approach is that of manufacturing-based quality. Quality is measured by the conformance to a set of requirements, design specifications, or general specifications. In order to measure against the requirements, a clear and acceptable set of requirements or specifications needs to be established. The measurements are very specific, such as *zero defects*. Expressions like "get it right the first time" are also used with a manufacturing-based approach. "Quality means conformance to requirements."[8] Whether procedures are being followed is an indicator used by healthcare professionals to relate to a "manufacturing-based" quality attribute.

Value-Based Approach

Value-based quality is based on price. In this view, in order to have high quality, the product or service must perform as advertised and it must conform to the expectations of the stakeholder at an acceptable price. The interesting part about the value-based approach is that quality can be viewed across a wide variety of prices relatively evenly. An expensive product or service that delivers on the advertised (or for that matter perceived) performance is viewed as having the same quality as a less expensive product or service that also performs as advertised depending on the price charged and the value perceived or expected for that product or service. "Quality means best for certain customer conditions. These conditions are (a) the actual use and (b) the selling price of the product."[9] In today's market, with the variety of financial responsibility methods, it is hard to get a handle on whether or not the services rendered are worth the cost of those services. However, the "life-saving" factor of some procedures will heavily influence a positive response.

Quality of Service Approaches

Healthcare is a service-based industry. Primary stakeholders, the patients, are looking for certain aspects of service quality. There are several aspects of service quality to be considered: reliability, responsiveness, assurance, empathy, and tangibles. Stakeholders' expectations are for these services to be provided reliably and dependably, that there be a willingness to provide the services, and that the services be provided promptly. They want competence, confidence, understanding, and courtesy. Additionally, stakeholders want clean and modern facilities and equipment. Finally, stakeholders are looking for their providers to have a professional appearance.

So what do these approaches to quality have to do with the healthcare professional? To best serve the stakeholder (patients, other healthcare professionals, the community, administration, and more), it is imperative that you understand the stakeholder's approach to quality. Each stakeholder may have his or her own approach to quality; therefore, if you are trying to satisfy one approach, but another approach is more relevant to a specific stakeholder, then you are missing the mark. Missing the mark can lead to a loss of confidence in the healthcare provider's quality. As a result of that loss of confidence, the stakeholder will seek an alternative. It is therefore imperative that all quality approaches be considered when planning, organizing, and implementing healthcare projects.

The qualities of service approaches are more obvious. What they do, however, is provide a basis for a number of service improvement projects. Examples of some of the projects undertaken are facility improvements (from new paint to new hospital wings), new equipment and equipment upgrade projects, educational programs for helping healthcare personnel with patient handling skills, and increased competence training.

Basic Statistical Concepts Used in Quality Assessment

While not required in detail, the project manager needs a basic understanding of statistical concepts.

Attributes and Variables

Two elements of data collection are attributes and variables. An attribute can be defined as something that is inherent, something that never changes. The place and time you were born are some of your attributes. A variable is a data point that can change. Hair color and eye color are human variables.

Mean, Median, Mode

The mean is the average, the median is the mid-point, and the mode is the most common data point in an array of data points. For the numbers 1, 2, 3, 3, 4, 4, 5, 5, 5, and 6, the average is 398/10 = 3.8, the median is 38/2 = 19, and the mode is 5.

Range, Variance, Standard Deviation

Range, variance, and standard deviation are all used in the measurement of dispersion.

The range is the simplest measure of dispersion. Numbers are ranked from the highest to the lowest, the lowest number is subtracted from the highest number, and the difference is the range.

Variance is the squared average of a number of values. The square root of the variance is then taken to determine the standard deviation. The standard deviation is the "spread' or distribution of the values around the mean. As an example, you may want to find the standard deviation of the weight of women who used the emergency room over the last day to use for a study. The chart data shows the following weights: 110, 150, 155, 170, 100, 160, 190, 100, 105, 130, and 120. The average weight is 145.46 (1490 – the total divided by 11 – the number of observations). To find the variance, take each weight, subtract the average (i.e., first weight, 110–145.46 = –35.46), square it (i.e., 1257.41), and add the squared differences together and divide the total by the number of observations. For example, (1257.41 + 20.61 + 91.01 + 602.21 + 2066.61 + 211.41 + 1983.81 + 2066.61 + 1637.01 + 239.01 + 648.21)/11 (number of observations) = 983.99 and then take the square root = 31.37, which is the standard deviation between the weights. By using three standard deviations from the mean, and by inferring that the samples taken are representative of all women who visit the emergency room, 99% of the women will weigh between 176.83 pounds and 115.09 pounds. One of the best quotes I've seen and something to keep in mind when using statistics is from Andrew Lang (1844–1912), a Scottish poet, novelist, and literary critic, who said "He uses statistics as a drunken man uses lamp-posts—for support rather than illumination."[10] So, when using statistics, use them for illumination.

THE COST OF QUALITY

It is one of those "pay me now or pay me later" scenarios. There is a cost associated with quality or with non-quality. There are prevention costs, appraisal costs, and rework/failure costs. Prevention costs, those costs incurred in an effort to meet a customer's expectations and avoid defects, rework, and errors, includes training, process, and procedures developed to increase effectiveness, and meetings/reviews to ensure conformance to the customer's requirements. Appraisal costs, those costs incurred by measuring the performance of processes, products, or procedures against acceptable standards, include quality control, quality assurance, and the evaluation of products, processes, and procedures. Failure costs are inevitable. That is why products have warranties. However, with increased vigilance, and prevention and appraisal processes, failure costs can be greatly reduced. If quality standards are not followed, additional failure costs will be incurred including waste, cleanup, rework, fines, lawsuits, lost business, and moral issues.

SUMMARY

Managing a project's quality, whether it is the high quality of the product of the project or the low quality of the project management processes, is one of the most important tasks that a project manager can undertake. Managing quality has been compared to project management as really being the same thing. When you look at the aspects of project management (cost and schedule control, risk management, and the procurement process, for instance), the ultimate goal is to successfully manage those aspects to increase the chances for a successful project. Successfully managing those aspects means that they are executed with the highest quality achievable. Therefore, managing projects is managing quality.

KEY REVIEW QUESTIONS

1. Why should quality be *planned in* rather than *inspected in*?
2. What are the *four* fundamentals of quality management according to the Project Management Institute?

3. What is the *key* difference between quality control and quality assurance?
4. Name *four* quality management tools and explain their uses.
5. Name *two* quality *approaches* and explain their *key* differences.
6. What is the difference between an *attribute* and a *variable*?
7. What are the *three* costs of quality?

ENDNOTES

1. Skymark, *Walter Shewhart—The grandfather of total quality management*, http://www.skymark.com/resources/leaders/shewart.asp
2. Skymark, *Joseph M. Juran*, http://www.skymark.com/resources/leaders/juran.asp
3. Skymark, *Joseph M. Juran*, http://www.skymark.com/resources/leaders/juran.asp
4. Project Management Institute, IC, 14 Campus Boulevard, Newtown Square, PA, www.pmi.org
5. Pirsig, Robert M., *Zen and the Art of Motorcycle Maintenance*, Bantam, New York, 1984, pp. 185–213.
6. Abbott, L., *Quality and Competition*, Greenwood Press, London, 1973, pp. 126–127.
7. Keuhn, A. A., and Day, R. L., "Strategy of Product Quality," *Harvard Business Review*, November–December 1954, p. 831.
8. Crosby, P. B., *Quality Is Free*, Mentor Press, Seattle, 1980, p. 15.
9. Feigenbaum, A. V., *Total Quality Control*, 4th edition, McGraw-Hill, Princeton, NJ, 2004, p. 1.

7

Communications

As in real estate where it is about location, location, location, for project management it is about communication, communication, communication. Communication is about being heard, being understood, creating actions, and following up on those actions. It is about fields of experience—that field in which you live and that field in which others live. Where those two fields overlap is the area of shared experience. The larger the overlap, the larger the shared area of experience and the easier it is to communicate. That is why people who are very familiar with each other can finish each other's sentences. Their area of shared experience is so large that they can almost think and, more importantly, be understood without any further explanation. In contrast, if the area of shared experience is very small, it is more difficult to communicate. I always use the example of when I was learning mathematics and I asked my father for help. Being a budget analyst for a major defense contractor, he had to add at least three zeros to the problem to be able to help me. His field of experience and mine did overlap, but not so much as to be able to communicate without adding those zeros. Teenagers and parents seem to have a very small area of shared experience, although if communications are conducted carefully, that area can expand exponentially. Table 7.1 is provided to help you understand which communication methods are the most effective.

Elizabeth Harrin[1] provided the following case study for your review:

Healthcare Case Study: Building a Consultant Database

One of the projects I did when working for a healthcare insurance firm was to launch an online database of specialists and hospitals. The project involved giving Web access to all the consultant and hospital information to customers. We had a lot of the information internally anyway, and all the

TABLE 7.1

Table of Communications

	Oral Effectiveness	Written Effectiveness	Oral and Written Effectiveness
General overview	Med	Med	High
Immediate action required	Med	Low	High
Future action required	Low	High	Med
Directive/order/policy change	Low	Med	High
Progress report to supervisor	Low	Med	High
Awareness campaign	Low	Low	High
Commendation	Low	Low	High
Reprimand	High	Low	Med
Conflict resolution	High	Low	Med

consultants were contacted and asked if they would be willing to have their information publicly available as part of the database. The objective was to offer insurance customers an extra benefit—a searchable, online directory of places they could go that would be covered by their insurance, and of people they could see for their treatment under their insurance plans. This would help them plan their treatment accordingly.

As the project manager, I worked with both the marketing and technical teams to co-ordinate the production of the database. The look and feel was developed by communications experts to fit with the existing corporate Web site. My role was to project manage the successful launch. I was a relatively new project manager and reported to the e-commerce Program Manager—the database project was part of an overall initiative to revamp our online presence both internally (through intranet developments) and externally.

The biggest challenge was coordinating the creative minds of the marketing and communications stakeholders. Once they had seen the prototype database there were several requests for changes that unfortunately would have meant significant technical re-writes. Where I could accommodate changes, this was managed through a change control process, where the implications of any change were noted and assessed before a decision was taken.

I was fortunate to be working with an excellent technical team. The technical lead provided updates and kept me informed of any difficulties she encountered, which meant I was able to revise the plans and the schedule accordingly.

As the project formed part of a larger program, I provided updates at the program meetings on a weekly basis. Risks and issues were discussed as part of the program monthly risk review meeting. The Marketing Manager responsible for the Web site was available for me to consult on the details of the project as and when required, which was invaluable.

Something I learned through working on this project was that it is essential to have stakeholder buy-in from the specialists concerned. There is a raft of data protection legislation that needs to be considered and we had to be sure we were only sharing information online that we had permission to publish. All the data had to be checked to ensure it was up to date, and we had to consider how we would keep data up to date on an ongoing basis.

Once the database was live it was great to be able to show colleagues and family, and say, "I made that happen." While I didn't code it, design it, or even come up with the idea, I know that good project management practices helped us as a team deliver a great service to customers, and I was pleased at the part I had to play in making the database a reality.

THE PROCESS OF COMMUNICATING

As I said before, communication is all about fields and shared experiences. An idea is generated. That idea goes from thought to words, and those words are composed in a message and sent to a receiver. The words are sent either in written format or spoken format. The receiver then translates those words into thoughts and understanding and prepares a feedback message. The feedback words are transmitted via some media, probably in the same format as the original transmission. The sender of the original message goes through the same process of translating the feedback, and the conversation continues. The communications process uses a channel to carry the transmissions. That channel can be affected in many ways. We'll talk more about things that can affect a channel in the section Barriers to Communications later in this chapter.

Methods of Communicating

All methods of communication take on a different meaning in our high tech world. In the past, the most influential method of communication, face-to-face, included vocal, tone and pitch, nonverbal, body language, and verbal, the actual words of the message. However, the actual words only carried about 10% of the message. Tone and pitch influenced about 40% of the message and nonverbal about 50% of the message. Vocal and nonverbal added together influenced about 90% of the message. In order to be "heard" one had to be cognizant of the vocal and nonverbal much more than the actual words. However, with written communications there is really no vocal and nonverbal, so the choice of words is much more important. With the advent of e-mail, texting, and social media, and the brevity of those communication methods, extreme care must be taken when choosing words in order to accurately communicate.

Meaning is much more easily distorted by the receiver's perceptions. Those perceptions include some of the *barriers to communications* that we will talk about later in this chapter, like whether or not the receiver trusts the senders. The third method to communicate is on the telephone. While there are no nonverbal communications, I believe that the vocal piece makes up the majority of the message, about 60%, and the verbal piece about 40%. It is therefore important to focus on tone, inflection, volume, rate of speaking, quality of your voice (clarity), semantics, and grammar, as the focus is on the words of your message. And, in this instance, your words carry much more of your message that they do in face-to-face communications. The reason (or meaning) for the verbal piece of communications is to inform, instruct, and explain. It should be much easier to do that with written communications, secondly with telephone conversations, and hardest with face-to-face communications.

Conditions of Communications

The conditions of communications depend on the message and the audience. It should be a conscious choice, not driven by emotions, although emotions do play a role in good communications. In project communications there will be times when all of the communication conditions occur at the same time. The conditions are empathy, respect, warmth, concreteness, genuineness, self-disclosure, and supportive confrontation. To communicate with empathy, one has to be able to relate to the situation. Communicating with respect is always the best way to communicate. Always relating to your audience as human beings may seem like something that should be ingrained, but mean-spirited communications occur frequently, and the lessons learned by the receiver are not easily forgotten. That makes the next course of communications even more difficult. Genuineness and warmth, like empathy and respect, are conditions that not only help the receiver "listen," but also help the sender formulate the true message of the communication. Picking the words that form the message using the conditions of empathy, warmth, respect, and genuineness will allow the receiver to feel safer and therefore more open to the message.

Concreteness is a necessary condition of communications in healthcare. The ability to communicate the message accurately and with a minimum of "fluff" is important to help patients and patients' families understand exactly the issues that are being addressed. People do not have a tendency to ask questions of their physicians for clarity; therefore, that clarity needs to be provided up front in the message.

A final condition for communications occurs when there is confrontation. The reaction to confrontation should be support. In order to gain the confidence of the receiver, to get the receiver to listen, supportive confrontation should be practiced. When you need to be confrontational, do it in a way that

BARRIERS TO COMMUNICATIONS

There are so many barriers to communications that sometimes I wonder why we even bother trying to communicate. But we all know why we must not just communicate, but be accomplished communicators.

Preconceived notions, ideas, or screening through our own expectations at times can prevent us from getting the right message. Sometimes we want to look at information through a different "lens," for instance, an environmental lens if we want to keep an environmental awareness about our communications. We also screen communications based on some notion or idea about a subject, and therefore are not open to listening. We will also *deny* information if it is contrary to what we believe or if it doesn't fit the stereotype we were expecting. The use of *personalized meanings* at best is distracting and at the worst makes communications not comprehendible.

Certainly *lack of motivation or interest* plays an important role in both sending and receiving communications. It can be very obvious when the sender lacks the enthusiasm or interest in the subject being communicated. Equally obvious is the apparent lack of interest or enthusiasm about the communication being received. The sender's issue of *lack of communications skills* could be a major cause in the receiver's lack of interest. It could also cause the sender, because of the anxiety about not having good communications skills, to appear unenthusiastic. *Noise, distractions,* or *multi-tasking* could manifest themselves as appearing to have a lack of interest for both the sender and the receiver. *Distrust* or *lack of credibility* of the source of the information, whether or not it is directed at the sender, can be a barrier to the receiver. There is a *halo effect* and *reference group influence.* Both can be barriers or enhancements to communications. They can be barriers in that they can influence the meaning of the communications, i.e., make them more believable when they are not. They can be enhancements in that, if the communications are accurate, they are enforced by the credibility of the "haloed" one or by the respectability of the reference group.

Information overload can be a barrier to communications. The amount of information absorbed during a communication may be limited. It is important, therefore, to *always consider your audience.* For instance, if you are communicating with high-level executives, your communications should be brief and to the point. The executives usually have a lot of business to conduct and are looking for a "snapshot" of information, an "executive summary." Engineers, on the other hand, may want excruciating detail because they may need to make a decision based on your information. Finally, a *poor organizational climate* can be a major barrier to communications. Communicating within functional organizations or those that are organized into silos is notoriously difficult. Communications usually go bottom to top, following a "chain of command," and then across functions and down the chain. Messages are often garbled by the time they reach the intended audience because of the layers through which they've had to pass.

Whether it is a poor organizational environment, information overload, or any number of other barriers to communications, communications under the best of circumstances is difficult. But understanding those barriers and overcoming them will lead to improved communications.

IMPROVING YOUR COMMUNICATIONS

The more comfortable you are with yourself, the more comfortable you will be when communicating with others. One way to improve your self-comfort level is through self-efficacy. Self-efficacy "is the belief that one is capable of performing in a certain manner or attaining certain goals."[2] "It is a belief that one has the capabilities to execute the courses of actions required to manage prospective situations. Unlike efficacy, which is the power to produce an effect (in essence, competence), self-efficacy is the belief (whether or not accurate) that one has the power to produce that effect. For example, a person with high self-efficacy may engage in a more health related activity when an illness occurs, whereas a person with low self-efficacy would harbor feelings of hopelessness."[3] It is not self-esteem, a person's sense of worth, but rather the way a person perceives his or her own abilities to reach a goal. Self-efficacy beliefs are what drive how we think, feel, and motivate ourselves, and our ability to motivate others. Remember, communications does one of three things: informs, instructs, or explains. In order to do any of those things, you must be able to "sell" your message. From an article by Albert Bandura,[4] the following are ways to improve your self-efficacy, which will improve your communications (interpersonal) skills:

- Set challenging goals and maintain a strong commitment to them.
- Heighten and sustain your efforts in the face of failure.
- Recover your sense of efficacy after failures or setbacks.
- Attribute failure to insufficient effort or deficient knowledge and skills, which are acquirable.
- Approach threatening situations with assurance that you can exercise control over them.

Self-efficacy is all about having faith in your abilities; if you doubt those abilities seek improvement (like education), don't take things personally (it's only business), be persistent, constantly challenge yourself, and take everything head-on.

Practicing *assertive* communications is another way to improve your communications skills and keep yourself healthy. Without assertive communications there is a tendency to hold onto anger, turning it inward, which leads to feelings of hopelessness, helplessness, frustration, and anxiety. It can lead to poor relationships and tension-related ailments like headaches, ulcers, and high blood pressure. The ability to communicate effectively not only gets your message out, but can keep you healthy. Some of the more effective methods of assertive communications include the following:

- Broken Record – repeating your point over and over until you are sure it has been heard.
- Fogging – not being provoked by criticism, but rather acknowledging the criticism and agreeing that there may be some truth to it.

An example could be, "I can agree that there may be times when I haven't been listening."

- Negative Assertion – reducing critics' hostility by accepting your issues without apology. "You are right; I do have a tendency to disagree too often."
- Negative Enquiry – seeking more criticism to both diffuse the situation and also to perhaps get to the bottom of the criticism. "So you believe that I'm not listening?"
- Free Information – information is power when you share it. Assertive communication includes the principle that information should be shared without the paranoia of, "If I give them the information, I won't have anything to leverage."
- Self-Disclosure – be able to communicate and include something of yourself in the message. It allows the sender to own the communications.
- "I Messages" – closely related to self-disclosure. Putting some of you in the communications. "I am concerned that you are not doing the necessary work to protect the patients. I need you to help me do that."

Additionally, you can improve your communications by resolving conflicts effectively, developing better communications skills, running meetings more effectively, and using a template for communications so you don't forget anything.

VARIABLES OF COMMUNICATIONS

Remember our discussion in Chapter 6. A variable is a data point that can change. Add the variables of communications to the barriers of communications and the odds against being able to effectively communicate seem astronomical. That's not really true unless you are unaware of the barriers and the variables. Just being aware of them gives you an edge. You know what to expect. Physical constraints are one of the variables. Distance from receiver to sender, either across the room or across the country, is a variable that needs to be considered. Whether or not the receiver is physically able to "hear" the message is a variable.

How much or how little education communicators have is another variable. No two people have the identical educational background. I'm not just talking about formal education, but also informal or experiential education. A person's social status and place in the power structure are two more variables. I have an American colleague who works for a French company who has seen the following concept firsthand: "So in France, the concept of the 'honor each class,' in which there is clear separation of superiors and subordinates, differs from the U.S. concept of 'fair contract' between employer and employee where managers have only certain prerogatives within limits."[5]

The way each of us understands/processes information is a variable because each of us processes data differently. "Human cognition is central to clinical decision making. Clinical information involves histories that can be biased by the manner in which questions are asked, vague clinical signs that are assessed with several senses, and diagnostic laboratory tests that are not perfect. If clinicians have a fundamental understanding of the process of cognition and inherent weaknesses in the process, they will be better able to compensate for weaknesses in this process and arrive at better clinical decisions in the long run."[6]

Finally, technical constraints are a variable to communications. Not everyone is comfortable with the technology of communications. For instance, there may be people who won't use e-mail or the other spectrum of people who insist that all communications be done on their handheld computing device. Variables to communications must be considered to make communicating more effective.

COMMUNICATIONS MANAGEMENT PLAN

Every project needs a communications management plan, no matter how large or how small the project is. The *communication management plan* defines what data is being collected and filtered for distribution, the filtering techniques to eliminate extraneous information and highlight key information, and how often data will be collected for the communications plan. A primary input to this plan is the stakeholder analysis we did in Chapter 3. Generally, the complexity of the communications management plan will increase as the size of the project increases. Developing a communications management plan is the roadmap for developing a communications infrastructure. That infrastructure includes all of the tools:

- E-mail

- Project management software
- Shared resources
- Document management systems
- Intranet
- Telephones
- Teleconferencing service
- WebEx,[7] Go-to-Meeting,[8] and similar services
- iPhones, iPads, and similar devices

Communication techniques include the following:

- Templates
- Reporting guidelines (sometimes specified contractually and by stakeholders' needs)
- Decision-making processes
- Problem-solving processes
- Conflict resolution
- Negotiations

Both tools and techniques are used to positively influence communications. Another necessary component to a good communications management plan is the final communications on the project, or project closure communications. The communications management plan must include how project artifacts, lessons learned, and formal acceptance are to be communicated. Sometimes those communications may be as simple as an invoice to be paid now that the project is complete. More often it is more complex than that, with contract closure including all of the addendums.

Communications Plan

Within the communications management plan is the *communications plan*, the execution vehicle for the communications management plan. The communications plan uses all the inputs, such as the stakeholder analysis, and specifically defines what information is going to be communicated (from an external view), who will receive the communication, how the information will be communicated, and when the communications will be conducted. The basic concept of a communications plan is to get the right information to the right people at the right time in a useful format. Technology (remembering the variables of communication) should be used to enhance communications. As our communications devices get more and more complex, the ability to communicate will also get more difficult. There is a large variety of devices available, and few standard protocols. While we've emphasized the formal methods of communications, there is that informal piece that can be considered in the communications plan: face-to-face or phone.

IMPROVING COMMUNICATIONS

Apart from the obvious, get training to be a better communicator, there are many ways to improve communication skills. Conflicts can be very disruptive to communications. Additional baggage occurs with unresolved conflict. That baggage can be a barrier to communication, causing distorted views from both sender and receiver. Being able to effectively resolve conflict is a way to improve communications by removing those obstacles. Meetings can take up an inordinate amount of communications time. Managing meetings with maximum efficiency is a way to control that time. One of the more effective ways to manage meetings is to scrutinize each one to see if it is truly necessary. If it is not, then *don't meet.* If the subject of the information to be gathered at the meeting can be communicated in any other way, *don't meet.* If participants have agendas other than to gather information, *don't meet.* Speaking agendas *always have an agenda* no matter how small the meeting seems to be. Once you have your agenda, *stick to it.* Hand in hand with an agenda is a statement of objectives. They may be one and the same, especially if a decision is expected as a result of the meeting. Outline that objective first so that people will have some time to consider it.

Don't let people come to the meeting unprepared. This is easier said than done, but one of the first things to do is to communicate the meeting's objectives. That way, people can be thinking about those objectives and see where they fit in the scheme of things. Provide leadership in the meeting by imposing time limits when appropriate. This is where an agenda can help. It can be used as a mechanism to portray the time limits assigned to each item. Remember to leave a little extra time in case an interesting subject overruns the time allotted. Provide templates for communications. This is similar to providing an agenda except that templates are more specific and require action on the part of meeting participants. An example of this would be the distribution of a progress report—we'll talk about the different reports a little later in this chapter. Stick to the times and topics specified by the agenda, and start and finish on time. I use the example of Newark Airport for starting a meeting on time. Once the planes begin not taking off on their scheduled times, the airport starts to back up. Once that happens, the backup continues to get worse at an exponential rate, just like a person's schedule. If the person is late getting out of one meeting and the next one runs long, the person continues to get further behind as the day goes on. It is acceptable to leave the meeting if you have to, to take a call, for instance (and cell phones are on silent mode only), but the meeting will continue without you. You will have to ask someone after the meeting to get you caught up.

Finally, *always* have a sign-in sheet. With a sign-in sheet it is easier to recall who was at the meeting and to document who accepted an action item and when the follow-up to the item will occur. Manage conflicts, because they will happen. Conflicts are disagreements, differences of opinions. However, if they are not controlled, a meeting can quickly get out of control and end up as a waste of time. Limit side conversations and listen to speakers rather than texting or preparing your statements and questions. If the meeting is managed correctly, there will be ample time for your opinion and questions, especially if the meeting is limited in attendance. When thinking about the meeting's agenda, think about who can effectively address the issues. Only invite those who can effectively address the issues and discourage those who cannot. Table 7.2 is a checklist for running effective meetings.

TABLE 7.2
Meeting Checklist

1. Prepare an agenda with topics and times.
2. Prepare attendees list.
3. Prepare action register.
4. Speakers notified to comply with time limits.
5. Meeting started on time.
6. Participants requested to return on time from breaks.
7. Participants notified that it is okay to leave, but meeting will proceed.
8. Participants notified to turn off cell phones.
9. Participants notified to sign attendees list.
10. Attendees list collected.
11. Participants notified of agreements and delivery dates of actions.
12. Meeting ended on time.

SOCIAL MEDIA AND HEALTHCARE

The following is from a blog from Green Buzz Agency (http://www.greenbuzzagency.com/) by ***Anna Heather, an Account Executive at Virilion (http://www.virilion.com/) in Washington, DC, used with permission.***

SOCIAL MEDIA AND THE HEALTHCARE INDUSTRY: STATS – INSIGHT

Many clients in the healthcare industry have recently come to us with questions about social media. Many of them want to know why social media matters and where it should fit into their marketing plans. Others want to know where to get started and how to build and maintain a successful Facebook Page, Twitter Account, YouTube Channel, or blog. But more and more, clients are simply looking for help understanding the social media landscape and how it impacts healthcare decisions.

While there is no easy answer to any of these questions, there are a few things you should know if you're thinking about developing a social media strategy for your hospital or organization:

61% of American Adults Look Online for Health Information

The number of American adults who looked for health information online has doubled in under a decade. That's according to a 2009 Pew Internet Research study, which found that 61 percent of adults look online for healthcare information, while only 25 percent of American adults looked online for this information in 2000.

Three-quarters of American adults aged 18 or older have access to the Internet either at home or at work. Eighty-three percent of those users have looked online for information about health topics ranging from information about a specific disease, treatments, alternative medicine, health insurance, healthcare providers, medical facilities, and ways to stay healthy.

24% of Patients Have Consulted Reviews of Medical Facilities Online

Just as more Americans turn to the Web to find recommendations on restaurants and local vendors, patients visit blogs and Web sites to find rankings and reviews of doctors, hospitals and medical facilities. According to Pew, health consumers looking for information, inspiration, and support often turn to blogs or Web sites with user-generated rankings or reviews to find solutions:

- 41% of patients have read someone else's commentary or experience about health or medical issues on an online news group, Web site or blog
- 24% of patients online have consulted rankings or reviews of doctors or providers
- 24% of patients online have consulted rankings or reviews of hospitals or medical facilities

More than 700 U.S. Hospitals Use Social Networking Tools

More and more patients look to connect directly with healthcare providers via social networking platforms like Facebook, Twitter, and YouTube. In addition to using the Web for health information and disease support, patients want information and updates in real-time, just like they get from others in their online communities.

Hospitals have started to get the picture, using social networks to connect with consumers, making it easier for patients to better understand products and services, and allow health providers to demonstrate clinical expertise, build trust, and deliver valued information to an engaged audience.

In June 2010, Found in Cache, an online resource for healthcare professionals, determined that 744 U.S. hospitals were active on Twitter, Facebook, and YouTube: 549 Twitter Accounts, 513 Facebook Pages, and 337 YouTube Channels.

60% of Patients Active Online Say Using the Web Affected a Medical Decision

Online health queries impact medical decisions. Among patients who researched health information online, the majority of respondents said the Internet had an impact on their own health or the way they care for someone else. Of the information found online:

- 60% said it affected a decision about how to treat an illness or condition
- 56% said it changed their overall approach to maintaining their health or the health of someone they care for
- 53% said it led them to ask a doctor new questions, or to get a second opinion
- 49% said it changed the way they thought about their diet, exercise, or stress management
- 38% said it affected their decision to see a doctor
- 38% said it changed the way they cope with a chronic condition or manage pain

Takeaway for Healthcare Professionals: Social Media Is Part of Our Culture

"It's time to get rid of the term 'social media' and call it 'media,' because there really isn't a difference," according to Shel Holtz, principal of Holtz Communications and the media manager for the Mayo Clinic. Today, eight of the top 20 most visited Web sites in the U.S. are social media based.

As you can see, social media connects healthcare providers to patients, while helping to accomplish marketing goals. While the Internet is no substitute for healthcare professionals and the care they provide, it can help hospitals and healthcare providers reach patients who are deepening their engagement with the online world.

Can information about your hospital, clinical expertise, or services be found in the places people are looking?

If not, now is the perfect time to get started!

REPORTING

There are three types of performance reporting that should be done on any project: *status reporting*, *progress reporting*, and *forecasting*. *Status reporting* describes where the project stands at a specific point in time. An example of this for the NCMC EMR Project would be, "As of today, we have received all of the hardware needed for our system." *Progress reporting* describes what the project team has accomplished during a certain period of time. For instance, "The accomplishments for December include receiving the hardware for our EMR system, hired a consultant to start developing training material, and sent out a brochure to all hospital staff explaining the pending changes. Next month we intend to install the hardware and receive the software. There was a compatibility issue between our new hardware and some of our old hardware that was resolved. We wrote a change order to our original proposal to include the necessary hardware to upgrade some of our old computers." Within this report are the accomplishments for December, what is expected to be accomplished in January, issues that arose during the month and resolutions of the same, and any change orders or project changes for that period. *Forecasting* is predicting future project status and progress based on the performance of the past using trend analysis, change orders, or any other past information gathered from action registers, for instance.

Communication is more than just sending and receiving. It is making those messages appropriate, relevant, understandable by the audience, and timely. Using the tools and techniques described can help unravel the mysteries of good communications.

KEY REVIEW QUESTIONS

1. In a face-to-face conversation, as a percentage, how much are the actual words of your message worth?
2. Name five barriers to communication. How would you overcome each one?
3. What can you do to improve your communication skills?
4. Does your organization use social media? If so, what social media does it use? If not, should it, and why or why not?

ENDNOTES

1. Elizabeth Harrin, http://www.pm4girls.elizabeth-harrin.com/
2. Ormrod, J. E., *Educational Psychology: Developing Learners*, 5th edition, Merrill, Upper Saddle River, NJ (companion Web site), "glossary," 2006.
3. Sue, D., Sue, D. W., Sue, S., *Understanding Abnormal Behavior*, 8th edition, Wadsworth Publishing, Cengage Learning, Inc, Florence, KY, p. 214.
4. Bandura, A., "Self-Efficacy." In V. S. Ramachaudran (Ed.), *Encyclopedia of Human Behavior* (Vol. 4, pp. 71–81), Academic Press, New York, 1994. (Reprinted in H. Friedman [Ed.], *Encyclopedia of Mental Health*, Academic Press, San Diego, 1998.)
5. Holfstede, G., "Cultural constraints in management theories," *Academy of Management Executive*, 7(1), 1993, pp. 81–94.
6. *Human cognition*, Draft 1.1, Initiated 7/8/04 – Updated 6/18/10, http://www.vetmed.wsu.edu/courses-jmgay/Cognition.htm
7. Webex, www.webex.com
8. Go-to-Meeting, www.GoToMeeting.com

8

Change

The only constant on a project is change. The sooner that is understood, the better prepared you will be for change. No one really likes change no matter what they say, but it is part of life and certainly it is part of projects. There are two change aspects to projects. The first is the changes resulting from the project itself. It can be changes to the way you do business because of undertaking a project, or it could be the changes caused by the project. The second aspect of project change is a change to the project, including changes to configuration, schedule, costs, contract, and quality, and how to handle those changes (see Figure 8.1[1]).

DEALING WITH CHANGE

The first aspect of project change is the impacts resulting from the project itself, and how to deal with those impacts. As said before, no one really likes change, but in reality, changes occur on a daily basis, whether they are significant changes, like buying a new house, getting married, or starting a new job, or minor changes, like a restaurant not having the menu item that you have your heart set on or the impact of putting up new curtains in your house. Minor changes can be dealt with easily; major changes may require major intervention. The focus is on minimizing the impact of change.

One of the most important ways to minimize the impact of a change is through communications: *the more the better* is the rule. The biggest complaint from people who are impacted by a change is that they never heard about the change until it was forced upon them. Increasing communications has two purposes: (1) to serve as an early warning system and (2) to

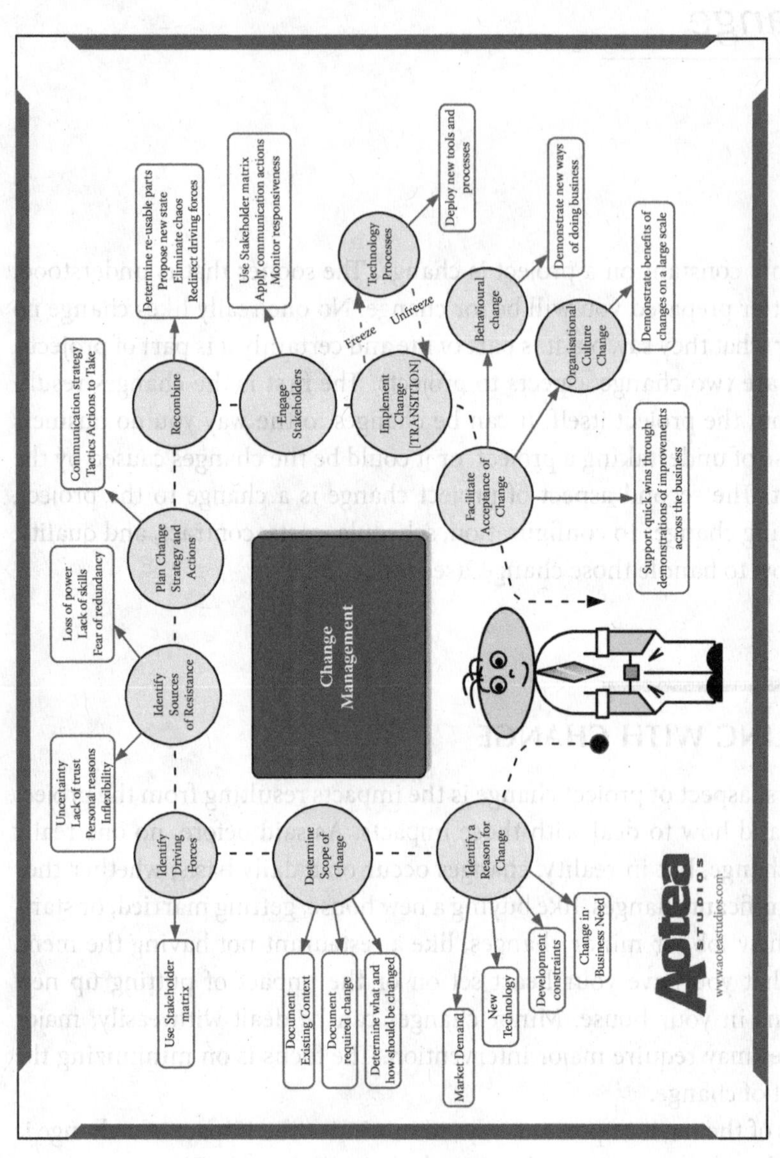
Change Management
Identify Driving Forces
Use Stakeholder matrix
Uncertainty
Lack of trust
Personal reasons
Inflexibility
Identify Sources of Resistance
Loss of power
Lack of skills
Fear of redundancy
Plan Change Strategy and Actions
Communication strategy/
Tactics Actions to Take
Recombine
Determine re-usable parts
Propose new state
Eliminate chaos
Redirect driving forces
Engage Stakeholders
Use Stakeholder matrix
Apply communication actions
Monitor responsiveness
Implement Change [TRANSITION]
Freeze
Unfreeze
Technology Processes
Deploy new tools and processes
Determine Scope of Change
Document Existing Context
Document required change
Determine what and how should be changed
Identify a Reason for Change
Market Demand
New Technology
Development constraints
Change in Business Need
Facilitate Acceptance of Change
Behavioural change
Demonstrate new ways of doing business
Organisational Culture Change
Demonstrate benefits of changes on a large scale
Support quick wins through demonstrations of improvements across the business
Aotea
STUDIOS
www.aoteastudios.com

FIGURE 8.1

provide a method for people to comment about the change. Whether or not those comments are incorporated is another issue, but the fact that people have a chance to comment gives them a sense of participation. Participation leads to a feeling of ownership, which leads to changes more easily being integrated. People who feel they participated in the decision to make the change feel that they have bought into the decision. It is difficult for people to reject a change once they have bought into it.

As mentioned in Chapter 11, communications can come in the form of formal or informal, and communicating change should be done using both methods. Formal (or written) communications provides the platform for more detailed communications. The more complex the project, the more emphasis there should be on formal communications, and the larger the project, the more emphasis there should be on formal communications. When I talk about large projects, I don't necessarily mean projects with long implementation intervals. I consider a project "large" if it is costly or critical to an organization. In those instances, communicate frequently and formally with key stakeholders. You certainly don't want them to have any surprises.

Help people with change by being an advocate for change. By nature, project managers are change merchants. That's what we do, change things. There are a couple of things you can do to help people with change, besides communications. Keep a positive attitude about change. There are always the "glass half empty" people. Don't be one of them. Change is good. Embrace change. First of all, recognize that people think about change in relation to buckets: the *no* bucket, the *let's make a deal* bucket, and the *get out of my face* bucket. The essence of the "no" bucket is that people flatly deny that there is a change. This happens most when there is an unpleasant or perceived unpleasant change occurring. The best way to deal with this is through understanding and persistence. "I understand where you are coming from, but this change is necessary for …"(fill in the blank—growth, profitability, safety). The "let's make a deal" bucket brings out people's instincts to try to return to the status quo before the change was instituted. Using all of their reasoning and persuasion, people will try to deal out the change and deal back to the way it was. When people are in that frame of mind, it is difficult to convince them that the change is better than changing it back to the old way of doing things. This is a place when fact-based logic is one of the tools used. The "get out of my face" reaction usually occurs when the "no" and "let's make a deal" buckets have been emptied. With the emptying of those buckets comes a feeling of hopelessness that leads to anger. "No one has listened to me. I'm being railroaded into accepting these changes. I'm angry!" This is the type of anger than will burn out on its own. The caution is not trying to force the release. Even when time is of the essence, let the anger dissipate on its own. Let the other person vent.

Change may also occur when using the project management discipline because it is a new way of doing business. Companies, especially entrepreneurial companies, like to be in a freewheeling, virtually unstructured mode. Putting structure into projects is like dragging your nails on a chalkboard (remember those?) for some people. One way to deal with that reaction is to show how many resources are saved when there is a structure in place and you don't have to "reinvent the wheel" each time. The use of project templates, lessons learned, and historical information about previous projects can save a considerable amount of time, particularly when personnel turnover occurs.

MONITORING AND CONTROLLING CHANGES

While some may advocate that each of the major processes (scheduling, costs, and quality) has its own change control process, I believe that one consistent change control process should be used for all of the project changes.

One of the processes used to control changes is the gate process, to use the generic term. Some call it Stage-Gate®,[2] some call it a gate review process, and some call it a phase-gate process. Whatever you call it, the structure is basically the same. At a point in time, or a relevant point in the project (see Figure 8.2), a gate is inserted. That gate will have criteria attached to it. Usually a list of events will be completed. In order to continue through the gate, the completion of those events will be confirmed and documented, or, if the parties agree, documented as exceptions to be completed at a new specified time. A gate process is only as good as the discipline employed. If the exceptions become the rule, then the effectiveness of the process is greatly diminished. The number of gates within a project-specific gate process will vary. However, I recommend a minimum of four gates, one each at the end of an idea phase, a planning phase, a design phase, and an implementation phase. The gate process will also be an important addition to the project's lessons learned in that how and when the individual criteria are met will be helpful when developing project plans for similar projects.

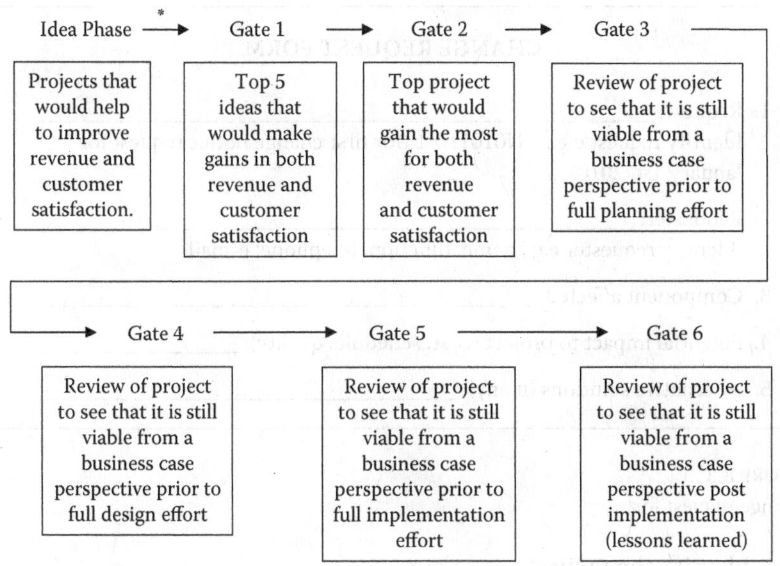

FIGURE 8.2
Gate process of NCMC.

The gate process or whatever process you use to monitor and control a project should include the following areas of project:

- Configuration
- Scope
- Time
- Cost
- Quality
- Communications
- Risk

While a gate process is one of the ways to monitor and control a project, changes are still likely to occur. Again, rather than develop change processes for each major project component, one consistent change control process is all that is needed. I am generally not in favor of a "one size fits all" solution, but in the case of change control, a consistent approach is best. The best change control process is the simplest. The key to the process is the change control request form (see Figure 8.3). The form should include places to

CHANGE REQUEST FORM

1. Request: ______________________________
   Identify request e.g., CN010110-1 (for first change notice request for January 1st, 2010)
2. Requester: ______________________________
   Identify requester e.g., name, function, telephone, e-mail
3. Component affected: ______________________________
4. Potential impact to project (cost, schedule, quality): ______________
5. Alternative solutions (if any): ______________________________

FIGURE 8.3
Change request form.

- Identify the request.
- Identify the project component affected (could be more than one).
- Document the proposed change and justification.
- Identify the impact to the project (could affect multiple components).
- Document the impact to the project if the change is not accepted

Once the form is complete it then goes to the next step in the process, the review. The size of the project will determine the methodology for the review process. For instance, in the case of NCMC, the review board will include the CEO (Michelle Michaels), CFO (Elaine Dumont), and Director of IT (Maryann Lords). However, in a smaller project, the project manager may be the approver/disapprover for project changes. The entire process may start and end with the project manager, but the process will be iterative (see Figure 8.4).

The change control process efforts need to recognize that there will be changes. Those changes can be divided into types (cost, schedule, and quality), and also the sources of those changes—external (customer, vendor) or internal (project team, executive). The process also includes evaluating and authorizing the changes, as well as implementing them. The process documentation is important as a record of those changes and to be able to easily identify them for lessons learned and application to the next project. Changes may be made with the product of the project as well as process changes within project management.

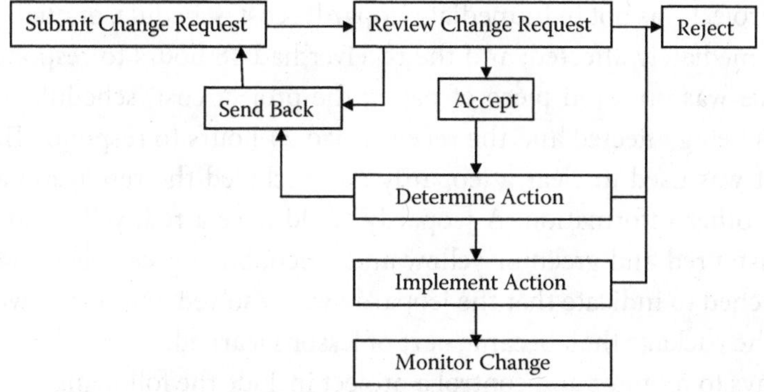

1. Submit complete change request (may got to project manager for small project or may go to Change Control Committee for large project–process should be defined as part of a project office–either way, project manager should be involved)
2. Review completed change request for completeness and action–may need to send it back to requester for additional or more complete information or reject it
3. Determine action that needs to take place–may need clarification or may reject it
4. Implement Action–may not be implementable
5. Monitor Change to make sure it does what it is supposed to do.

FIGURE 8.4
Change control process.

Another process that is part of the monitoring and controlling of projects is the escalation process. No matter what the size of the project is, there should be an escalation process in place to help resolve issues that may not be resolvable at the review board or project management level. If you don't have the process in place prior to starting your project, precious resources (your time) will be wasted trying to put a process in place on the fly. And a rushed process is probably not going to be effective. When dealing with a vendor, the process should include escalations for both sides of the equation. When developing your implementation process, identify the next several levels of management. If it is a joint effort with another organization, make sure you identify the equivalent levels of management in the other organization as well.

Another process that should be in place is a jeopardy process. Similar in nature to an escalation process, the jeopardy process includes the element of time, which an escalation process may or may not include. A simple jeopardy process I developed included three pieces of colored paper: green, yellow, and red. Each piece of paper contained the same information about the issue, the explanation of the issue, the impact to the project, and the requested action. If a yellow piece of paper was used, it is considered an alert. The project was not in immediate jeopardy; cost, schedule, or quality was not immediately affected; and the receiver had 48 hours to respond. If the notice was on a red piece of paper, the project cost, schedule, or quality was being affected and the receiver had 24 hours to respond. The green sheet was used to clear a jeopardy and included the resolution as well as the other information. A jeopardy could have a red, yellow, and green or just a red and green or yellow and green, but a green sheet was always attached to indicate that the jeopardy was resolved and how it was resolved. The package then became part of lessons learned.

Other ways to monitor and control a project include the following:

- Periodic risk reviews – looking at identified project risks and determining if new ones were added to the list and previous ones removed (risk is discussed in Chapter 13)
- Status and progress reviews
- Product performance measurements – testing at different stages to make sure that the product of the project is meeting its performance requirements
- Any formal actions taken to ensure that the project is on track

So with all of this monitoring and controlling, how do you know when a project is really in trouble? There are a couple of things you should look at, especially during a gate review. The business case is one of the criteria examined during a gate review. Some of the questions asked are as follows:

- Is there still sufficient return on investment?
  - Has the business climate changed?
  - Has the pricing structure changed?
  - Have the project costs changed?
- Is there still demand for the product of the project?
- Are there new regulatory requirements that may change costs?
- Is the product of the project still viable or has it become obsolete?
- Is the product of the project still technically feasible?

If the answer to any of these questions puts the project in doubt, then it is time to either reevaluate the project to see if it makes sense to continue, or terminate the project. Terminating a project becomes harder and harder as the project progresses through its life cycle, because more and more resources have been expended. However, if termination is justified, the project should be terminated. Remember from our cost discussion, sunk costs can be used to justify continuing a failing project. But sunk costs should not be considered in the decision to terminate a project.

So what are some of the signs of a failing project?

1. During a periodic project review it is noted that there is an extraordinary number of changes being recorded. This could indicate that the project is not meeting expectations.
2. Action items are being added to the action register at an alarming rate. This could also indicate that the project is not meeting requirements.
3. The personnel on the project are
    a. Requiring large amounts of overtime, indicating poor estimation of time or a poor understanding of the project requirements
    b. Requesting to be reassigned, indicating that the personnel feel the project is going to fail and they don't want to be a part of it
    c. Lacking interest in the project, when there was interest in the beginning
    d. Failing to deliver on milestones, even the small ones
4. Resources are being moved off of the project, indicating that someone believes the project is doomed
5. Constantly changing scope means that the project is poorly planned

Remember, these are just signs and don't necessarily mean that the project will fail. They do indicate that immediate action should be taken, probably a red jeopardy situation.

CHANGE AS A GOOD THING

Change can be a good thing when a project, although well planned, needs a correction because the original conditions under which the project was operating changed. Without a change in focus, the project would continue to point to the original outcome and certainly would fail to meet the new requirements.

From a vendor's point of view, changes are almost always good. It is called "up scope" from that point of view. When I was managing projects as a vendor, I was always looking for ways to increase the scope of work for the customer. From a customer point of view, then, it is very important to spend the proper planning time to fully understand and articulate the project's requirement to the vendor so that up scope or scope creep (from the customer's point of view) did not occur during the project. It is difficult to go back and ask for additional money because of a change in scope when the plan should have included the requirement.

Change, just like everything else a project manager does, is all about managing the expectations of stakeholders. Whether those stakeholders are your internal customers, your project team, or the executives to whom you report, change will occur and you will have to manage those changes. Good communications and well-planned escalation and jeopardy processes, as well as good upfront project planning, can help manage those changes.

Support and Authority

A very important success criterion for change is the level of support and authority the project manager enjoys. As the level of support and authority goes up, there is a greater chance that the change can be successfully implemented. Although this is not to say that without support and without authority the project can't be successful, it will just be more difficult to implement. Generally, however, project managers work in a more matrixed environment, meaning that project team members are not dedicated and solely under the authority of the project manager. As mentioned in Cohen and Bradford's seminal work on the subject, "You are more powerful than you think."[3] This means that you have advantages and should use them. As an example, your training and experience as a project manager, whether accidental or not, gives you the tools and techniques to communicate a comprehensive plan or at least a logical idea of how to proceed with a project. One of the key management skills talked about is the ability to communicate. This adds to the project manager's ability to help stakeholders understand the rationale behind the need to change.

Project Managers as Change Agents

The pressure is on. All projects create changes in some way, as mentioned before—changes are either the way an organization does business due to the introduction of the discipline of project management, or as a result of the project. Successfully managing changes therefore will be the primary reason that projects succeed or fail. So accept that change is good; that no one likes change, except you; and that it is your job to convince everyone else that the change is good for them. That is the key to successfully managing projects because it is only human nature to ask, "What's in it for me?" In order to answer that question, the project manager has to (1) buy into the change and really believe in it, and (2) sell it to the stakeholders. The only way to do that is to become an advocate for change and the change agent that defines project managers. As an advocate for change, you not only have to believe in the change, but you also have to campaign for the change, and show excitement and enthusiasm for it. After all, it is for the betterment of the organization; otherwise you wouldn't be undertaking it, especially when resources are scarce. Your infectious enthusiasm for change has to influence your project team, too. How your project team reacts to your being a change advocate is one of the issues to monitor. It can tell much about how the change is being perceived and what you may need to do to make your advocacy more effective. You need to have the consensus of your project team to make the change successful.

Projects/Change Are One and the Same

Although I've been advocating change, I want to remind you that change and projects are one and the same. To illustrate, let's looks at some changes/projects that an organization may undertake:

- Instituting project management discipline
- Buying equipment
- Upgrading equipment
- Enhancing a project—change control
- Changing project direction due to obsolescence, technical, or regulatory issues
- Instituting "green efforts"
- Developing new processes or procedures
- Updating old processes or procedures
- Patient safety initiatives

SUMMARY

It is important not only to think about the project, but also to think about how the change, because that's what a project is, will affect your stakeholders. Remember, you are a stakeholder, too. When looking at all of the new projects that will be undertaken by an organization, think about it as a change and about how it will affect everyone involved. Go back to Chapter 2 and think about why projects are chosen, and to Chapter 3 and who the key players are. Understanding the reasons for the change and who is affected are the keys to advocating for the change.

KEY REVIEW QUESTIONS

1. What is a way to *minimize* the impact of a change?
2. People think of change in three buckets. What are they?
3. Explain the *gate process* as an effective tool to manage change.
4. What are the *five* key areas of a change control request form?
5. In a paragraph, explain why project managers are *change agents*?

ENDNOTES

1. Sergey Korban, aoteastudios.com, used with permission.
2. Stage-Gate is a registered trademark of Stage-Gate International, http://www.stage-gate.com/knowledge_pipwhat.php
3. Cohen, Allan R., and Bradford, David L., *Influence without Authority*, John Wiley and Sons, New York, 1991 p. 129.

9

Risk

Probably the most significant of the issues that the project manager will have to deal with is risk, especially in the healthcare field. Why? Because on a daily basis, healthcare professionals are dealing with life and death situations. To state the obvious, any time you deal with life and death situations on a daily basis, it is very risky—all the more reason that the discipline of project management is so important to the healthcare professional, because project managers, besides being advocates for change, are also risk managers. It is not the project manager's job to decide on what projects an organization should spend its resources, although project management input can help make better decisions, but it is the project manager's job to anticipate issues that could arise in both the process planning, implementing, and controlling the project as well as the impacts of the product of the project.

WHAT IS RISK?

A concern to be evaluated as a potential risk is literally any issue about which some doubt exists. According to BusinessDictionary.com[1] it is the "probability or threat of a damage, injury, liability, loss, or other negative occurrence, caused by external or internal vulnerabilities, and which may be neutralized through pre-meditated action." I like this definition for a couple of reasons. It includes the word "liability," something that is very important to healthcare administration. Additionally, many times internal threats, because they are easier to access, are the ones that are considered, but external threats can be very significant. Finally, "neutralized through pre-meditated action" clearly defines what the project manager, as risk manager, must do.

NCMC from time to time deals with patients who potentially can hurt themselves or others around them either from a reaction to drugs, medical conditions that could cause seizures, or psychosis. Dr. Chimers, the Medical Director, proposed a project to take one of the larger examination rooms in the hospital and turn it into a "safe room." During the planning process, the project manager identified a potential risk condition. Because it is an existing room, the only way to protect the patient and healthcare workers in case of a fall during a struggle or seizure was to add padding to the floor. The padding would elevate the entry threshold to a point where it would be a tripping hazard. The potential risk was identified, evaluated, considered, and accepted by the medical director.

The Project Management Institute's PMBOK® guide divides risk management into six categories: plan risk management, risk identification, qualitative analysis, quantitative analysis, response planning, and monitoring and controlling risks.

RISK AND REWARD

Before discussing the six categories of risk management, there several techniques that can aid in the process of managing risks that should be discussed. One of the techniques used to determine risk is make versus buy considerations. It may be as simple as evaluating whether or not your IT department can effectively install a new software package, or whether this should be done by an outside contractor. If you decide to "make it" and have your IT department do it, there are several questions you need to ask:

- Do we have the money that an outside contractor would charge?
- Does our IT department have the skills and availability?
- Does the IT department have any prior experience in installing software packages?

- How does it fit with the organization's mission?
    - Are we a healthcare facility or a software installation group?
- Do we need total control over the project or can we delegate it to an outside contractor?
- Do we want our IT department to get experience in software installation?

INTERVIEWING

Discussions with stakeholders, project team members, and subject matter experts can have a profound influence on your risk identification ability and accuracy. Risks can fall into four categories:

1. Known by you, known by others (known/known)
2. Know by you, unknown by others (known/unknown)
3. Unknown by you, known by others (unknown/known)
4. Unknown by you, unknown by others (unknown/unknown)

Projects risks are usually known by someone, either you or others. Very few, if any, project risks fall into the unknown/unknown category. You just have to ask the right questions of the right people to discover the potential risks to your project. That is also part of the art of risk identification. One of the more popular interviewing methods is the Delphi Method, which is based on the oracles of Greek mythology. This technique focuses on a solution to a specific problem based on the results from a panel of experts. One of the keys to this method is to find subject matter experts who have experienced a similar problem. Each expert is then polled for information about the solution. The information from each expert is correlated and the results are returned to the experts for iteration until a convergent solution is found.

RISK MATRICES

By developing a risk matrix, you can help determine which risks will have the most significant impact on the project, and therefore their priority. In

Risk Analysis		
Project Name:		Date:
Project Manager:		
Probability	**Impact**	**Risks Identified**
High, Medium, or Low	High, Medium, or Low	1.
		2.
		3.
		4.
		5.
		6.
		7. etc

FIGURE 9.1
Risk Analysis template.

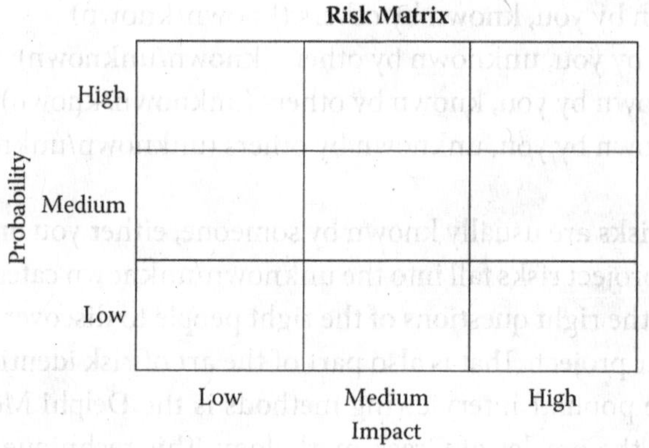

FIGURE 9.2
Risk Matrix template.

order to populate the risk matrix (Figure 9.1), a risk analysis (Figure 9.2) must be conducted. This occurs at a much higher level than the qualitative and quantitative risk analysis discussed later in this chapter, because its function is to determine the level of risks at a high level. It allows you to then pick the risks that should be further analyzed. At this stage, risk analysis is more of a sophisticated brainstorming session where the risks are identified *and* rated so that they can populate the risk matrix. Figure 9.3 shows the risk analysis for the purchase of some new x-ray equipment. Once the risk analysis has been conducted, the risk matrix can be populated. Figure 9.4 shows the risk matrix developed based on Figure 9.3. The

Risk Analysis		
Project Name: Purchase of New X-ray Equipment		Date: July 1, 2010
Project Manager: Dosey Madder, NCMC		
Probability	**Impact**	**Risks Identified**
M	H	1. Room not ready
H	L	2. Vendor ships early
L	H	3. Vendor ships late
L	L	4. Shipped to wrong location
L	H	5. Equipment Damaged
M	L	6. Education material not complete
M	H	7. No trained personnel available to operate equipment

FIGURE 9.3
Risk Analysis example.

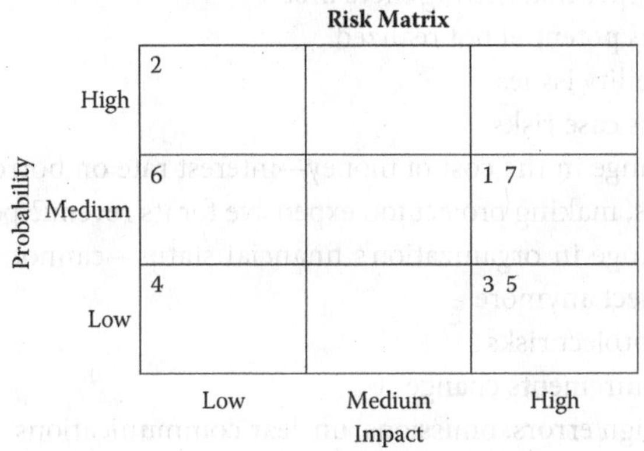

FIGURE 9.4
Risk Matrix example.

categories that can most influence risk management are the ones in the high impact and high, medium, and low probability categories. In this case, the higher priority should be given to tasks 1, 3, 5, and 7, with tasks 1 and 7 being the top priorities.

RISK IDENTIFICATION

The first task of the project manager is to define the project's risks. Risk identification is actually about defining the project's risk triggers, those events that need to occur in order for a potential risk to become realized.

In other words, in most projects there are key people, whether a lead engineer or marketing representative, involved. The risk trigger could be that one or more of those key people become unavailable.

What to Consider

Risks can come from everywhere or anywhere. It may seem like a daunting task to identify the risks to a project. The larger the project, the more potential risk triggers there are. As with any large task, it is better to break it down into manageable pieces. Some of the areas that are sources of risk triggers are as follows:

- Business risks
    - Competition getting there first
    - Sales potential not realized
    - Liability issues
- Business case risks
    - Change in the cost of money—interest rate on borrowed money rises, making project too expensive for its revenue potential
    - Change in organization's financial status—cannot afford to do project anymore
- Direct project risks
    - Requirements change
    - Design errors, omissions, unclear communications
    - No clear role and responsibility definition
    - Poor resource estimates (cost, people, schedule)
    - Wrong skill set for people on project
    - Leading edge (first time doing something is the riskiest)
- External risks
    - Acts of nature
    - Regulatory (especially with medical device manufacturers and biopharma companies)
- People risks
    - Poor communication skills
    - Poor conflict management skills (conflicts are inevitable)
    - Poor organizational structure
    - No leadership
    - Adversarial relationships
    - Inadequate quality control

So where do you look for the definition of some of these potential risk triggers? A good place to start is the Project Charter. The charter will give you a high-level and detailed view of what the project entails, how much it will cost, how long it should take, and what the expected quality of the outcome would be. The organization's risk policies are another place to explore. Whether the organization is conservative, like a healthcare facility, or risk taking, as entrepreneurial companies tend to be, will have an impact on your risk planning. Another place to look for potential risk triggers is the major stakeholder's risk tolerance. For instance, even though the organization is risk averse, the CEO of the hospital, in an effort to answer the competition, may be willing to take some risks to do that. Once the risks are identified to the best of your ability, a determination has to be made on two bases: likelihood of occurrence and impact of occurrence.

QUALITATIVE AND QUANTITATIVE RISK ANALYSIS

Qualitative risk analysis looks at a risk using some sort of qualification scale. The scale applies to both impact and likelihood. In some cases, there is actual data to compare it to; in other cases, the scale is subjective in nature. If no data exists, then the next best thing to do is to use comparison or a subjective scale based on expert judgment or an analogous method.

Using the analogous method of looking over past projects, I noticed that when there is an insignificant increase in cost or schedule the projects have been successful 95% of the time. Therefore, when I qualitatively analyze the risk to cost or schedule, I will consider that if the increase in cost or schedule is insignificant, 5% or less, the impact to the project's cost or schedule will be minimal. However, if I see that the potential risk would increase the project's cost or schedule by 20% and, using the same model, that there is an 80% chance of failure based on previous projects, I will determine that the risk is unacceptable and a contingency plan should be put in place.

Quantitative risk analysis requires that the value of the potential losses associated with the risk be determined. With quantitative risk analysis it is important to consider two factors mentioned previously: the likelihood that the risk will occur and the impact if the risk event does occur. A simple calculation can be used to determine the expected value of a risk: the probability that the risk will occur (in percent) times the value of the risk event on a scale based on the event's impact (1–10). If the likelihood that some event will occur is 50%, and the impact of that event to the project's schedule, for example, is 5, then the expected value of that risk event is $0.50 \times 5 = 2.5$. This type of evaluation is very helpful when trying to determine which of the risk events, those with higher expected value, you should commit your valuable resources to addressing.

LESSON LEARNED

Probably one of the most significant tools that the healthcare project manager has at his or her disposal is lessons learned. Valuable information is contained in lessons learned documentation: what risks were encountered and how those risks were mitigated. Not only will this information be useful in planning projects to avoid some of the risks from previous projects, but it will also be helpful when responding to risks. Being able to see results from previous risk responses will allow the project manager to better plan a response.

RESPONDING TO RISK

To properly respond to risk, you need the following information:

- List of potential risks
- Results of qualitative and quantitative risk analysis
- Risk tolerance thresholds from stakeholders and policies
- Lessons learned from previous projects

With this information you can begin to prepare a risk response plan. There are only three ways to respond to risk: avoidance, mitigation, or acceptance. Risk avoidance in today's world is practically impossible to achieve. "Progress always involves risk; you can't steal second base and keep your foot on first base."[2] With proper planning and significant risk identification, you may be able to avoid some risks. You may also be able to avoid risks by not taking any chances, but that implies no forward progress. Without forward progress, an organization is not likely to survive. That makes avoiding risk a non-starter.

By far, the best way to deal with risk is to mitigate it by taking out as much of the pain as possible or perhaps even eliminating the risk altogether. Risk mitigation is both a challenge and an art. Determining what risks to respond to is the challenge. Finding ways to deal with the risk once it has been identified is the art.

Mitigating Risk

One of the ways that risk can be mitigated is to transfer the risk to someone else. Insurance is one of the most popular ways to transfer risk. We use insurance every day to mitigate the risk of something happening to our automobiles, homes, or health. The more risk you transfer, generally the more costly it is. Almost anything can be insured, from a prominent entertainment show host's legs, to a race horse, to the chances of an oil spill, to our pet's health. In healthcare, one of the better-known forms of risk mitigation (insurance) is malpractice insurance. In most instances, healthcare professionals are either required or recommended to carry malpractice insurance, sometimes called personal liability insurance. Other ways in which healthcare professionals can use insurance is to insure the delivery of a product that is necessary to execute a project, especially if that product's arrival is crucial at a certain time in your project. By insuring delivery, if the delivery is not made for reasons covered by the insurance, then penalties would be imposed if requirements are not met. This doesn't guarantee that your project will be on time, just that if it is late because of the late delivery of one or more of the needed products, there would be some compensation to mitigate the risk. Bonds, specifically performance and completion bonds, and warranties are popular forms of "insurance." The difference between a performance bond and a warranty is that a performance bond can be used throughout the delivery process of a project, while a warranty is used after delivery of the project's product has been accepted.

Some other ways to mitigate risk is to change the planned approach for the project. If, during the risk identification or risk analysis phases, too many risks are uncovered, or those that are uncovered have extensive impacts on the project, perhaps a less risky approach to the project can be made. Subcontracting the project or parts of the project could also transfer that risk. A downside of that is you may lose control of that part of the project. If subcontractors are used, contractual controls may be prudent. A joint venture or even an acquisition may be a good strategy to mitigate risks. If there is a critical piece needed to successfully complete your project, then that piece or a similar piece is needed for future projects or for the long term, and if the organization has the resources, it may be advantageous to acquire the provider. Acquisition certainly has more control associated with it than does a joint venture. But a joint venture may be a good choice especially of the organization has limited resources.

Accepting Risk

"The very nature of project work is one laden with risk, and the primary mission of each project manager should be to reduce, transfer, avoid, or otherwise lessen the impact of risk in a manner consistent with the achievement of project expectations."[3] The very nature of project management is that some risk will have to be accepted. Mitigation costs may be too high, the organization wants to challenge employees or employ leading edge technology, or the nature of the risk will not allow mitigation. In this case, proactive acceptance may be the right policy. Proactive steps include the following:

- Contingency plans
    - Multiple sourcing of critical inputs
    - Adding personnel or shifts
    - Cross-training of personnel
    - Subcontracting
    - Trailing edge technologies
    - Overtime
- Contingency allowances – intended to reduce impacts due to cost overruns or schedule delays
- Management reserves – controlled at a higher organization level and span many or all projects

One other way to accept the risk is to passively accept the consequences should that risk occur. It is not a recommended strategy because it implies "doing nothing." Accepting risk may mean accepting lower profit should the identified risk be realized. If the impact of the risk is minimal, it may be prudent to do nothing and just accept it.

MONITORING AND CONTROLLING RISKS

If nothing else, one thing to remember is that *risks change throughout the project.* Risks that may have been identified during the design phase of a project may be eliminated as you move to the implementation phase, and new risks may appear. Risk identification is an iterative process that is never complete; therefore, controlling the identified risks becomes very important. Monitoring the risk triggers, signals that the event has taken place, or warning signs that the risk may occur is part of risk control. One place to look is at the actual versus planned budget, quality, and schedule. While it is important to monitor what is going right with a project, the focus should be on what may go wrong with the project. It is a more active approach to risk monitoring and control.

Earned Value Management

Earned value management (EVM) is used as a tool to discover variance in budgets and schedules to *warn* a project manager about a potential risk to a project. "EVM is an integrated management control system for assessing, understanding, and quantifying what a contractor or field activity is achieving with program dollars:

- Integrates technical, cost, schedule, with risk management
- Allows objective assessment and quantification of current project performance
- Helps predict future performance based on trends

EVM provides project management with objective, accurate, and timely data for effective decision making."[4]

EVM uses project data to calculate variances in the project schedule and the project costs. The key word is *variance.* That doesn't mean that it tells you what or where the problems are in the project, just that there is a *potential* issue that needs to be investigated. EVM uses data from the

TASK	A	B	C	D	E	F	Total
Planned value ($)	10	15	10	25	20	20	100

FIGURE 9.5
Earned value—baseline.

project to calculate those variances. It is a snapshot of project costs and schedule at a point in time. The data includes the following:

- Actual project costs
- Planned project costs
- Earned value

It is best not to look at a specific task, because for reasons I'll explain below, one task doesn't provide enough information to make a judgment. I define earned value as the cost of the work performed at a certain point in the project. If I had a task that was supposed to be complete on day 5 of the project, I would look at that task on day 5 and determine (1) if the task is complete and (2) how much I believe the task is worth to the project. My determined earned value may be more or less than the actual cost.

In the following example, I will look at six tasks at a particular point in time. To properly use EVM, it is necessary to establish a baseline (see Figure 9.5). Once the baseline is established for that point in time, use the planned value and the earned value to view schedule variance (see Figure 9.6). Looking across the six tasks, there is a –35% variance between the determined earned value and the planned value. The interpretation is that the project appears to be behind schedule.

To complete the assessment, I next look at the same six tasks, but use actual cost along with earned value determined during the schedule vari-

	A	B	C	D	E	F	Total
Planned value ($)	10	15	10	25	20	20	100
Earned value ($)	10	15	10	10	20	—	65
Schedule variance	0	0	0	15	0	20	−35 = −35%

FIGURE 9.6
Earned value—schedule variance.

	A	B	C	D	E	F	Total
Earned value ($)	10	15	10	10	20	—	65
Actual cost ($)	9	22	8	30	22	—	91
Cost variance	1	–7	2	–20	–2	0	–26 = –40%

FIGURE 9.7
Earned value—cost variance.

ance exercise (see Figure 9.7). Looking at Figure 9.7, there appears to be a cost variance of –40%, or the project is overrunning the budget by 40%.

Now that the analysis is complete it is time to do the interpretation. The result of the analysis warns that there is a potential problem. The interpretation will conclude whether action is needed or not. In Figure 9.6, Tasks A, B, C, and E have a 0 schedule variance. However, Task D, the value that the activity was planned to achieve, was not achieved, and Task F has not achieved any of its earned value. Therefore, Tasks D and F need to be further scrutinized. At a close look, Task F may not have started because of a necessary delay in obtaining the resources, for instance. While it shows up as a flag to the project, it may not necessarily cause a project delay if the task can be "crashed" or fast tracked (see Chapter 4) or if the task can be delayed without affecting the project's final delivery date.

Further examination of Figure 9.7 shows that Tasks B, D, E, and F have some variance. The cost variance of Task F is consistent with the task not being started, and therefore not consuming resources. Maybe further examination of Tasks B, D, and E may show *real* cost discrepancies that need to be addressed. As an example, during Hurricane Katrina the price of plywood in some areas of the county quadrupled. One way or another, that cost had to be passed on to the project. Management reserves or contingency allowances may need to be tapped.

Risk management is as much of an art as a science. While tools like earned value management can be used to gain further knowledge about a project's progress, there are still interpretation, subjectivity, and educated guesses that go into managing risks.

Specific Example of Risk Assessment

We talked about risk in some detail, but I want to provide you with a specific example of a risk assessment of the most common area of risk for the project manager, that at the requirements or specification stage of a project. One of the more important areas to consider when assessing risks is the requirements/specification-gathering process. Risks occur when there is no clarity or specificity with the requirements/specifications. Clarity and specificity of the requirements definition can be related to (1) ambiguity, (2) completeness, (3) verification, (4) focus, (5) related to project output, (6) technology, and (7) how changeable the requirements may be. It is helpful to not only analyze the potential risk, but also to place a value on it. That way, the total risks of the requirements-gathering process can be considered in the decision-making process. The following scale can be applied: no risk = 0, slight risk = 1–4, acceptable risk = 5–6, and high risk = 7–10. Some of the risks are noted as either a risk or not a risk. To assign values, including zero, review the requirements with the extended project team. Include key stakeholders in that evaluation. (See Chapter 3 for more information about stakeholders.)

Clarity and Specificity of Requirements Risks

- Ambiguity – If the requirement/specification has one clear interpretation, it would be considered "0" risk. If it can be misinterpreted or is confusing, assign the appropriate value.
- Completeness – Is the requirement defined so that the customer's expectations are defined? The requirements should clearly state what is expected and, just as important, what is not expected.
- Verifiability – Can the requirement be "tested"? If so, how easily can it be tested? If it cannot be tested, the risk then is in the 7–10 range depending on how critical the requirement/specification is to the project.
- Focus – Is the requirement/specification focused on one specific feature of the project? If so, the risk would be "0".
- Relationship – Is the requirement/specification directly related to the project's output (risk/no risk)?
- Complexity – Is this based on existing technology (0 risk), tested new technology (1–6), or yet to be developed technology (7–10)?
- Changeability – This is one of those risks that can be based on the analysis of the other risks. Given the high risk of verifiability, focus, and completeness, how likely is the requirement/specification to change?

By adding the scores of your analysis, you will have a good picture as to the risk during the requirements/specification-gathering phase of the project. If your risk scores are high during this process, you already have to deal with a multitude of issues before the project-planning phase is under way. At this point, the project may be deemed too risky to proceed. Should this occur, the major investment at this point is the analysis process. It is better to have to stop the project here than deep in the development stage after countless resources have been expended.

KEY REVIEW QUESTIONS

1. In your own words, *define risk.*
2. What is a *make/buy* decision and why is it important to risk management?
3. What are the *four* risk categories?
4. What are the *three* ways to deal with risk?
5. What are *three* ways to proactively manage risk?
6. In a paragraph, explain why risk management is considered an *art and a science.*

ENDNOTES

1. BusinessDictionary.com, http://www.businessdictionary.com/definition/risk.html
2. Wilcox, Fredrick (1881–1956), English footballer, is attributed with this quote.
3. Gilbreath, Robert D., *Winning at Project Management, What Works, What Fails and Why*, John Wiley & Sons, New York, 1988.
4. National Aeronautic and Space Administration, http://evm.nasa.gov/

10

Project Close-Out

While not one of the larger chapters, Chapter 10 is no less important. As a matter of fact, some think that properly closing a project is one of the most important functions of a project manager. That is because properly closing out a project can save an organization countless resources. Conversely, not closing out a project properly can cost an organization additional resources. Why, because it is all about reinventing the wheel, or not, and making the same mistakes over again, or not. Additionally, in the excitement of moving to a new project, closure of the old one becomes low on the priority list. So how do you close out a project properly?

Part of the answer lies with the question "How well was the project documented?" The obvious answer is "Very well, thank you." And, to prove it, the project manager will have at his or her disposal, all of the documentation required by all of the previous chapters in this book; the results of the use of any decision tools, the Project Charter, results of stakeholder analysis, the Scope Statement (requirements, expectations, detailed project description, milestones, deliverables, and acceptance/success criteria), the contract (if there is one), the Work Breakdown Structure, estimates and techniques used for both costs and schedule, the project schedule (network diagram, Gantt), the project budget, resource usage, roles and responsibilities, quality plan, communications plan, change management plan, and risk plan (including assumptions and constraints). Finally, lessons learned should be collected and added to the project documentation. Using the archived information from the project will allow similar projects to "hit the ground running." Much of the processes and procedures for those similar projects will already be in place. Some tweaking will need to be done, for instance, updating the cost of money for budget estimates, but the majority of the information will not have to be reinvented.

INTERNALLY FACING REASON

So many organizations undertake projects that are similar in nature that reusing previous projects information will save a significant number of resources. That is the internally facing reason for proper close-out. The collected lessons learned are critically important to the success of any future projects. Mistakes, missteps, and unknown risks will occur on any project. That's a given. However, what you don't want to do is have the same things occur on the next project. It is not just having those same things occurring over and over again, but also that the project management processes sometimes need a course correction. One size does not always fit and customizations to the various project management processes need to happen. Some examples of project management process changes are frequency of data collection, methods for collecting data (survey vs. focus groups), document formatting, correct use of media (wikis versus blogs), etc. Fortunately, once those changes are done, they will apply to similar projects. Forewarned is forearmed, and that's what lessons learned is all about. It is all about learning from mistakes.

EXTERNALLY FACING REASON

The externally facing reason for properly closing out a project is to gather all the information needed by external stakeholders or customers so that their expectations are met. This is especially true where there is a contract involved. Documented proof of the fulfillment of those contractual issues may be the trigger for payment. Proper closeout may include signoff, whether contractual or not. That signoff signifies that the external stakeholders or customers expectations have been met. It is the formal acceptance of the project.

CONTRACT CLOSURE

Contracts come to a close just as projects come to a close. Contract closure is concerned with completing and settling the terms of the contract.

It supports the project closeout process because the contract closure process determines if the work described in the contract was completed accurately and satisfactorily. Keep in mind that not all projects are performed under contract so not all projects require the contract closure process. Obviously, this process applies only to those phases, deliverables, or portions of the project that were performed under a contract. Proper contract closure ensures that the specific conditions of the contract, including the adherence to any contract clauses, are complete and documented as complete.

Contract closure is also the impetus for the "formal" notice to the stakeholder that the project is complete. Because it is externally focused, it is a two-way street. Closure also signals to the project team that the contract was successfully completed, and that the stakeholder is also satisfied.

A note about contract closure: in some cases the project may have a contract that is administered by another organization, perhaps a centralized contracting organization. In that case, the closure is the responsibility of that organization. If that is the case, while that organization may be responsible for contract administration, the accountability is still with the project manager. A copy of that close-out document should be included, for completeness and verification, with the project close- out documentation.

CLOSING OUT THE TEAM

While that has a ring of finality to it, it certainly isn't meant to be a bad thing. Part of project close out is also acknowledging the project team, preferably with a celebration. Whether or not the project was a rousing success, there was hard work done on the part of the project team and that hard work should be acknowledged. In addition, as you will see in our discussion of teaming in Chapter 11, one of those aspects of teaming was "adjourning." Adjourning is closure to the team. It is the signal that this project is officially concluded and it is time to move on. It is also the time to collect the lessons learned about the project personnel to assure that you will have that information when it comes to performance appraisal time. Whether you are asked or not, your input should be given to supervision for of your matrixed team members. Your matrixed team members may not have been as visible to their own management as they were to you, and it is important that their efforts be acknowledged.

KEY REVIEW QUESTIONS

1. What are the principle external and internal reasons for project closure?
2. Why is it important to properly close out a contract?
3. Why is it important to close out the team?

Section III

Management Skills as a Necessity

11

Motivation, Teaming, and the Project Team

One of the key management skills either in possession of or to be gained by the project manager is the ability to motivate people. Now, I'm not saying this in a derogatory sense, but the reality is that project managers are manipulators, but in a good way. In most cases, project managers do not have the direct power to influence others' behavior to get them to execute on project duties. Others will, however, execute those duties as part of their regular functions. But what the project manager wants to do is get people to execute their duties because they want to, not because they have to. And the project manager wants them to execute their duties based on the project manager's defined project plan.

HISTORY OF MOTIVATION

One of the ways to understand what motivates team members is to review the history of motivational studies and see what the early motivational "gurus" found. Elton Mayo was one of those motivational gurus. As with the quality efforts, motivational gurus also looked to the Hawthorne Works, AT&T's Western Electric Manufacturing facility in Cicero, Illinois. Once again, the reasoning was that the country was moving to a more high tech environment, although the word "high tech" did not appear until the 1950s. While he may not have known the word, Mayo did know something was happening. So he undertook a study between 1927 and 1932. His experiments were designed to measure what influenced workers' productivity. What he found was that group interaction, affiliation, and the personal attention of management were bigger influences than salary and benefits.

Frederick Herzberg, an American psychologist, worked a couple of decades later than Mayo. In 1968 he published "One More Time, How Do You Motivate Employees?" He developed the *motivation-hygiene* theory. His theory was that there were certain factors (motivators) that were the real stimulus for employees, while certain factors (hygiene) can be dissatisfiers if not present but do not, in and of themselves, stimulate employees. This theory was mainly targeted toward employee productivity and what truly stimulated employee productivity. The satisfiers Herzberg identifies were a sense of achievement, recognition by management for achievement, the work itself, responsibility, advancement, and personal growth. The hygiene factors he found to provide dissatisfaction if not present were the company policy, micromanagement, working conditions, and salary. When you look at both Herzberg and Mayo and, more to the point, when you think about what it takes to motivate your team members, it is certainly within your means even though you may not control their compensation. Giving attention to team members and congratulations for jobs well done are free. One other thing to remember is that, even though the project you are working on does not turn out as successful as it should be, your team probably worked very hard and still needs to be acknowledged.

One of the more interesting and useful studies of human behavior is from Abraham Maslow (1908–1970). If a project manager can ascertain where in the Maslow hierarchy a team member is, then the method of motivating that team member is more clearly defined. Maslow defined a five-level hierarchy of needs. It was purposely designed as a hierarchy, increasing in sophistication as one works his or her way up through the hierarchy (see Figure 11.1). The *physiological* or *bodily* needs include the basics needed for life: water, food, sleep, etc. *Safety* or *security* needs include things like

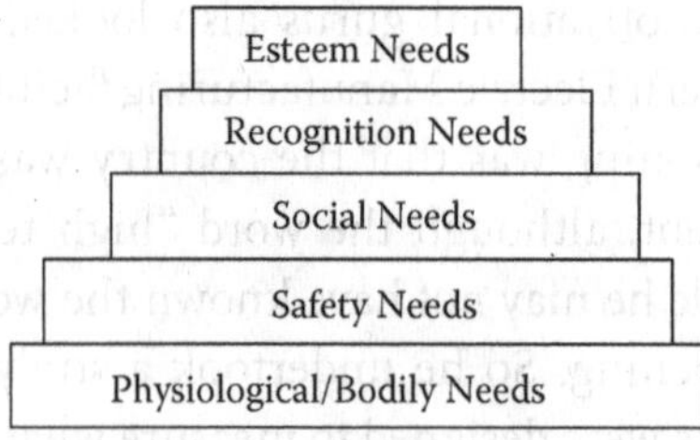

FIGURE 11.1
Maslow's hierarchy.

job security, a retirement plan, and life insurance. Working one's way up through the hierarchy, the next level encountered is *love* or *belonging*. That level includes affiliation (remember Mayo), being part of a community, club, or church, as well as being in a loving relationship, whether it be with a significant other, sibling, or friend. The fourth level of hierarchy is the *esteem* level, where recognition, appreciation, reputation, confidence, competence, and dignity are imperative. The fifth level is *self-actualization*, the uppermost and most advanced level an individual can strive to achieve. It is a very complex level that includes a rather hard-to-define concept of "becoming the most complete, fullest 'you.'"[1]

So why does the healthcare professional managing projects care about Maslow's hierarchy, and does he or she use it? With most projects, the project manager cannot and does not work alone. The key to working with people and helping to motivate them is to know them and what motivates them. By learning your team in terms of the hierarchy, you can then figure out where those people are in the hierarchy and then it is relatively easy to determine what motivates them. Once you have determined that the individual has reached the self-actualization level, he or she will be self-motivated. That doesn't mean that those individuals do not need the benefits of the esteem level or that they can slip down the hierarchy depending on life challenges. You still need to continually evaluate and reevaluate each team member. For more information see the Web site http://webspace.ship.edu/cgboer/maslow.html

WHAT MOTIVATES YOU?

It's not that you have the choice; it is just that you do! Motivation is a personal choice. In spite of all of the research and the motivational "gurus," it is difficult for anyone to "nail" what motivates you. Sometimes you don't even know what motivates you, until something does. For instance, the result from all of your own actions may be motivation enough. Being accountable for actions that yield other than positive results can be a powerful motivator.

The very tools that project managers live by can provide significant motivation. The judicious use of milestones in a project schedule is a great motivator. Having the milestones visible provides a visual stimulation, and meeting the milestones provides a satisfaction motivator. While detailed and specific communications are the cornerstone of project management, they may not seem to be a motivational tool. But in fact, precise communications will enhance your ability to achieve your project goals, thus increasing your own sense of satisfaction, which may be one of your motivators. Precise communications make it easier to understand what your project goals are, therefore defining much more clearly what it takes to achieve those goals. The ability to communicate clearly and concisely with a variety of project stakeholders provides a personal satisfaction that may be a motivator to some.

Motivation complements good leadership. There is personal satisfaction from the ability to team with others, trust and respect, and benevolence. Good leaders encourage creativity and create a motivational and stimulating environment, opportunities, challenges, and high expectations. These characteristics of leadership tend to provide motivation to those who stimulate that behavior.

Of course, there are always the "old standbys," the "harder" capabilities: incentives, salary, benefits, and bonuses. I tend to agree with Frederick Herzberg[2] and his motivation-hygiene theory that these standbys are hygiene factors that are dissatisfiers if not present, but in and of themselves they are not motivators. The hard capabilities coupled with the "soft" capabilities, including job restructure, job enrichment, job enhancement, and job advancement, can provide a motivational environment. It is therefore extremely important to learn your team, where they are in the hierarchy of needs, and what motivates them so that the motivational environment that a good leader (project manager) creates addresses the needs of those people.

TEAMING

> Coming together is a beginning. Keeping together is progress. Working together is success.
>
> **—Henry Ford**

Forming, storming, norming, performing, and adjourning are well-acknowledged principles of team development,[3] and I use them all the time to illustrate the process of team development. It is a process! When teams first come together, there is a period of searching that takes place.

Forming

- What are the real tasks?
- Who are the other people involved?
- Will I like working in this team?
- Will people in the team like working with me.
- What is expected of me?
- What do I expect from others?
- How will working in this team affect my daily work?
- Is there a leader?
    - If yes, who is it?
    - If no, am I expected to step up?

This is a conforming, non-confrontational phase of team development. As a matter of fact, confrontation is avoided at all costs. It may also be a time that is very uncomfortable for some, especially those who are highly introverted and more comfortable working by themselves. There also may be some who are more impatient than others to get to the action. However, this phase of team development is like the planning process in project management—ample time must be spent addressing the process issues of this phase in order to create a solid foundation for the team to move to the next, most difficult phase of team development. The planning process of project management provides a similar solid foundation.

Storming

Just as the name implies, this phase is like being in a lifeboat full of people for a couple of days when a gale blows in. The boat gets rocked, you are tossed around, and you have been in the boat long enough to have formed some opinions about the other people in the lifeboat. It can get ugly. There are those, however, who are very comfortable in this situation and like to watch and sometimes instigate the conflict. They are people I call "gasoline throwers." They will not start the fires, but merely feed them. Of course, there are also the provocateurs, the "fire starters." Fire starters and gasoline throwers for the most part are not interested in moving out of this zone and need to be encouraged by the true leaders to participate in the team. This is where learning about the motivators of these types of people can help to remove them as obstacles. This is also a good place for conflict management skills, which we will talk more about in Chapter 11. Because conflict is not necessarily bad, it can be creative, but it must be managed. A leader will begin to emerge at this stage, possibly by proposing some conventions on which to operate.

Norming

Not all teams will get to this point because they will get stuck in the storming phase. If a leader does not emerge during the storming phase, or the fires that have been started and fed become infernos, or the situation changes somehow and the original task becomes moot, there is either no need or no way to get to the performing phase. This phase is characterized by people starting to calm down from storming. Listening is a big indicator of reaching this phase. People begin to "get" each other. Respect for opinions and people is another indicator. People start to feel better and want to move toward accomplishing the task. The seas are calming.

Performing

Finally we reach a stage when *work can be accomplished*. There is a sense of trust, understanding, and maturity in the team. Morale is improving and loyalty is high. All of the previous energy put into forming, storming, and norming is now put into completing the task. There is interdependency, and all of the people are on the oars heading toward shore.

Adjourning

Now that we are all a team, and the task (or project) has been accomplished, the team as it is defined is no longer relevant. But the people are. After all of the hard work of forming, storming, norming, and performing, bonds have been formed. When faced with the dissolution of the team, some people may feel a sense of loss. Some will not want to leave the team and the friends they have made, particularly if the task or project was very difficult to accomplish and people put a big part of themselves into it. But as project managers we realize that projects by definition are unique, and the next one will probably not have the same resource requirements as the previous one. That's what makes project management such an interesting field.

The best way to handle the adjourning phase is to make sure that accomplishments have been recognized. Whether or not the project is a success, people have worked very hard trying to meet the project's requirements.

There should be a close-out celebration to instill a sense of accomplishment, and then you should move on.

WHY ARE TEAMS SO IMPORTANT?

Belonging to a team leads to a spirit of cooperation and understanding of the task at hand. Members who are more familiar with approaches to accomplishing a particular task can mentor those who are not. That mutual support will enhance the overall performance of the team. "Two heads are better than one" is a quote I believe may have been adapted from the Bible (Ecclesiastes 4.9, "Two are better than one"). Teams combine talents, skill sets, and knowledge to provide more innovative and creative solutions to issues that may arise. They are very attractive to management because there will be multiple sources of input to the decision-making process, making it more diverse, with the possibility of making a better decision.

THE PROJECT TEAM

Without a project team, there wouldn't be much project management. Unless it is a very small project that could be done through a single-person effort, a project manager could not possibly follow through with all of the planning, organizing, and controlling that has to be done to successfully manage a project.

CHOOSING A PROJECT TEAM

There are certain criteria used when picking a team. The first consideration is to determine the project's goals and objectives. The goals and objectives of a project are the first order of business to determine team members based on their experience level, personality requirements, and convenience. The project team may need to be comprised of people with technical expertise, particular business acumen, administrative experience, project management experience, or a combination of all of these. A project will usually include a leader; some followers; a cheerleader or two, who may also be one of the others; and a techie or two. Effective projects need both extroverted and introverted personalities. In some instances, convenience is an important criterion for choosing a project team, but sometimes it is not. Distributed teams are effective when the project is spread out across the country or across the world. But in the world of managing projects in healthcare, convenience is critical for communications, even with all of the modern communications conveniences. Nothing beats face-to-face contact in an environment that is so people oriented. Sometimes resources that are available are not consistent with the project needs, so what can be done?

PLANNING FOR THE TEAM

There are prerequisites (homework) the project manager needs to meet prior to developing a team. I like to put together a checklist (see Figure 11.2) of those criteria to keep them foremost in my mind.

- Clearly define the project's mission, goals, and objectives
- Align the project team with the project's mission, goals, and objectives
- Cultivate a motivational climate
- Be clear and precise with communications

√	Team Planning Checklist
	Have you clearly defined the project's mission, goals, and objectives?
	Is your project team aligned with the project's mission, goals, and objectives?
	Have you cultivated a motivational environment?
	Are your communications to the team clear and concise?
	Have you clearly defined the project's roles and responsibilities?
	Is there a responsibility assignment matrix?
	Do you have a conflict resolution strategy?
	Do you have methods to celebrate and reward accomplishments?

FIGURE 11.2
Team planning checklist.

- Clearly define roles and responsibilities
- Build in time for conflict resolution
- Listen to team members
- Recognize and celebrate accomplishments and individuals

DEVELOPING A PROJECT TEAM

There are certain criteria that have to be established during the project team development process. I cannot emphasize enough that a clear project definition is critical to the success of a project. Without a clear definition, the project manager will not be able to access the project's needs, especially from a personnel standpoint. Remember, one of the measures that defines the word "project" is that it is unique; therefore, every project will require different skill sets to successfully complete it. Reviewing the task list contained in the work breakdown structure will help define the personnel requirements. There is a theme here; I believe that creating a good WBS is crucial to a project's success. By reviewing an accurate WBS, the project manager can select a team to address those exact project requirements.

Now that there is a definitive WBS, all the project manager has to do is select the right people to accomplish each of the tasks, correct? In a perfect world, the answer would be "yes." In the imperfect world of project management, however, the majority of the time, some of the right people are available and some probably are not. So what do we do in that case? There are several options, and remember, options will include trade-offs, principally between costs, quality, and schedule.

Diane Westfield, the project manager for NCMC's EMR Project, is in the process of developing a project team. This project is considered a "leading edge" project for NCMC because it is a first-time deployment for them. As a result, there is not much in-house experience to draw from for the team. It is critical that Diane has a few people on the team who are familiar with EMR so that she can delegate some of the duties and she, being the good project manager she is, can keep her eye on the "big picture." She has planned a 2-day introduction to EMR for her team to have a better appreciation for the project, and a 5-day detailed seminar for a couple of her key team members to give them a more detailed view, bringing in outside consultants. She will need to review her budget and schedule in order to accommodate the increase in costs for the consultants and the additional time to train her team members. Diane believes that not training these people will add to the cost of quality. While the training will not guarantee that project mistakes won't be made, it is a risk mitigation strategy. If the training is not undertaken, the chances of rework, overtime, and scope creep will result in a greater increase in costs and schedule, as well as potentially damaging the quality of the project and the project's product, the new EMR system.

Training is one option. Choosing the right person or people to educate becomes a challenge. Some people seek education; some consider it a burden. Choosing the right education program is another challenge to be overcome. Bringing in consultants to review any part of the project is also an option. Consultants familiar with EMR systems could be hired to review the planning, WBS, schedule, or whatever process or interval the project manager has some concern about. For some of the requirements of the project, like ongoing support, hiring permanent employees with the requisite skill set is another option. As with any of these options, there has to be a consideration of the budget. Consultants and experts can add expenses to the project. There is also the issue of the less skilled people already on the team and what can be done with them.

KEY REVIEW QUESTIONS

1. In a paragraph, explain what Mayo and the other motivational *gurus* found when they studied the motivational factors of workers.
2. What are the *five* stages of team development and how do they differ?
3. Which stage of team development is the best for actually working on the project?
4. What is a *critical* task performed by the project manager to help achieve project success?

ENDNOTES

1. Boeree, C. G., *Abraham Maslow 1908–1970*. Personality Theories, http://webspace.ship.edu/cgboer/maslow.html
2. Herzberg, Frederick, "One More Time, How Do You Motivate Employees?" *Harvard Business Review*, 1987, p. 8.
3. Dr. Bruce Tuckman published his Forming Storming Norming Performing model in 1965. He added a fifth stage, Adjourning, in the 1970s.

12

Leadership and Power

Leadership and power in project management are inextricably intertwined. Just like one size probably doesn't fit all, one leadership style doesn't fit all situations. Depending on the power structure of an organization and the power bestowed on a project manager along with the type of project, project budget, schedule, and scope are all factors in determining the effectiveness of the project management effort. Complicated? You bet. Can it all be interpreted to help the project manager gain insight? You better believe it, because if the project leader does not understand the relationship, chances are that it will be more of a struggle than it needs to be to plan, organize, and control a project. Again, let's look at leadership and power from a historical perspective to see where we can "borrow" the best practices to apply to the healthcare environment.

LEADERSHIP

The question I always ask myself is what style of leader should be applied to this situation. Mind you, I'm not saying that you should not be true to yourself; what I am saying is that we can all take a lesson from others' successes. If you were to emulate a great leader who shows a penchant for motivation, who would you emulate? Who would you choose from modern history? How about some of the great coaches: Knute Rockne, Red Auerbach, Bobby Bowden, Leo Durocher, Mike Krzyzewski, or Vince Lombardi? I'm sure I left one of your favorites out. But using "coaching" as a leadership style, what do you need to be a good sports coach? First and foremost all of the good coaches I've ever met or read about had a *passion* for what they were doing. They also made me feel that they were interested in *my success* or the success of their players as individuals. As well as encouragement, they expressed that interest in the form of constructive criticism, and when I say constructive I mean that they had solutions to help me get better, not just critique. One of the dimensions when managing a project (coaching) is the team dimension: how individuals are helping or how they are hurting the *team*, just like players on a sports team. Also, to use the sports team analogy, critique should not only be project focused, but should also help the individual grow as a person—continual improvement, not just in project quality, but in personal quality as well. As an additional benefit I have found that by coaching others, I have been able to see areas of my own growth and improvement, making me a better coach (manager)—a vicious cycle.

What other leadership skills or qualities does a project manager in healthcare need to be successful? Due to the nature of the healthcare environment, as we've already discussed, compassion and empathy are qualities needed for the project manager to understand the context of the project, not necessarily the content. Projects are changes, and sometimes long-lasting changes. As a project manager, success is not just measured by whether or not the project "came in" on time, on budget, and with the scope as determined. It isn't, you ask? No—if you've burned out your project team or in some way hurt the organization in the process, is that considered a success? Especially in this environment, if you haven't shown compassion and empathy for those who need to implement the changes, those affected by the changes, and members of your team, then I don't consider the project a personal success, even if it meets all the financial goals.

Good leaders are also visionaries, which is one of the reasons why project management is a great breeding ground for future leaders. One of the primary skills of a project manager is to keep the "big picture" or the overall "vision" of the project. Good leaders, like good project managers, keep the vision in focus and in the forefront of the team's perspective. While keeping the vision in mind, leaders still need to act in a determined and resolute manner advancing toward the ultimate goal. Communication skills, the ability to use decision-making tools, negotiating, conflict management, stakeholder management, and other skills detailed throughout this book are also important. So then the question becomes, "Is leadership an innate quality, or can it be learned?"

There are countless studies that have been done relative to this subject. Arguments for both sides are credible. When I talk to groups about this subject, there are always parents who will insist that they knew which of their children were the instigators (or leaders if you will) and which of their children were followers. That would indicate to me that there is a leadership "chip" that some people have and some do not. I believe that there is some innate ability to lead, but I also believe that, whether or not you have the leadership chip, leading is, for the most part, a conscious effort. Of course there are "battlefield commissions," and I am sure that some of us have experienced that phenomenon, whether we've been in the military or not. Sometimes a leadership position is made available because of a particular situation. But pertaining to the conscious effort, people who want to lead need to accomplish a few things:

- They must want to lead.
- They must proactively seek leadership positions.
- They must know their strengths and weaknesses.
- They must learn others' strengths and weaknesses.
- They must have a strong sense of efficacy (believe in their capacity to achieve a goal).
- They must continually challenge themselves.
- They must seek continual personal improvement.
- They must be fearless in pursuit of their goals.

Leadership is *situational.* No one leadership style works for every situation. The ability of an individual to assess the situation and apply the necessary skills is critical for project or general leadership.

To see what kind of leader you may be, take the leadership quiz in Figure 12.1. Once you have multiplied and totaled the columns you will have a cumulative number. If the number is between 48 and 38, you have great utilization of your leadership skills; between 37 and 28, you have good utilization of your leadership skills; and 27 and under, you are underutilizing your leadership skills.

LEADERSHIP VERSUS MANAGEMENT

I believe that there has always been some misunderstanding about the differences between leadership and management. A *leader* is "someone who occupies a position in a group, influences others in accordance with the role expectation of the position and co-ordinates and directs the group in

	Seldom	Occasionally	Often	Frequently
1. I am aware of what I am feeling.				
2. I know my strengths and weaknesses.				
3. I deal calmly with stress.				
4. I believe the future will be better than the past.				
5. I deal with changes easily.				
6. I set measurable goals when I have a project.				
7. Others say I understand and am sensitive to them.				
8. Others say I resolve conflict.				
9. Others say I build and maintain relationships.				
10. Others say I inspire them.				
11. Others say I am a team player.				
12. Others say I helped to develop their abilities.				
TOTAL THE NUMBER OF CHECKS IN EACH COLUMN				
MULTIPLY EACH COLUMN BY:	1	2	3	4
TOTAL THE NUMBER IN EACH COLUMN				
TOTAL ALL FOUR COLUMNS				

FIGURE 12.1
Leadership quiz.

maintaining itself and reaching its goal."[1] Therefore, the term *leadership* would be an expansion of this definition, being the "process of influence between a leader and his followers to attain group, organizational and societal goals."[2]

Most people view leadership as being associated with the role of a manager. Nothing could be further from the truth. Leading and managing activities are separate and distinct, particularly with respect to interpersonal style. "Leaders ... are often dramatic and unpredictable in style. They tend to create an atmosphere of change, ferment even chaos. They are often obsessed by their ideas, which appear as visionary and consequently excite, stimulate, and drive other people to work hard to create reality out of fantasy. ... Managers are typically hard-working, analytical, tolerant, and fair-minded. They have a strong sense of belonging to the organization, and take great pride in perpetuating and improving the status quo."[3]

There is an opposing view that says that leadership is but one aspect of management. I tend to agree that managers and leaders come from different perspectives. When I think about a leader, I think more about vision and mission than I do about day-to-day operation. I think about inspiration, stimulation, and creativity. When I think about managers, I think about the day-to-day operations and managing them. I believe that project managers, in spite of the name, have to be both leaders and managers. The leading aspect of project management involves being able to influence project team members to achieve the desirable goals of the project. In slight contrast, the management aspect of project management involves the process activities of planning, organizing, and controlling the project through the use of the tools available: WBS, schedule, budget, etc.

Leadership Theories

While there are many leadership theories, I will only cover the three more interesting ones. The first is the Great Man/Great Woman Theory. "Much of the work on this theory was done in the 19th century and is often linked to the work of the historian Thomas Carlyle, who commented on the great men or heroes of history saying that 'the history of the world is but the biography of great men.' According to him, a leader is the one gifted with unique qualities that capture the imagination of the masses."[4] It also says that there are major events, both national and international, that are influenced by those in power. "A sudden act by a great man could, according to this theory, change the fate of the nation."[5]

The second theory is the "Trait Theory." This theory concentrates on personal characteristics. It includes traits like physical appearance, intelligence levels, and communication skills. Adler,[6] in 1991, said that "the research on trait theories of leadership has shown that many other factors are important in determining leader success, and that not everyone who possesses these traits will be a leader." Both of these theories tend to purport that leaders are born.

"Rather than a great man causing a great event to happen, the situational approach claims that great events are the product of historical forces that are going to happen whether specific leaders are present or not."[7] This approach is based on the premise that the events are the focus and it doesn't matter who is in charge. The events make the leader. One could reasonably conclude that leaders were made.

In conclusion, "Leadership thus implies something more than a mere supervisory responsibility or formal authority. It consists of influence that accompanies legitimacy as a supervisor. Therefore, it can be said that leadership is the incremental influence that a person has beyond his or her formal authority. Incremental influences can exist to varying degrees in every member of a work group. As a result, it is not uncommon to find situations in which a subordinate who lacks formal authority, actually possesses substantial incremental influence. We would call such an individual an informal leader."[8]

Whatever the reasoning, the leader must achieve a balance and that may require a combination of the powers defined below.

POWER

As I said in the introduction, leadership and poise are inextricably intertwined, and in the conclusion of the leadership section, leadership is situational. In order to properly assess the situation to be able to apply effective leadership, you have to know (1) the power structure you are working with, and (2) what power you "wield." To understand these conditions, some explanations of power structure and power may help.

Power Defined

There are two types of power people can have, *positional* and *personal*. Positional power, also known as "formal" power, is power that can be granted by an organization. Those powers include the power to reward or not reward people, punish people, have access to the organization's information, and grant a position of power within an organization. Personal power includes your own skills and knowledge as well as a more ethereal power: referent power.

Reward or not and punitive power can be lumped in together. Both of these powers granted by an organization to an individual are powerful, excuse the pun, motivators, especially those that are on the lower end of Maslow's pyramid. Employees at the bottom of the pyramid's primary concern are to have shelter and food. The inability to supply those bodily needs has a profound effect on your motivation. However, elements higher up in the pyramid can feel the effect, too. Safety (security of employment), the feeling of belonging to an organization, respect, self-esteem, and sense of achievement can also be affected by reward/punishment power.

The access to the organization's information or withholding of that information is another indication of where an employee is in the "pecking order." Unlimited access shows that the person can be trusted. The organization has confidence that the information will be used to forward the mission and goals and that the information is a critical part of doing business. Withholding of that information has the opposite effect and message. Granting of positional power is the ultimate formal power. We'll discuss referent power, a power **not** granted by the organization, next.

Referent power is the power one person has over others merely by being who they are. This is an oversimplification, but it is true. It is that inherent ability that some people possess that may be called "admiration," "respect," or "charisma." Whatever it is called, there are people who have or had it, and use it for good or for not so good. Adolph Hitler is one example of a person with referent power, and initially he may have had some of it. However, as time went on, fear of retribution (the ability to punish) was more likely the source of his power. John F. Kennedy, General George Patten, Martin Luther King, and others had powers more in line with the ideals of referent power. Allan Cohen and David Bradford wrote a book in 1989 called *Influence without Authority*,[9] a sentiment familiar to project managers. It a great book for project managers (and others) to help understand referent power and how a project manager can use what he or she has, which is usually not formal power. Finally, expert power is the ultimate in personal power. It is controllable because the skill sets and knowledge base can be obtained. Education, formal or informal, can increase expert power. Whether you go to school for an advanced degree, take a certification course to increase specific knowledge, or do it yourself by reading books, blogs, researching Web sites, etc., you can control your own expert power.

Power Structures

As discussed in Chapter 2, there are some organizational structures that influence power. In a functional organization, there is a definitive power (or command) structure. It is structured purposely by the organization to provide some with positional powers, and those will have the reward and punishment powers. That structure drives the behavior of those who follow such leaders. In the military, as in law enforcement, this structure is not only acceptable, but it is critical to the goals of the organization. Orders and procedures *must* be followed to protect individuals who are performing the duties and those who they are there to protect. The emphasis is on accomplishing the "mission." The manufacturing environment and certain organizations that require a high sense of safety, like the mining industry or the Alaskan crab fishing industry, need to be organized functionally. Procedures *must* be followed, a chain of command must be identified, or, as with the crab industry, there can only be one captain.

"Power tends to corrupt, and absolute power corrupts absolutely."[10] In an effort to limit the "corruption," or at least spread the power to have some checks and balances, organizations will use a matrixed structure. In a matrixed organization, power is distributed among the various functions and project teams are managed using the "softer" skills: knowledge, persuasion, communications, negotiations, and relationship building. The bad news is that there are no "formulas" or rules to guide the project manager. The good news is that this type of management style is fully controllable by the project manager. It is really up to you. It will be your efforts that make this a successful strategy. It will be up to you to acquire the skills necessary to provide the basis for this type of management in a matrixed structure. Of course, it will be necessary to access the structure. Organizations must have some elements of a functional organization like coercive and reward powers, and you need to determine how much influence you have with those powers.

This is particularly true in the healthcare industry where there can be no definitive power structure, but rather it has to have a combination of functional and matrixed organization because of the diversity of issues that healthcare professionals have to manage. For instance, in an operating theater, the surgeon is supreme. He or she has the ultimate power and the other functionaries are subservient to the surgeon. All major decisions come from the surgeon, of course with input from other "project" team members. But the final accountability lies with the surgeon. In contrast, patient evaluation is done in a more collaborative environment. Looking at a patient for potential weight loss surgery, the patient will have to undergo many evaluations by many different specialists: psychological and psychiatric, nutritional, as well as a physical evaluation, for example.[11]

There is a "buzz word" in organizational structure that has some popularity, although I'm not sure it really has merit. It is a "flat" organizational structure. The theory behind this structure is to eliminate as much of the management structure between worker bees and the top of the food chain as possible. It also provides rotational responsibilities among the workers, i.e., designated "project" or "team" leaders that periodically change. While flat organizational structures seem to be a good idea, I think they are about as effective as the "bottom-up" structure of the 1990s. In theory, in a bottom-up structure the power structure in an organization is flipped. The executives, or whatever the visionaries of the organization are called, support the workers. Decisions are driven from the bottom up. Again, while this may seem like an interesting idea, it is chaotic. Decisions need to be driven and projects need to be chosen based on the vision or mission of the organization. That mission/vision has to be defined and implemented from the top down. Input may be, and should be, accepted from the bottom up, but in order to keep the ship on an even keel, critical decisions relative to the mission/vision must be made at the visionary level and then communicated downward.

So what can limit your organizational currency or power? We've already talked about some of the limitations of the organizational structure. There are many other limits being imposed on those in the healthcare industry. The U.S. Department of Health and Human Services has instituted the Health Insurance Portability and Accountability Act (HIPAA). This Act details how the privacy of consumers' health information is protected, including who is covered by HIPAA, what information is protected, and how that protected information can be accessed and used. The Joint Commission on Accreditation of Healthcare Organizations (JCAHO) is an independent, not-for-profit organization that accredits and certifies healthcare organizations throughout the United States. By evaluating and accrediting healthcare organizations, they fulfill their mission "to continuously improve healthcare for the public ..."[12] The National Union of

Healthcare Workers (NUHC) and the Service Employees International Union (SEIU) are two of the unions that could limit your power. State and local regulations may also be power-limiting factors. As you can see, the healthcare industry certainly doesn't exist in a vacuum—just the opposite. Given the current and future scrutiny that healthcare is and will be under, the need to consider various restrictions on power will be critical to understand what you can and cannot do.

KEY REVIEW QUESTIONS

1. Discuss whether leaders have an innate quality that makes them a leader, or can anyone become a leader?
2. Name and define *formal power.*
3. Name and define *informal power.*
4. Define a "flat" organizational structure.
5. What can limit your power?

ENDNOTES

1. Raven, Bertram H., and Rubin, Jeffery Z., *Social Psychology,* John Wiley and Sons, New York, 1976, p. 37.
2. Rost, Joseph C., *Leadership for the Twenty-First Century,* Greenwood Publishing Group, Menlo Park, CA, 2000, p. 76.
3. French, J. P. R., Jr., and Raven, B., "The Bases of Social Power." In *Studies in Social Power,* Dorwin Cartwright (Ed.), University of Michigan Press, Ann Arbor, 1959, p. 475.
4. Management Study Guide, *Great Man Theory of Leadership,* http://www.managementstudyguide.com/great-man-theory.htm
5. Wrightsman, Lawrence S., *Adult Personality Development: Applications,* Sage Publications, University of Kansas, Lawrence, 1994, p. 638.
6. Adler, R. B., and Rodman, G., *Understanding Human Communications,* Holt, New York, 1991, p. 267.
7. Adair, J., *The Skills of Leadership,* Gower, Aldershot, Kant (England), 1984, p. 8.
8. Vecchio, Robert P., Hearn, Greg, and Southey, Greg, *Organisational Behavior,* Harcourt Brace, Sydney, Australia, 1996, p. 334.
9. Cohen, Allan R., and Bradford, David L., *Influence without Authority,* John Wiley and Sons, Inc., New York, 1989.
10. Acton, John Emerich Edward Dalberg (1834–1902), first Baron Acton. The historian and moralist, who was otherwise known simply as Lord Acton, expressed this opinion in a letter to Bishop Mandell Creighton in 1887.
11. *Preoperative Patient Evaluation: Lap Band and Laparoscopic Gastric Bypass,* http://www.lapsurgery.com/BARIATRIC%20SURGERY/PatientEvaluation.htm
12. The Joint Commission, http://www.jointcommission.org/AboutUs/

13

Contracting and Procurement

You may wonder, "Why in the world do I need to learn about contracting and procurement? I am not involved in contracts and I don't buy anything. After all, I am a charge nurse," or "I'm a phlebotomist," or "I'm a medical technologist." The answer is fairly simple. You may not be aware of the contracts you are involved with, but there are many. As far as procurement goes, I believe that future trends will dictate that everyone in healthcare will be "cross-functional" in their work and may be called on to manage the purchase of equipment or a renovation or one of the many projects in healthcare.

WHAT IS A CONTRACT?

There are five elements that define a contract: offer, acceptance, exchange, capacity, and legality. If any one of those elements is missing, *you do not have a contract.* The offer is simply that, an offer to do or not to do something. It may be an employment contract that spells out the terms of your employment, such as wages and benefits. It may be a confidentiality agreement that indicates what information about your job or organization you cannot share. Yes, that can be contracted also—not to do something.

The acceptance of the terms of a contract can only be done by *the offeree* or the *offeree's agent.* No one else can accept the terms of a contract. In most cases, an *agent* is someone who has the express power to act in the interests of another. To be positive of the relationship, agency should be defined by a written document, and as you have probably deduced, that is a contract. Acceptance itself, however, does not have to be written. There are plenty of enforceable oral contracts.

One of the key principles of a contract is *consideration*. Something must bind the contract, and that is consideration. It may be an exchange of goods, services, or money. It could also be a promise to do or not to do something. It doesn't really matter what the exchange is; it just has to be there to have a valid contract.

Capacity is another element of a contract. Capacity can be either "de jure" or "de facto." If the capacity is de jure, the authority to enter into a contract is granted by the organization. Sometimes it is positional. For example, a chief operating officer of a company is given contractual authority by the board of directors of a company. There may be a monetary limit on that authority. Managers in an organization are often given de jure authority to enter into smaller monetary projects, based on a formula that says that it is less expensive to allow the managers to enter into smaller contracts than to utilize more expensive organizational resources to negotiate.

A more nebulous authority is that of de facto, and organizations and individuals must be very careful of this type of authority. De facto capacity is when one organization *feels* that, because of the way an individual has purported his or her authority, either by actions or words, the individual has the authority to enter into a contract, whether or not that individual really has the authority. Of course, this can't be a frivolous decision. The affected organization must perform due diligence prior to assuming the individual's authority, but if the organization does its due diligence and truly believes that the individual has the capacity to enter into a contract, then the contract may be valid, whether or not the individual is authorized.

Finally, the contract is only valid when it is *legal*. According to Lawyers.com,[1] there are three essentials needed for a legal contract: competence, consent, and legality. A person must be of legal age and sound mind, and must agree to the terms of the contract, which implies that he or she understands the contract and its terms and cannot violate existing laws.

Note: All five elements must be present to have a legally binding contract. If you have a question about a contract or authority issue, see your organization's legal representative.

One other item that should be considered is contract clauses, which are legal additions to a contract. Some of the clauses that should be considered are as follows:

- Title/ownership change – when the organization becomes responsible for a product or service

- Specifications – the actual specifications/requirements of a product or service
- Jurisdiction – where the contract is to be enforced; perhaps some states have caps on punitive damages or more advantages to the supplier organization
- Change orders – the actual change order process is contractually defined
- Termination – the circumstances if the contract needs to be terminated
- Damages – defines both punitive and actual damages
- Dispute resolution – can be related to jurisdiction, i.e., in what venue the dispute will be resolved (the state, the court)
- Warranties
- Data rights – for instance, the owner of the source code of a software product
- Force majeure – acts of God or nature

CONTRACT TYPES

There are really only two basic types of contracts: fixed price and cost reimbursable. All other contracts are a hybrid of these two types.

Fixed Price Contracts

A fixed price contract is just that, a contract in which the price is fixed. The price is given and accepted with the understanding that it will not change throughout the contract, unless there are specific, agreed upon reasons for the change. For instance, the contract may include an escalation or reduction clause that may be invoked for reasons such as an unforeseen increase or decrease in raw material costs that can be passed on to the buyer. Fixed price contracts may also include incentives, for instance, finishing a project earlier would invoke a "bonus," or finishing a project under budget could trigger an additional payment of a percentage of the retrieved costs.

The major advantage of a fixed contract is that because the price is fixed it can be included in a budget with a high degree of certainty. A disadvantage of the fixed price is that the price given must take into consideration any anticipated increases that could occur in labor charges, raw materials, or the cost of money. The price, therefore, may be higher because of anticipated increases that are not necessarily realized.

Cost Reimbursable Contracts

The premise of a cost reimbursable contract is that all costs of the contract are collected, documented, and submitted for reimbursement. Generally, it is not enough to reimburse costs, but there has to be an add-on to the cost reimbursable contract to provide some profit. The *Government Contract Guidebook*[2] identifies cost-plus-award-fee, cost-plus-fixed-fee, and cost-plus-incentive-fee contracts. Cost-plus-award-fee contracts allow for costs to be recovered with a two-part fixed fee. The first of the award fee is a fixed amount that does not vary with performance. The second part of the award fee is provided as a motivation for increased quality, coming in under budget or ahead of schedule, or some other contract performance improvement.

A cost-plus-fixed-fee contract "provides for the reimbursement of all allowable costs expended by the contractor, as well as payment to the contractor of a fee that remains fixed regardless of the contractor's actual cost experience."[3] With a cost-plus-incentive-fee the contractor is provided with all of the allowable costs plus a profit (fee) that varies with the costs of the project. There is usually a minimum and a maximum range for that fee.

It is important for healthcare professionals to be aware of the different types of contracts available to them in order to have the information to make the right contract choice for the situation. It is situational. There is not one type of contract that will fit every need.

ORGANIZING FOR CONTRACTING

There are two elements for organizing for contracting: centralized or decentralized. Both have advantages and disadvantages.

Centralized Contracting

Most organizations are organized centrally for their contract activities. Their contracting efforts are managed by one organization. The personnel in a centralized contracting organization are highly specialized and knowledgeable in the contracting process. It may be more economical to have a centralized contracting organization, rather than utilizing more expensive project resources for the task. While the process allows for a more structured approach to contracting, the project manager does not have as easy access to the process, and therefore may not have the details needed to properly manage the deliverables. It probably means that the project manager did not have access to the upfront negotiating process, which could be detrimental to the quality, costs, and schedule of the project. By not knowing the details of the upfront planning, unrealistic commitments could be made, which is a common complaint by project managers. Further, there may be delays in approving contracts caused by a clogging of the funnel, because all project contracts flow through the central organization. The project manager may have to use manipulative strategies to get the contracts through. Centralized contracting organizations are most effective and efficient when utilized to purchase non-specialty items, particularly office supplies where they can use bulk purchasing to their advantage.

Decentralized Contracting

Decentralized contracting efforts are more expensive than utilizing centralized contracting efforts in some instances, but just don't make sense in other instances. For instance, in most cases there is a specialization or detail that needs to be considered in larger healthcare projects. The effort needs to be project specific and tailored to the project's needs. In order to properly assess the impacts on time and costs of the project, the project manager needs to actively participate in the contracting process. Later in this chapter I will discuss exactly the phase of the procurement process in which the project manager needs to be the most active. While I already said that the cost of decentralized contracting is greater than that of centralized contracting, the decentralized contracting structure is more flexible and more responsive, making it a better process for the healthcare professional project manager. The next question is, "Where in the procurement process should the project manager be involved?"

THE PROCUREMENT PROCESS

I am going to split the procurement process into three parts: pre-purchase, purchase, and post-purchase. I will share some information about all three phases, but concentrate on the pre-purchase phase, which is the phase most important to the project manager.

Pre-Purchase

The reason that this phase in the process is most important to the project manager is because this is the phase where the need is determined, the item and supplier are selected, and the contract is written. Part of the project planning process, under the direct responsibility of the project manager, is the development of the project plan. In the project plan, stakeholders, requirements (project quality or scope), budget, and schedule are determined. As defined in Chapter 3, some of the tools to properly plan a project for success are the scope statement and the work breakdown structure. To populate these tools, the project manager needs to know what is being purchased and needs to be a part of the selection process. Without that information, the project manager cannot make an accurate estimate of the time it will take to procure the item or how much the item will affect the budget. Some of the decision points that will be determined during this phase are as follows:

- Price
- Technical requirements
- Sourcing (single or multiple)
- Which suppliers meet the requirements (rank order—price, schedule, quality)
- Negotiations
- Comparable estimates

As part of NCMC's attempt to increase customer satisfaction, the board has requested that more comfortable chairs be provided for the waiting room. CEO Michelle Michaels has asked Daniel North, Director of Housekeeping, to research appropriate chairs and report back to the board in 2 weeks with some recommendations. The intent is to have the chairs included in the overall project. After about a week, Mr. North has investigated several chair manufacturers and has some alternatives. He calls Diane Westfield, Project Manager, for her input. She then constructs a simple spreadsheet with costs, quality recommendations, and availability. The spreadsheet will allow her to see how the purchase of the chairs will affect the overall project budget and how their availability will affect the project schedule. The project quality decision will be made by the board with the cost and availability recommendations by the project manager.

In this example, the need and selection of a product (the chairs) was determined by the board, and the project manager supplied her input into the vendor/supplier selection as well as the contract by providing the spreadsheet showing the effect of the product on the schedule and budget. If the chair with the most quality is the most expensive and has a lead time that will adversely affect the project's end date, then a decision will have to be made by the board to move forward. Either way, a change request (see Chapter 8) for the project will need to be filed because there will be some impact on the project.

Purchase

The second phase in the procurement process is the actual purchasing of the product or service identified in the pre-purchase phase. In this phase, the project manager may or may not be involved. In some organizations, the purchasing is done by a specialized department that only does purchasing for the organization. That department is responsible for the purchasing, the inspection of the product or qualification of the service, and the actual expenditure for the product or service. The project manager has some vested interest in this phase and should therefore monitor the process to ensure that the phase is accomplished satisfactorily. In some instances, the project manager will take the lead in this phase, especially if it is a highly specialized product or service that needs to be monitored by an expert on the project team, or if it is expensive and will have a significant impact on the project budget. *This is one area that can have a significant influence on the success of a project.*

Post-Purchase

There is some controversy over this final phase. Traditionally, the project manager would be involved with the first part of the process, ensuring that the product or service is utilized in the manner planned, but not in the second part, disposal. However, as detailed in *Green Project Management*,[4] the assertion is that project management continues or at least provides for life cycle assessment of both the product of the project and the processes involved in the project itself.

Contract Administration and Close-Out

The final aspects and responsibilities of the contracting/procurement process are administering and closing out the contract. This may or may not be the total responsibility of the project manager, depending on whether the project is organized centrally or decentrally. However, the resulting impact of these aspects will affect the project manager. If a contract is poorly administered, for example, if payments are not made on time, there may an effect on delivery or even costs as there may be a penalty. Early payment may result in a discount that could positively affect the project budget. If the contract is not closed out effectively, future negotiations with the supplier could be jeopardized. *Contracts are not written or executed in a vacuum. It is likely that the same vendor/supplier will be considered in the future. How that was treated could affect that relationship.*

KEY REVIEW QUESTIONS

1. List and explain the *five* necessary elements of a contract.
2. What are the ways an organization can *organize for contracting*? What are the advantages and disadvantages of each?
3. What are the steps in the *procurement process*?

ENDNOTES

1. http://consumer-law.lawyers.com/Contract-Basics.html?page=2, pp. 1–2.
2. Arnavas, Donald P., and Ruberry, William J., *Government Contract Guidebook*, Federal Publications, Inc., Washington, DC, 1994, pp. 4–19 to 4–21.
3. Ibid, pp. 4–21.
4. Maltzman, Richard, and Shirley, David, *Green Project Management*, CRC Press, Boca Raton, FL, 2010, pg. xxiii.

14

Negotiating and Conflict Management

Probably one of the most important project management skills is negotiation/conflict management. I lump them together because they both have basically the same roots, definition, and resolution tools and techniques. Keep that in mind as you read this chapter. Before you enter a negotiation or try to resolve a conflict, there are certain steps you should take. You should plan the session. My axiom holds: the size of the planning effort is commensurate with the size of the task. If you are negotiating resources, and those resources involve a large amount of money or a long length of time, it is best to spend a significant amount of time preparing for the negotiation. So the first thing to do in preparation for the negotiation is to plan. Planning should include answering the following questions:

- How much time will I need to devote to this effort?
- Is it a win/win situation or can I turn it into a win/win?
- What are the goals of this effort, both mine and theirs?
- What information do I have about the issue(s)?
- What information do I need?
- What are my competitive advantages?
- Do I have a strategy?
- What is my "walk-away" position?
- What are the possible outcomes?

The second activity is to do your research, particularly to know what your limits are. It could be time (for example, you need to get this negotiation complete within 30 days), or it could be money (you need to keep the budget under $100,000, for instance). Another part of this second activity is to know what is acceptable and what is non-negotiable. Is there anything that is off the table? Also, do all negotiating partners know their limits and the limits of their counterparts in being able to make the deal? Taking the time to negotiate with someone who needs to bring in a third party to make the deal can be frustrating and, in certain instances, a waste of valuable resources (time). The third thing to remember is to keep your emotional distance. We'll talk further about this point a little later in this chapter. The fourth activity is to listen more than talk. There are some tactics and techniques for listening that we will discuss later in this chapter that are also discussed in the communications chapter, Chapter 7. And finally, once again, communications are key and they must be clear and concise.

WHAT IS A NEGOTIATION?

Negotiations can be anxiety producing, emotional, and stressful, *if you don't have the tools to deal with them.* The objective of good negotiating skills is to be able to assess the situation and hold your emotions in check while getting what you need. There are two components to keep in mind when negotiating: the logical component and the emotional component.

The Logical Component

The easier of the two components, and the most understandable, is the logical component. It is your focus, your need that has to be fulfilled by the negotiations. It may be as simple as the product you need to acquire. As a good project manager you will plan for your negotiating session. Take the example of the purchase of a new automobile; you should have your requirements—type of vehicle, color, options, the dealer, and a price—in mind. *You have done your homework.* This is a common element in *all* negotiations. You are clear on those requirements and have organized your thoughts. *Make sure you have some written notes to help you remember. During the "heat" of a negotiating session, you'll want to refer to your notes.* You have set the limits: how much you can spend on the vehicle, what you are willing to negotiate on and what you will not. Safety is one of those items on which you may not want to compromise. You are prepared to keep your emotional distance, and I'll discuss this later in this chapter. You will *listen* to the other side and be clear with your desires. Clarity of communication in negotiations can set the tone.

The Emotional Component

This is the more complex and least understood, least definable component of negotiation, and it is also a major component in conflict resolution. The emotional component revolves around *feelings*. Those feelings can either help your cause or hurt your cause depending on how you, as an individual in the negotiation, respond to them. For example, how you feel about the other person or persons in the negotiation will have a major influence on how you approach the negotiating session. If you are comfortable, have a high degree of trust and respect, refrain from making unfounded assumptions, and have interests in common (other than the ones at hand) with the other party, it will be easier to keep your emotions in check. However, if you distrust the other party and feel that they are taking advantage of you, your emotions may rise to the surface, clouding your judgment. Whenever your emotions come into play, you are more likely to lose control of the situation, thereby allowing the other party to gain an advantage. The ability to "push your buttons" is a tactic or technique used to gain that advantage. You can either allow it to happen or take control of the situation by being aware of the tactics used by others. I won't recommend using any of these yourself, but just be aware of them. So what are those tactics?

- The close talker – crowding your counterpart can make him or her uncomfortable. In some instances, being uncomfortable is an emotional response to the situation and can lead to a quicker agreement in order to stop the behavior.
- The temper tantrum – when dealing with someone you perceive as being a reasonable person suddenly flies into a rage over some negotiating point. It is an effort to get you caught up in the emotion of the situation in order to appease the person throwing the tantrum. Don't get caught up in this tactic, and I do not recommend using this as a tactic either.
- The appeal to your "soft side" – uses an emotional appeal to help gain an advantage. Of course, there are legitimate soft side issues, but you should be careful not to allow those issues to help you make a bad decision.
- The deception – making you believe people are being honest and opening themselves up to you when, in fact, they are trying to manipulate you and they have no intention of showing their "real" side.
- The almost there – when you believe that the final deal is about to be realized and the other party either brings in someone totally new

to the situation or raises a totally new issue to be resolved, hoping that your resolve has been weakened and they can use it to their advantage. Another iteration of this is to bring in another person at a late stage in the game who asks for additional concessions. A lot of the time, you are battle weary, ready to settle, and may jump at the chance to close the deal, even though it costs you more.
- Finality – the deal is only good for the next 30 minutes, or you need to make the decision right now.

I will probably say this many times: *you need to set your own stage.* Whether it is a "now or never" or the "show you the money" situation, or they try to push your buttons, doing your homework ahead of time can help you set your own stage.

TYPES OF NEGOTIATIONS

There are really only two types of negotiations, a win-win or a win-lose. Successful negotiations in business are all about getting a good agreement, not whether you win or lose. You should approach all your negotiations with the attitude that it is a win-win situation; you and your counterpart are collaboratively working toward a mutually satisfying conclusion. There are several ways to approach negotiations, but only one way that keeps your integrity intact.

- **Accommodation** – You can choose to use an accommodation strategy in order to "keep the peace." However, a disadvantage to this strategy is that it is not a win-win situation for you. You will have to give up too much to accommodate. If the issue is of no importance to you or has relatively little impact on you, you may want to use an accommodating strategy.
- **Competition** – While we know that competition is sometimes good, in a negotiation it is not the best strategy. It is certainly a strategy focused on win-lose, or getting the most for you out of the negotiations no matter what the consequences. The problem with this type of negotiation is that it leads to contempt and resentment. Remember, *negotiations are not done in a vacuum.* According to Dr. Dorothy Neddermeyer, the old cliché, "What goes around, comes around," is

the American definition of karma.[1] To me, in negotiations, it means that taking a competitive strategy can haunt you in the future. People have long memories. If they feel that you treated them badly in the past, it will set an unpleasant tone for future negotiations.

- **Compromise** – While not the best strategy, because it still isn't a win-win situation, it is better than competing. By compromising, neither party will get what they want, but the strategy does indicate a cooperation or searching for a solution even though neither gets what they really want. I like this quote from Winston Churchill about compromising or, as he says, appeasing: "An appeaser is one who feeds the crocodile—hoping it will eat him last."[2] Remember, *the most important outcome of a negotiation is a good, solid agreement.* Accommodating, competing, and compromising may not be the best way to get a good agreement.
- **Collaboration** – Collaboration is by far the most productive way to approach negotiations. Collaboration is *always* win-win. By nature, collaboration is just that—an effort between two or more individuals to reach a mutually satisfying agreement. Because it is mutually satisfying it creates value for all sides of the negotiation, and thus creates a stronger agreement than most all other methods of negotiation. The agreement is strongest because of the buy-in of the parties involved. Each of the participants has been instrumental in crafting the agreement and will assume greater ownership of the solution.

NEGOTIATION STYLES

I advocate that most situations call for principled negotiations (looking for that win-win). However, in business, and the healthcare field is a business, personalities are as varied as the types of jobs there are. I'm not talking about Myers–Briggs or Jung Typology; I am talking about how personalities manifest themselves. In negotiations, for some, it is impossible to leave those manifestations out. You'll notice I shift from using the term "counterpart" to using the term "opponent," because that's what happens in a win-lose situation. When I was with Bell Laboratories, I worked with highly skilled and educated engineers. The main function of one of the groups I worked with was mathematical modeling. Thus we had several individuals with doctorate degrees in mathematics. Those individuals probably had one of the more effective win-lose negotiating tactics I've ever witnessed, that of questioning everything. They certainly did their homework when it came to researching an issue and approached all of the negotiations by asking detailed questions in order to work their opponents into a corner and then pounce. By doing that, they were able to get into the heads of their opponents and convince them that they hadn't done enough homework. By doing that they were able to manipulate the outcome to meet their own desires. The style rarely failed to yield the results those mathematicians wanted.

Another tactic they used, and that I have seen many others use also, is befriending. The tactic is to appear to befriend the opponent and gain their trust prior to making demands. Usually it involved seeking some common ground apart from the actual issues or what I call "cocktail conversation." But it was all meant to manipulate the opponent into a false sense of security in order to get a favorable agreement.

Another technique is to purposely keep quiet. It seems that people, especially Americans, do not like a cone of silence around them. In an effort to fill that void, they will have a tendency to keep talking. If you are a good listener and can control yourself by not feeling the need to talk, you have a definite advantage in negotiations. By seemingly pondering each and every word from your opponent, you encourage them to continue to talk. As they continue to talk, more and more information is revealed. There is a classic expression in negotiations: "Whoever speaks first loses." You can also stimulate some of that talking by asking questions for clarity so that your counterpart continues to simplify and simplify, usually continuing to reveal more and more information. In most cases it is much better to listen than to talk.

Again, I don't advocate using these techniques. Negotiation, like conflict management, should be conducted in an ethical and principled manner. You do, however, need to be aware of other methods that people will try to use to gain advantage.

People Who Are Different

There are some types of individuals who can influence the way that you should proceed with a negotiation. The *hostile aggressive* individual is a person who appears to be angry all the time. They can be verbally or physically threatening, or argumentative or defiant. It can be very unnerving dealing with some of these types of individuals, especially a hostile aggressive person. The best way to deal with this type of person is to stand up for yourself. Don't slouch. Make direct eye contact. Physically stand your ground and don't back down. There is a balance between assertive behavior and aggressive behavior. You certainly don't want to mimic the person's aggressive behavior. Give the aggressor time to run down. Sometimes the posturing is short-lived. Use "I" messages. For example, personalize your messages: "I am concerned with your behavior," rather than, "We are concerned with your behavior." That ubiquitous "we" tends to trivialize your message. It is always best to communicate in a direct manner. There are people who are always complaining about something. Complainers can effectively derail a negotiation or the resolution of a conflict. It is very easy to get caught up in the complaining web. Don't do it. Listen attentively to the complainer, acknowledge the person's feelings, but carry on with the facts without an apology. Try different methods of problem solving like brainstorming to get the person back involved with the issue and out of the complaining mode. As with complainers, there are people who are always negative in their thinking. The first word out of their mouth is "no" or "can't." Don't join in the negativity, and realize that you probably can't talk them out of it. Be ready to take action without them if you want to get anything done. More about communicating with different people's styles can be found in Chapter 17.

SPECIFICALLY MANAGING CONFLICT

Sooner or later everyone has to deal with conflict. It is inevitable in business. It is nothing more than a difference in opinion or views, and the conflict over them. Conflict is not inherently bad. It is part of the creative process. No two people view the world exactly the same and those differences can cause conflict. Disagreement is normal. The problem comes with the emotional baggage. Conflicts are usually personally meaningful and are disagreements over principles, ideas, or interests. The occurrence of conflict is easily detected. In personal relationships it manifests itself as sudden avoidance or rudeness toward an individual. The best way to deal with this issue is the same as dealing with all issues, and that is head on. If you believe there is a problem, there probably is. Set up a private meeting with the individual you believe is having a problem and ask whether there is a problem. If the answer is yes, then find out what it is and discuss possible solutions, win-win. If the answer is no, then it gets a little more complex. Let the individual know that you think there is a problem and explain why. Be careful not to attack, just ask for feedback. Keep an open mind and work collaboratively on a solution.

Conflicts in meetings can be very productive, if managed, or very disruptive if not managed. However, if the conflict does get out of hand, then the meeting can get out of control. As a result, all of the time spent by everyone in the meeting could be compromised. There are several approaches you can take to minimize the "damage" of an out-of-control conflict. The first thing to do is identify the area of disagreement. By doing that, you may be able to determine your best course of action.

- Defer the subject to a later meeting.
- Document the disagreement and set it aside to be dealt with at a later time.
- Ask to speak to the individual or group in disagreement after the meeting.
- See if there is anyone else in the meeting that could mediate the issue.
- Create a compromise (although compromise is not necessarily win-win).

Conflicts in the midst of a negotiation can have a devastating effect on the outcome. Both parties should be seeking a win-win, but that is not always the case. If one or both parties have a win-lose mindset, negotiations will be contentious. Someone will have the feeling that he or she is being taken advantage of, and no one wants to feel that way. As a result, there will be no collaboration; therefore, there will be no possibility to get a good agreement. The best way to deal with a conflict in a negotiation is to hold your emotions in check. It is easy to get caught up in defend-attack behavior. However, a better approach is to try to clarify the issue by asking questions, trying to understand the other party's perspective, and keeping the communication lines open.

When disagreeing, make sure that the other party knows that you value their opinion and value them as an individual. Use "I" messages. Make sure you are true to yourself and make your opinion known. Never ever shy away from a conflict. Conflicts are natural and a part of everyday life.

There are also creative ways to provide solutions to contentious issues. You can seek additional resources to divide. Even with tight budgets, particularly with a project that is being executed successfully, there may be some contingency resources available. You never know until you ask. You may also seek something different. For instance, if a subordinate is asking for a raise, as a manager, it may be an issue. If you can't get the money being asked for, perhaps you can offer a company car, new computer, or other nonspecific compensation.

You may also be able to compromise on an item that is not so important for an item that is more important. To carry on with the previous example, perhaps the subordinate needs a computer more than the company car. Additionally, you may be able to create some other alternative not proposed before, like working from home rather than a company car. The objective is to resolve conflict in an amicable way that leads to a good agreement, a happy employee, and elimination of any possible baggage for future dealings.

The skills required for successfully participating in a negotiation and resolving conflict are very similar in nature. Both skill sets require the individual to be knowledgeable of the situation and know the limits of the parties involved. It also requires keeping an emotional distance, listening carefully, and being able to communicate both questions and alternatives clearly. Following the steps outlined above can greatly increase your success in either situation.

KEY REVIEW QUESTIONS

1. Define a win-win situation and explain how it affects the strategy of your approach.
2. Define a win-lose situation and explain how it affects the strategy of your approach.
3. What is the best way to gain consensus: accommodating, competing, compromising, or collaborating? Why?
4. If you were the moderator of a meeting and a "know-it-all" was trying to hijack it, how would you handle it?

ENDNOTES

1. Neddermeyer, Dorothy M., PhD., http://ezinearticles.com/?What-Goes-Around-Comes-Around&id=180369

2. Churchill, Winston (1847–1965), British politician. This quote is said to be attributed to Churchill at the Munich Conference in 1938 where representatives from Russia, Germany, Britain, France, and Italy met to decide what action, if any, to take concerning Germany's aggression in Czechoslovakia.

Section IV

15

Program Management

A discussion about project management would not be complete without a discussion of program management. *A Guide to The Project Management Book of Knowledge* (PMBOK) defines a program as "a group of related projects managed in a coordinated way to obtain benefits and control not available from managing them individually. Programs may include elements of related work outside the scope of the discrete projects in the program. A project may or may not be part of a program, but a program will always have projects."[1] Another definition is, "A long-term undertaking which is usually made up of more than one project, sometimes used synonymously with *project*."[2] I would further define it as a philosophy and methodology for integrating a major stakeholder's application, need, or desire, rather than in terms of a task. It is a relationship to the desire, much like quality and customer satisfaction, rather than a logistical undertaking. The philosophy behind program management is to establish the relationship to stakeholder desire early in the process and provide the "golden thread" that ties all of the various deliverables together. Program management is the instrument through which that coordinated approach to their implementation is made. The major stakeholder in this instance would be the visionaries or strategic managers who are responsible for the "Five-Year Plan" or "Mission" of the organization. The program, therefore, could be the Five-Year Plan or Mission of an organization. It appears as a custom design for each implementation, but in fact, it is the manifestation of a set of guidelines established for all implementations of projects related to the program. In its simplest form, a program is the cradle-to-grave management of the Five-Year Plan or the Mission, for instance. A program could easily be a major renovation of a healthcare facility planned to occur over an extended period, or it could be a healthcare facility's Five-Year Plan to become the area's leading transplant facility. The basic concepts outlined below can be used in any program, no matter what the scope.

PROGRAM PHASES

Setting Customer Expectations

The most important phase for setting realistic expectations is the Pre-Planning Phase, which is no different from that which we discussed (as the idea phase) in Chapter 8 except it is at the program level. It is in this phase that the program is defined. This is the phase that establishes the tone and the basis for success of the implementation of the program and all associated projects. In this phase, the program definition is at a "50,000-foot" level, and it will be the stakeholder's basic program understanding. It is impossible to clearly define the stakeholder's program at this time. In some cases, the stakeholder does not have a clear direction. The stakeholder may have established a business philosophy, perhaps identified square footage requirements, which areas are targeted for renovation, or which buildings will be demolished. At this point it is up to the program manager to provide the stakeholder with a representation of the program. The Program Team, core and extended, can provide the necessary direction to the stakeholder to begin the expectation-setting process.

Core Program Team Elements

At a minimum, a *core* program management team should be established. The disciplines included are as follows: (1) program director, (2) program engineer, (3) planner/scheduler, (4) site project manager(s), and (5) program clerk. If the program is extensive enough, the team can be dedicated to one program, as in this case. Otherwise, the team may be deployed across many smaller programs.

Program Director

The program director (PD) is responsible for ensuring the flawless implementation of the stakeholder's program. Working with the core program team and the extended team, the program director works to define and implement the stakeholder's program.

Program Engineer

For lack of a better term, the program engineer (PE) is the technical expert for the program. For the construction project the PE should be experienced in healthcare construction projects, and may in fact have been a construction project manager. For the transplant program, the PE should be familiar with the qualifications of physicians who perform transplants and may lead the selection team, as well as having familiarity with the requirements for equipment, operating suites, and transportation logistics needed for transplants.

Program Planner/Scheduler

Because of the complexity of programs and the need to coordinate the different projects that compose a program, a planner/scheduler is needed. The planner/scheduler (PS) has the responsibility to establish the "cradle-to-grave" program timeline, as well as helping to identify and coordinate the processes necessary to achieve a high level of stakeholder satisfaction. For instance, if any of the processes are cumbersome and time-consuming to the stakeholder, to the point that they affect the implementation, the PS should effect changes in the process by working with a process team formed to establish uniform processes across all teams. The PS will also have the responsibility to tie the program implementation to the master program plan or vision. That connection is needed to ensure that the success metrics, schedule, quality, and finances for the program are considered, recorded, and evaluated.

Site Project Manager

The site project manager (SPM) is responsible for the day-to-day operations of the specific projects included in the program. This doesn't necessarily mean that there will be an individual project manager assigned to each project, just that a project manager will be assigned to each project. The number of projects and their complexity will determine how many project managers are required within the program. Additionally, the timing

TABLE 15.1

Core Program Team

Title	Function
Program Director	Overall responsibility for program, coordination of individual projects, and Core Program Team
Program Engineer	Technical expert for program, coordination of project engineers (Core Program Team)
Program Planner/Scheduler	Coordination of Program Schedule and its relationship to the individual project schedules (Core Program Team)
Site Project Manager	Responsibility for individual project elements and coordinating with Planner/Scheduler (Core Program Team and Project Team Leader)
Program Clerk	Clerical support functions (Core Program Team)

of the projects will influence the number of project managers. A single project manager may be able to manage sequential projects, but may be at a disadvantage when it comes to multiple parallel projects. The primary function for the construction program's project manager is to insure that the necessary equipment, personnel, and permits are available when the different construction project phases occur, and that the raw materials are properly ordered and delivered in sufficient time.

Program Clerk

The Program Management Team will be supported by the Program Clerk, who will create and maintain a log and files of official program correspondence; create and maintain a log and library of official program documents; and create, maintain, and publish program organization charts, contact information, and distribution lists. The clerk will also be responsible for distributing program correspondence and documents per distribution lists and support the PM and core team with common clerical support functions (see Table 15.1).

Program Documentation

The Integrated Plan

In order to establish realistic expectations with the stakeholder, the program team should provide an integrated plan to the key stakeholder led by the Program Director. The integrated plan includes the understanding of four critical elements: the program's statement of work (SOW), work breakdown structure (WBS), cost, and schedule. The cost and schedule should be all-inclusive of the program, as defined in the WBS. The WBS defines the scope of execution details for the program's phases: PE input, planning, organizing, and controlling (see Project Life Cycle section in Chapter 1).

Statement of Work

The SOW will define, at a high level, the work to be performed for the stakeholder. The Program Engineer (PE) will facilitate this stage in the process. The Program Director (PD) will provide a sketch of the stakeholder's program to the PE for review. The PE will request additional reviews by other functional areas, including the Site Project Manager (SPM), as necessary. The result will be a program description that is understood by the key providers of the program, including the key stakeholder. The PD should also provide the SPM with the program's description. This is critically important with multiple SPMs on a project so that each may understand what the other is doing.

The SPM will begin initial discussions with those functional areas to gain understanding of the work effort involved. With the configuration and the understanding of the work involved, the program team can start to establish the standard intervals for that work. As a result, a preliminary *integrated plan* can be provided to the PD to be shared with the key stakeholder. A certain stakeholder expectation for the work to be performed and the schedule will be established. As more details are available, the program team will continue to refine the schedule and the work definition. The next step in establishing the customer expectations is to develop a work breakdown structure.

Work Breakdown Structure

The work breakdown structure (WBS) is the defining documentation of a program. The high-level understanding of the stakeholder's request is critical at this juncture. This is the first attempt to define the *scope* of the program. It will contain "targets" for support from all of the identified functions from planning, to organizing, to controlling, to program completion. This WBS should be positioned as preliminary at the same level of detail as the preliminary scope statement (PSC). (See Chapter 3 for more information on the scope statement.) Again, the stakeholder's program is not solid at this point, and therefore it is difficult to predict the final supporting structure that will be needed. The information in this step and how it is presented to the stakeholder will help determine the next level of stakeholder expectations. Information can be presented in several ways, depending on the function to be defined. If the function lends itself to high-level description, like Program Management, then that can be included in the PSC in detail. The information provided for each function, whether menu or specific, must be *clearly* understood by the internal team, and then *clearly* specified in the detailed scope statement so that there is no misunderstanding.

An important element during this stage is the stakeholder deliverables definition. The Program Team should have some idea of any tasks that are required of the stakeholder to complete before and during the program implementation, such as funding availability.

The timeframes may not be available, although the standard interval may. While the Program Team will not manage those stakeholder deliverables, unless specifically asked to do so, the milestones will be included in the detailed schedule. The internal team and the stakeholder should be tested constantly, in order to ascertain whether the members understand and agree to the terms. *Silence should not indicate acceptance.* In some cases, silence is deliberate and can lead to serious implications during the implementation phase for the Program Team. Once an agreement is reached, understandings and conversations contrary to the words in the agreement are inconsequential. The word of agreement should be considered *law.* The effort here is to make the agreement as clear and easily understood as possible. Conflicts due to disputes over ambiguity in agreements are never easy and are often painful, win or lose. (See Chapter 11 for information on conflict resolution.) This, too, is a "living" document and details will be added as they become available. The next step in setting the customer expectations occurs after the agreement is finalized. Ideally, all the details outlined below would be defined prior to finalizing the agreement, but, in most instances, that is not the case.

Costs

There are certain major components to the cost of a program. Some, like equipment, engineering, and installation, are well known and well understood. Stakeholder expectations are set via those known costs, even though some may be discounted by negotiations. Others, like the cost of program management, may not be well known, but can be proposed as a fixed price, based on salaries and overhead. However, integration services (the integrating of the new processes, procedures, or facilities into the organization) and ongoing operations can be usage sensitive and are therefore more difficult to quantify early in the program implementation. The most effective way to set stakeholder expectations is to provide clear definitions of each service to be provided and the associated price. The stakeholder can then pick and choose the level he or she wishes or that is minimally necessary and the associated costs, thereby setting his or her own expectations.

Working the Detailed Schedule

At this point, with a high-level understanding of the stakeholder configuration, schedule, and cost as specified in the SOW and the WBS, the "preliminary" stakeholder expectations are set. The stakeholder should expect the schedule to be a "ballpark" schedule. For instance, the stakeholder may know the quarter, but not the month. Or, he or she may have targets quite different from the agreed upon dates. Either way, it is time to begin to work intervals and resource issues with the key stakeholder and others to refine the schedule and reach a win-win for the team and the key stakeholder. At this stage in the process, leadership begins to swing from the individual PD to leadership shared with the Program Team. Team composition at this point expands. It includes members across all the interfaces to assure buy-in, particularly on the schedule. A "strawman" schedule should be presented to the internal team. This is an iterative process, so the schedule will be discussed and modified until the team can agree in principle. The PD can then socialize the proposed schedule with the stakeholder. If there are any minor changes to the schedule, the PD and the key stakeholder can make the modifications. If there are serious differences, negotiations will have to take place with the key stakeholder, and additional resources may have to be provided to the program to make the schedule more aggressive.

In parallel, the detailed configuration plan will be drafted. The configuration and the schedule are "finish-to-finish" tasks (see Chapter 4 for more information on scheduling). When those two activities are finished, it is advised that an external kickoff meeting be held. During the external kickoff meeting, a detailed configuration and schedule can be discussed with the customer. Again, the PD is the lead, but the PE, PS, and SPM will be closely involved. Specifically, the SP will develop the detailed implementation schedule with input from the team, which now includes the key stakeholder's representatives. If this groundwork is set with discipline, clarity of communications, and program understanding, *the implementation is set for success.* Lack of any of these objectives could be a basis for failure. The reason that this upfront planning as a stakeholder expectation-managing tool is so critical becomes clearer as we move to the next phase.

Plan, Obtain, Execute

I will use the terms plan, obtain, and execute (PO&E) for the next phase of the program. This is applied at the individual project level. The first sub-phase of the PO&E Phase, planning, is based on the configuration established in the preceding phase. The accuracy of that configuration will determine how much churn will occur during planning. Churn is inversely related to the efficiency and the ability of the PE to quickly and accurately determine the planned requirements for individual parts needed to satisfy the needs of the program's projects.

A key issue during this phase is the understanding of the program. Because we are so used to seeing things in a parochial way, this mindset is difficult to overcome. It is not impossible, and there have been great strides made by some organizations to be able to see beyond their immediate needs. The PE is instrumental in this phase to help the individual team members understand the application and how the various elements interact with each other, external needs as well as internal needs. That understanding can eliminate, or at least reduce, the churn I mentioned earlier. Of course, changes will not be completely eliminated, but they should be reduced significantly. (See Chapter 8 for more information about change.)

The PS is also involved at this stage to coordinate the interface handoff specification and understands, from the timing perspective, what is required to execute the project. What is required includes the time needed to implement internal and external elements as well as any interconnectivity and testing required between the elements. For instance, if the project is a new electronic medical record system (EMRS), then the PS needs to account for any hardware/software or old system/new system compatibility testing.

At this phase the PS, PE, and SPM have a detailed understanding of the total program across PO&E to testing and to final turnover.

All inputs and outputs to the project have been identified, scheduled, and documented. Checklists for the handoffs across the disciplines are established (and agreed to). With accurate ordering information, established interface requirements, and final schedule approvals, ordering and execution of the projects required for the program's ultimate success become routine.

However, there always seem to be shortages, modifications due to stakeholder or internal changes, or other factors that require the full attention of the PS. But, with the detailed planning and engineering complete and accurate, the need for "firefighting" should be greatly reduced. It allows the SPM to be involved with multiple projects if required.

Integration

One of the most important functions performed by program management, as opposed to project management, is the overall integration function. Allowed to proceed on their own, projects tend to become relatively internally focused. That focus can lead to issues if the integration function is ignored. Just think about the Chunnel Project, which was actually a program. For simplicity we'll just look at one aspect and divide the program into two projects. Digging was done westerly from France (one project) and easterly from England (one project). If the projects weren't coordinated as a program with the program manager being responsible for the two projects, they would not "integrate" together and the two tunnels would not have met in the middle. The SP, PE, and SPM oversee the handoff to integration. Although there is final preparation work taking place during this phase, the transition should be smooth. A critical part of setting the expectations for this stage is the *Integration Checklist*, which is a good tool to be used by the program manager to make sure all parties are aware of the final integration. High-level stakeholder expectations have been set because of the definitions contained in the SOW. However, to execute on them, the defined customer deliverables have to be met. The deliverables can be captured in a checklist proposed by each project manager and shared with the PE. After the PE reviews the checklist, it is shared with the stakeholder for concurrence. By gaining the stakeholder's concurrence, the expectations are once again validated. Once integration is complete and the checklist is satisfied, the next handoff occurs to the individuals who have to monitor and maintain the projects and ultimately the program.

Ongoing Operations

A checklist similar to the integration checklist containing the operational requirements should be established using the above-mentioned process. Integration and the individuals responsible for operations execute on that checklist. If the program has been managed as defined in the previous steps, everything necessary for monitoring the program has been established. The projects and the program are in a steady state. The program team is in the position to establish a close-out meeting.

Close-Out

The close-out and the Stakeholder Satisfaction Survey are key elements to verifying that expectations have been met. The survey will indicate the success of the Program Implementation. It will cover the entire experience from the requirements specifications to the handoff to ongoing operations. It can be used as a program "post mortem" for the purpose of continuing improvement. The expectation is that if the methodology outline is followed, the survey results should be more than satisfactory, exceeding stakeholder expectations. The close-out process should also include the accumulation and filing of all documents and artifacts, both program and projects within the program. The artifacts should included, but not be limited to, the schedule, budget, risk logs, action item registers, and lessons learned, those issues that have been documented throughout the planning, implementation and closing-out phase of the program and associated projects. This process should also be followed for any project close-out.

SUMMARY

There are two key areas for setting stakeholder expectations: (1) the initial phase of the program and (2) the collection of functions during the ordering, implementation, and integration phases of the projects and program. Stakeholder expectations are like first impressions: no matter how hard one tries to ignore them or change them, chances are that the first impression is the lasting impression. It is very important to set the correct ones up front in customer interactions. Program Management can help establish those expectations by coordinating all the issues and forming the integrated picture of the stakeholder solution, and translating internal commitments to stakeholder expectations, specifically with a realistic schedule. To establish a realistic schedule, all project (program) participants must be part of the discussion and part of the commitment.

A valid schedule cannot be constructed without the individual contributors agreeing to the intervals. Too many times schedules are proposed to the stakeholder that meet a strategic intent, but have not been socialized with the key providers of the services. And while winning the battle, the war may be lost. A favorite expression of mine is, "With a strong wind, even turkeys can fly." While the market demand is high and competition is low, slips in schedules may be tolerated, but when competition enters the market, developing realistic expectations becomes more critical. Setting the schedule with input and buy-in from the functional areas is the key to establishing a realistic schedule and managing stakeholder expectations. Program Management is not without cost. In some cases, the core team is dedicated to a program. As with project management, it is usually an expense item. The benefits of both project management and program management are realized through the coordination efforts. Reducing redundancy because of having the "big picture" and managing all of the expectations, not just those of the key stakeholder, potentially can reduce the resources required, and thus reduce the costs and contribute to the bottom line. There is no doubt that undertaking most projects and programs is expensive. Saving costs can go a long way to justifying the reasoning behind the management.

It is the Program Team's duty to bring those savings to light to help manage the stakeholder's program expectations. By being in the process early, the Program Team can help identify all dependent tasks required to successfully deploy the program, set the stakeholder's expectations for the delivery and performance of those tasks, and then be able to successfully execute on them.

KEY REVIEW QUESTIONS

1. What is the *major* difference between *program management* and *project management*?
2. List the *five* disciplines of the core program management team.
3. What is the *primary* responsibility of the *planner/scheduler*?

4. Define the *integration checklist*?
5. What is the *key element* of the close-out phase?

ENDNOTES

1. *A Guide to the Project Management Body of Knowledge*, Project Management Institute, Standards Committee, Newtown Square, PA, 2008, p. 9.
2. Archibald, Russell D., *Managing High-Technology Programs and Projects*, 2nd edition, John Wiley & Sons, Hoboken, NJ, 1992, p. 24.

Section V

16

Project Management—Pharma and Medical Device Manufacturing

Managing projects in the pharmaceutical and medical device manufacturing industries doesn't have a direct bearing on the audience of healthcare professionals this book is intended to address. However, because of the potential interactions between those professionals and these industries, a working knowledge would be helpful. Project Management in the pharmaceutical and medical device manufacturing industries follows a more technical/formal path, especially in the design stages of the products. Of course, the "discipline" of project management, whether you are managing projects in healthcare or for a medical device manufacturer, is still a disciplined approach. There needs to be a charter, stakeholder analysis, work breakdown structure, etc. So let's look at the differences and some of the formalities of those other industries, not that their methods can't be used by the healthcare professional as defined in this book. It is just that those methods may be overkill for the healthcare professional. As you will see, there are some similarities in the processes, and some of these lessons can be applied to your projects.

PROJECT NEEDS AND INITIATION

Just like in your projects, the following needs should be considered, with some exceptions noted:

- Competitive advantage
- Fits with the overall organizational mission

- Return on investment – although not as critical in healthcare because there are some different drivers; may not need to include profit in the calculation, for example
- Time to market – more so in pharma and medical device manufacturing because of the critical need to be first to market and the additional time required for regulatory testing
- Technology – may not be as critical to healthcare because healthcare doesn't necessarily have to be on the leading edge of the competition

I am not saying that project initiation activities in the healthcare industry are not intense, but I do believe that the initiation activities for projects within pharma and medical device manufacturers is particularly extreme due to the intensity of the competition, particularly when there are billions of dollars at stake that a new drug or new device can add to an organization's bottom line. Look at Pfizer Inc., the world's largest pharmaceutical company. Its annual revenues in 2009 were $50 billion dollars,[1] up $1.7 billion from 2008. The drug Lyrica, a pain reliever, alone produced $267 million in revenue. While that is a large sum of money, you have to realize the amount of time and effort that goes into developing a new drug, and the appreciation of the project managers who have to manage those types of projects. To better appreciate what goes into the drug manufacturing process, the California Biomedical Research Association, a non-profit medical advocacy group[2] provided the following "fact sheet":

> **New Drug Development Process**
>
> At one time or another everyone has relied on prescription drugs to help treat or cure a symptom or illness. In fact, approximately 2 billion prescriptions are filled each year in the United States, but few know of the complicated and lengthy process involved in creating and providing a new medication to the public—humans and animals.
>
> *Who Is Involved in Developing New Drugs?*
>
> Many various scientists and researchers are involved in the development of a new drug. For many years, traditional organic chemists, scientists, physiologists, and statisticians have been involved in the research process. In more recent years, they have been joined by new kinds of specialists. For example, biochemists study the chemistry of life processes. Molecular biologists study the molecules that make up living matter. Toxicologists

investigate chemicals' potential for harm. Pharmacologists look at how drugs work, and computer scientists apply the power of their sophisticated machines to analyze and assess new chemicals. Each of these individuals plays a critical and necessary role in new drug development.

How Long Does the New Drug Development Process Take?

It takes an average of 12 years for a drug to travel from the research lab to the patient. In addition, only 5 in 5,000, or 10%, of the drugs that begin preclinical testing ever make it to human testing. Only one of these five is ever approved for human usage.

How Much Money Is Spent on the Development of One New Drug?

On average, it will cost a company $800[3] to develop a new drug from the research lab to the patient.

Who Regulates the New Drug Development Process?

The new drug development and approval process may be one of the most difficult processes in the world. The Food and Drug Administration (FDA) monitors and regulates the new drug development process. The FDA's role in the preclinical research stage is minimal. However, once a company finds sufficient evidence that a drug is successful in animals, human trials will begin. The FDA plays a much more crucial role during the various clinical trial phases. If the drug shows successful effects in humans and the FDA approves it to be prescribed by physicians to humans, the FDA will determine what information should be placed on the label, including directions for use, potential side effects, and other necessary warnings.

What Are the Various Types of Drugs Currently Being Developed and Tested?

At any one time, thousands of new drugs are being researched and developed to treat and cure the diseases that affect both humans and animals. New drugs for diseases such as AIDS, cancer, diabetes, arthritis, asthma, Parkinson's disease, feline leukemia, and other chronic diseases are continuously being researched and developed. That is why it is critical to support biomedical research. Continuous and ongoing research is important also to the discovery of new treatments and unexpected benefits. For example, the popular hair growth treatment Rogaine began its existence in a research lab as a potential heart medication.

What Steps Are Involved in Developing a New Drug?

There are many steps researchers take when developing a new drug, which can be divided into seven different phases.

Preclinical Research

The first place researchers start is in the lab. Preclinical research is the process where scientists and researchers determine what germs, viruses, or bacteria cause a specific disease. Once this is accomplished, researchers and scientists will work to break down the different components that make up a disease to find out what abnormal events or processes are taking place in the body.

Scientists then work to develop a drug that will treat these abnormalities by conducting experiments in test tubes where they will add various compounds to enzymes, cell cultures, or cellular substances. The goal is to determine which compound additions result in some sort of chemical effect on the disease. Whenever possible, scientists will use computer models to test different compounds; however, computers don't provide any final answers. These compounds still have to be placed into a living biological system to see if they work. Therefore, after successes in the "Benchtop" process (test tubes and cell cultures), scientists then test these compounds that have shown some desired effects in living animals. The entire process of preclinical research can take up to three and a half years. Once the process is complete, a pharmaceutical company will then file an Investigational New Drug Application (IND) with the FDA.

Investigational New Drug (IND) Application

The IND becomes effective if the FDA approves it within thirty days. At this time a pharmaceutical company can begin to test the potential new drug in humans. This process includes three phases of clinical trials.

Phase I Trials

A new drug is administered to approximately 20 to 80 healthy volunteers to study the activity and monitor potential toxicity in people. This process takes about 1 year, and if successful, will lead to phase II clinical trials.

Phase II Trials

During the phase II trials, the drug is given to 100 to 300 volunteers with the disease being studied to determine the drug's effectiveness. Proper dosages are established during this time. This process can take about 2 years to complete before moving to phase III clinical trials.

Phase III Trials

This phase involves anywhere from 1,000 to 3,000 volunteers with the specific disease who are in clinics or hospitals. Physicians will monitor these patients closely to determine the effects of the drugs and determine if any side effects are involved. This phase confirms if the drug is effective and safe and can take about 3 years.

New Drug Application (NDA)

After all three phases of clinical trials have been completed successfully, a pharmaceutical company must file a New Drug Application (NDA) with the FDA. The pharmaceutical company must be able to clearly demonstrate the effectiveness and safety of the drug and must provide all of the scientific information the pharmaceutical company has collected on the specific drug. The FDA can take up to 6 months to review the application. Oftentimes, this process takes longer than 6 months.

Approval

If the FDA approves the drug, it is then made available for physicians to prescribe to patients. The pharmaceutical company is still responsible for submitting periodic reports to the FDA regarding any unknown side effects that may occur after approval. For some medications, the FDA requires additional studies after approval. These are known as Phase IV Clinical Trials and serve to determine if there are any long-term side effects.

(Please note: Some of the above information was obtained from the FDA Special Consumer Report, The Beginnings: Laboratory and Animal Studies; Drug Safety Testing Fact Sheet; Alliance Pharmaceuticals Corporation; and the Congressional Office of Technology Assessment.)

As you can see, it is quite an extensive, time-consuming, and expensive process, thus the more formal project management required.

PROJECT DEVELOPMENT

To better familiarize you with the product development process in the medical device and pharmaceutical industries we'll look at two significantly different processes, the "waterfall" and the iterative development processes.

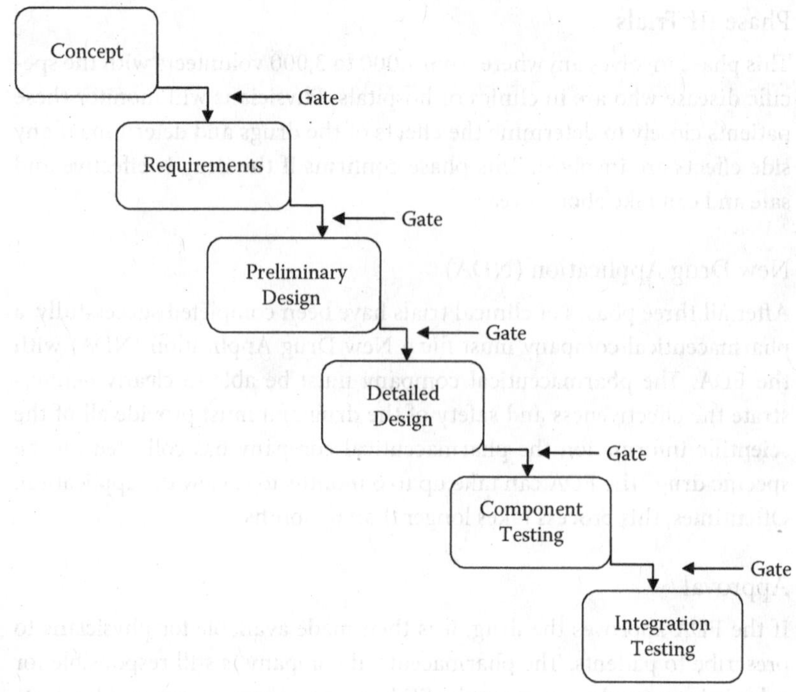

FIGURE 16.1
Example of waterfall process.

Waterfall

Just as the name implies, the waterfall process flows in a logical sequence from the familiar project phases of requirements gathering to project close-out. We've seen something similar to this in Chapter 1 in planning, organizing, and controlling a project. This process is outlined in Figure 16.1 and is more detailed and formalized. As they are completed, each task in the "clear" boxes "falls" to the next task. However, prior to the next task beginning, a gate review should take place to ensure that the requirements of the task have been met. Also, the prototype, or beta, and the final product will be checked against the customer expectations (requirements). The verification process must consider the original user requirements, again to ensure that the original requirements have been met. In today's development world, a major drawback to the waterfall process is the sequential element. One task is completed prior to another one finishing.

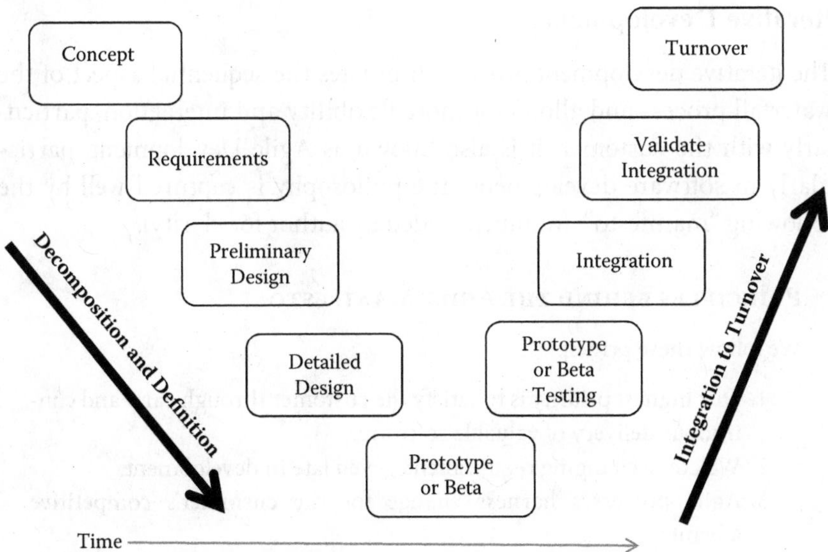

FIGURE 16.2
Example of a Vee Chart.

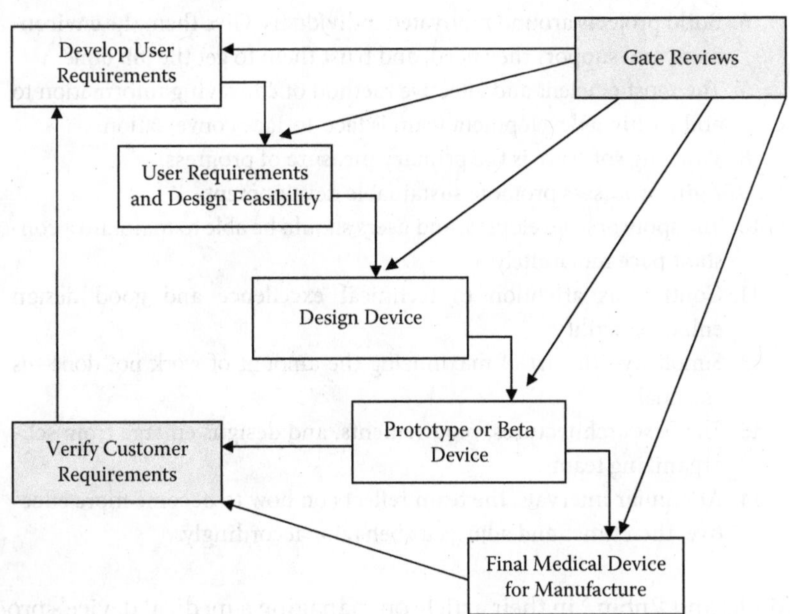

FIGURE 16.3
Example of Project Life Cycle for medical device.

Iterative Development

The iterative development process eliminates the sequential aspect of the waterfall process and allows for more flexibility and interaction, particularly with the customer. It is also known as Agile Development, particularly in software development. The philosophy is captured well by the following "manifesto"[4] (numbers added by author for clarity).

Principles behind the Agile Manifesto

We follow these principles:

1. Our highest priority is to satisfy the customer through early and continuous delivery of valuable software.
2. Welcome changing requirements, even late in development.
3. Agile processes harness change for the customer's competitive advantage.
4. Deliver working software frequently, from a couple of weeks to a couple of months, with a preference to the shorter timescale.
5. Business people and developers must work together daily throughout the project.
6. Build projects around motivated individuals. Give them the environment and support they need, and trust them to get the job done.
7. The most efficient and effective method of conveying information to and within a development team is face-to-face conversation.
8. Working software is the primary measure of progress.
9. Agile processes promote sustainable development.
10. The sponsors, developers, and users should be able to maintain a constant pace indefinitely.
11. Continuous attention to technical excellence and good design enhances agility.
12. Simplicity—the art of maximizing the amount of work not done—is essential.
13. The best architectures, requirements, and designs emerge from self-organizing teams.
14. At regular intervals, the team reflects on how to become more effective, then tunes and adjusts its behavior accordingly.

Matlis and Rubin,[5] in their article on managing a medical device's product life cycle, list the functional obstacles encountered by what they consider a "reactive" and undesirable approach:

- Requirements Management

- Software Source Control Management
- Mechanical Computer Aided Design Data Management
- Electrical Computer Aided Design Data Management
- Portfolio Management
- Laboratory Information Management
- Document Management System
- Clinical Data Management System
- Submission Management and Publishing
- Quality Management System
- Inquiries and Adverse Event Reporting
- Learning Management System

These obstacles do not allow the more interactive approach needed to increase the speed to market of medical device products.

A much more flexible product development environment embraced by Matlis and Rubin is the Total Product Life Cycle (TPLC) approach developed by the U.S. Food and Drug Administration's Center for Devices and Radiological Health (CDRH).[6] CDRH states the following:

> In keeping with our mission, the Center for Devices and Radiological Health (CDRH) is responsible for protecting and promoting the public health by assuring the safety, effectiveness, and quality of medical devices, assuring the safety of radiation-emitting products, fostering innovation, and providing the public with accurate, science-based information about the products we oversee, throughout the total product life cycle. We seek to continually improve our effectiveness in fulfilling our mission by planning strategically and regularly monitoring our progress.[7]

Part of "fostering innovation" is encouraging medical device manufacturers to streamline their approach to product development. It requires the manufacturers to work more closely with stakeholders. In order to do that, the development processes have to be more open to the stakeholders. It is a give-and-take situation where the developer will be developing and testing the product in real time with the stakeholders. All bugs and errors will be visible. However, the agreement must be that there will be bugs and errors visible, and stakeholders have to realize that. Along with customers as stakeholders, the regulatory agencies are also stakeholders and have to have the same flexibility in order to make this process work.

In 1991 there was an unprecedented case of stakeholders and a drug manufacturer signing a cooperative research and development agreement. The subject of the agreement was for the development of the cancer drug Taxol®. The agreement was between the National Cancer Institute and Bristol-Myers Squibb, and was reviewed by the Food and Drug Administration. Taxol® is an anticancer agent that showed great promise. The primary reason behind the agreement and the review was to "fast track" the development of Taxol®. To quicken drug development, several important factors have to be present. "A significant factor in the ability to get a rapid review of the Taxol® dossier by the FDA was the fact that regulatory affairs personnel established a good rapport with agency personnel through regular communication throughout development of Taxol®. This communication not only included BMS personnel, but also those from NCI."[8] In addition, it didn't hurt that the drug was in such high demand, which points to another factor that probably has to be present: *urgency*. There is significant risk in fast tracking any project, as discussed in Chapter 4. In order to fast track a drug, there may be some compromise in the clinical trials, shortening them if necessary. Long-term effects of the drug may not be well understood. Another factor to consider is that in order to fast track, additional resources need to be added to the project. Those resources may have to be diverted from other, not as critical, projects.

Managing projects such as the development of medical devices or new drugs, whether traditional or "proactive," has its own set of issues and procedures. While the discipline of project management used by healthcare professionals and medical device or drug manufacturers will have some of the same elements, the abbreviated cycles will probably not be used by the healthcare professionals for whom this book is intended.

ENDNOTES

1. *Pfizer Inc. 2009 Financial Report*, http://media.pfizer.com/files/annualreport/2009/financial/financial2009.pdf, p. 4.
2. California Biomedical Research Association, a non-profit medical advocacy group, *Fact Sheet: New Drug Development Process*, http://www.ca-biomed.org/pdf/media-kit/fact-sheets/CBRADrugDevelop.pdf, used with permission.
3. Updated August 2010 to reflect latest costs—Amanda Carson Banks, PhD, CRA President/CEO, California Biomedical Research Association/California Society for Biomedical Research.
4. *Twelve Principles of Agile Software*, http://agilemanifesto.org/

5. Matlis, Daniel R., and Rubin, David, *Managing the Total Product Life Cycle: The Changing Face of Medical Device Product Development Medical Products Outsourcing*, July 1, 2009, http://www.mpo-mag.com/articles/2009/07/managing-the-total-product-life-cycle.
6. FDA, *Total Product Life Cycle (TPLC)*, http://www.fda.gov/AboutFDA/CentersOffices/CDRH/CDRHTransparency/ucm199906.htm
7. FDA, *CDRH Strategic Planning*, http://www.fda.gov/AboutFDA/CentersOffices/CDRH/CDRHVisionandMission/default.htm
8. Crabtree, Gerald W., *PMI Seminar/Symposium Proceedings*, Project Management Institute, Newtown Square, PA, 1993, pp. 616–622.

Section VI

17

Sustainability and Green Efforts in Healthcare

Sustainability and green efforts are two concepts that are gaining in both popularity and substance. Certainly not new concepts, serious sustainability and green efforts began in 1970 with the creation of the National Environmental Policy Act. It "established as a national goal the creation and maintenance of conditions under which humans and nature can exist in productive harmony, and fulfill the social, economic and other requirements of *present and future generations of Americans*."[1] Also, in 1970, the Clean Air Act was enacted, followed by the Clean Water Act in 1972. There have been many updates to those acts since. The impetus to be sustainable and green became regulatory driven, to some extent. In the eight years or so I have been teaching in the healthcare environment, I have seen marked improvement in the efforts of healthcare facilities and healthcare professionals to strive for a more sustainable and green environment. I believe that by nature, healthcare organizations and professionals strive for sustainability, that of prolonging and preserving an individual's quality of life. But recently, sustainability efforts aimed at facilities, processes, and procedures are being instituted in greater numbers.

There are some solid reasons for healthcare organizations to consider their "green" or sustainability efforts. According to an article by Brett Willis,[2] there are six economic benefits gained by "going green":

1. Direct cost savings – saving energy, for example
2. Increased customer loyalty and attraction
3. Increased employee attraction and retention
4. Ability to grow – saving resources and gaining efficiencies

5. Innovation and development of new technologies
6. Increased profit and shareholder value – not for profits still need to make money

When you think about the business you are in, these benefits can easily apply.

SUSTAINABILITY

Sustainability is about the long-term view. It is about working in the present, and doing what we can to not sacrifice the future by our efforts. The first question you should ask is, *do we have an environmental policy?* If the answer is, "I don't know," then the next step is to find out. If the answer is, "No," then the next step is to work to institute one. This can be one of the more important contributions that a project manager can make.

Here are some basic questions to ask yourself about whether or not your facility is acting with sustainability in mind:

- When doing new construction or renovations are we using
  - The most energy efficient design?
  - The most energy efficient materials?
- Are we considering the greenality[3] of our vendors/suppliers?
- Have we read and considered the Natural Step Framework and the Four System Conditions?[4]
- Are we doing everything we can to redesign our process and procedures to make them more sustainable?
- Are we reusing what we can, realizing that there are things that just cannot be reused safely?
- Are we reducing what we are using and recycling what we cannot reuse?

More and more project stakeholders are making sustainability and green efforts priorities in their decision-making process. Indices have been developed to help consumers decide whether or not an organization is being responsible when it comes to sustainability. The Roberts Environmental Center at Claremont McKenna College in Claremont, California, publishes the Pacific Sustainability Index. The index scores

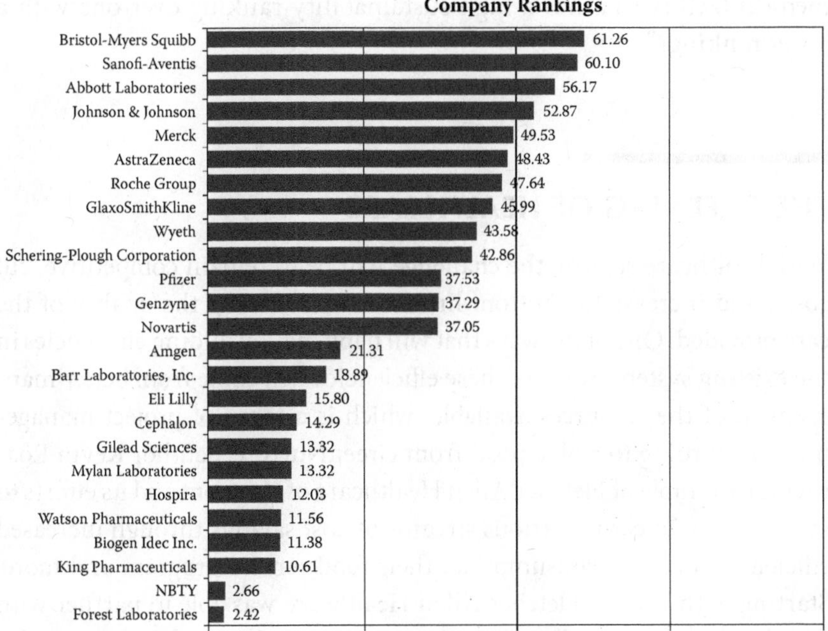

FIGURE 17.1
Overall large pharma rankings (analysis 8/11/2008–4/14/2009). (Source: Pacific Sustainability Index Scores, http://www.roberts.cmc.edu/PSI/PDF/Pharmaceuticals 2009.pdf)

are reported by industry. While they have yet to include healthcare providers, I am sure they are on their radar. There is a score for the pharmaceutical industry and medical device manufacturers (see Figure 17.1). According to the index, Bristol-Myers Squibb (U.S.) to Merck (U.S.) are in the "A+ to A−" range, and the others scored lower, digressing to Forest Laboratories with an "F" rating. For the full report details, go to http://www.roberts.cmc.edu/PSI/PDF/Pharmaceuticals2009.pdf. Dow Jones also has a sustainability index (http://www.sustainability-index.com/). Reporting since 1999, the index allows investors to evaluate companies on the basis of their sustainability. The Global 100 List (http://www.global100.org/annual-reviews/2010-global-100-list.html?sort=company) is another index that presently includes big pharma and medical device manufacturers. Of course, there are many more indices out there, and it won't be long before there are indices or lists for sustainability on the order of *U.S. News and World Report* list of the "best hospitals."[5] The question then becomes, "As a stakeholder and being more and more concerned about sustainability and the environment, would I choose a medical facility that has a high sustainability ranking over one with a lower ranking?"

THE GREENING OF HEALTHCARE

With healthcare reform, the challenge will be to remain competitive, cut costs, and increase the bottom line without reducing the quality of the care provided. One of the ways that will happen is by finding efficiencies in the existing system. Some of these efficiencies will come from better management of the resources available, which is a focus of project management. According to a blog post[6] from GreenNurture™, author Kevin Rose uses the example of Fletcher Allen Healthcare of Vermont and its efforts to save costs by "creating various streams of cost savings through increased efficiency in energy consumption, their food service program and more. Starting with energy, Fletcher Allen Healthcare was able to partner with their local utility provider while investing $2.2 million in facility upgrades to lighting and HVAC systems. By reducing electricity consumption by 350,000 kilowatt-hours and natural gas usage by 4,000 kilowatt-hours annually, the $2.2 million invested was paid back in energy savings in just 3 years. Most importantly the energy reductions have been a source of added available capital for the hospital ever since. In addition, the organization has put forth quite a bit of effort in increasing the efficiency of their food service program. The facility now features a roof garden, growing its own fruits and vegetables to serve for consumption by both staff and patients. Various natural herbs are also being grown for medicinal purposes in the garden, as well as their first honey harvest produced in 2009. Fletcher Allen has also been specific in where the remainder of their food provided comes from. By sourcing all food locally from a variety of growers and ranchers, they have been able to see even further cost savings from their food service program."

Mandy Weist, a floor nurse with NCMC, has noticed that whenever she goes into the nurses' lounge the lights are on, even during days when there is plenty of ambient light shining through the windows. She proposes the idea to Dr. Chimers, the Medical Director, that if a motion sensing, photoelectric switch was installed in the lounge, it would save a sufficient amount of energy to cover the cost of the switch in a very short time, therefore saving energy costs in the long run. In addition to that, she proposes that energy efficient light bulbs (CFLs) be installed. Dr. Chimers likes the ideas and asks Mandy to investigate the cost savings. (Mandy has just become an accidental project manager.)

Upon further investigation, Mandy discovers that the cost savings of those two simple fixes will pay for the installation of the switch and the bulbs within 2 months. Dr. Chimers asks that Daniel North, Director of Housekeeping and Facilities, institute the changes as soon as practical and asks Mandy to monitor the cost savings for six months.

There are many ways healthcare project managers can green up their facility, organization, processes and procedures, and themselves. It is certainly on everyone's mind these days because not only can it save precious resources (dollars, for instance), but it is also the right thing to do. You might ask yourself, "I'm only one person, what can I do?" All it takes is one person to start a snowball down a hill before it becomes an avalanche.

The Organization

How do we use paper? Remember, it is redesign, reduce, reuse, and recycle, in that order. Can we redesign our communication processes to use less paper? Perhaps we can use more electronic media, like iPads or Kindles™. If we must use paper, is there a way to use both sides of the paper? Is there a way we can reuse some of the paper? Once we have finished using the paper do we recycle it? If it is sensitive material, we can shred it before recycling it? Yes, that will use more electrical energy, which is a consideration.

What about our IT Department? Does our computing facility have a large physical footprint? If it does, can we reduce the footprint? There are many options available to reduce a computing footprint. Using virtual servers or shared hosting is one way. While I realize that there is sensitive data that needs to be protected, there are other methods of protecting data other than behind your own firewall. Electronic medical records (EMRs) are the wave of the future. Not only will they be necessary for instantaneous record retrieval, there has to be a way to access those records remotely. If I were injured in California and in an emergency room and unconscious, I would like to have a way for the emergency room doctor to know if I have any conditions that will affect my treatment.

Another advantage of moving data servers out of your facility is the decreased need for administrative personnel to manage the data center. Scarce resources (money) can be reallocated to patient care.

If the facility has its own data center, the following questions can be asked:

- Is there a survey of power use?
- Are we taking advantage of external air for heating and cooling?
- Can we recycle some of the heat produced by the servers?
- When upgrades are considered, is potential growth taken into account?
- Is power management software installed on the servers?

The following questions can be asked about the computing environment:

- Is there power management software installed on all computers?
- When we upgrade can we purchase laptops rather than desktops, because laptops require less power?
- Do we run our laptops on battery as much as possible to both reduce power grid consumption and to extend battery life?
- What kinds of ink are we using: natural inks or toxic inks?
- Do we recycle our ink cartridges? If we do, how are we getting compensated for that?

How does the organization do business? Do personnel attend a lot of conferences? If your organization does do a lot of traveling, perhaps virtual meetings (at least some) are the answer. With increased bandwidth and reliability, webinars and other Web-based meeting protocols are almost as good as being there and reduce the carbon footprint as well as giving back all that travel time. Additionally, some of the social media tools mentioned in Chapter 7, as well as wikis and intranet documents, can also save time and money. Caution, however, should be exercised when using these tools. They take the "personal" out of personal communications. Time must be set aside for the occasional face-to-face or video teleconferences, and interactions like "ice breakers" can help team members get to know each other, even in a virtual environment. If you have to fly to a meeting or conference, take direct flights. While it may cost a little more, direct flights use less fuel. Takeoffs particularly are fuel intensive.

The Facility

Saving energy costs seems to be the number one topic on people's minds these days. Some of the things that you may want to consider are as follows:

- Is the lighting in areas that are not used 24/7 on motion sensors?
- Are computers and other equipment, as appropriate, turned off when not in use? Are they unplugged to save "phantom power" when appropriate?
- Are we using natural light when possible?
- Are we using energy efficient lighting?
- Are we using low-flow bathroom fixtures?
- Are the appliances used ENERGY STAR® rated?
- Are we using as much locally produced food supplies as possible? (Twofold advantage: saves transportation [energy] costs and adds to local economy.)

While I believe that there are many ways to save energy, I also believe in being reasonable. Some facilities are older and cannot be compliant with the latest energy saving technologies until the facility is upgraded, and that is expensive.

If the campus is large, as with some major hospital complexes, or spread out over several city blocks, are there ways to get around the facility without driving? For instance, some organizations, like Google, provide shared bicycles to get from building to building. Other ways I can think of are electric golf carts, solar-powered vehicles, and scheduled bio-fuel shuttles, based on organizational needs.

Other questions to ask and consider in the facility are as follows:

- Are we using water coolers and encouraging reusable water bottles when practical and safe?
- Are we using environmentally friendly packaging? Are our vendors using the same?

Deidre Imus, wife of radio personality Don Imus, has been interested in greening hospital environments for the main reason that it is healthier for the patients. Her Web site, http://www.dienviro.com/, has a number of tips, tools, and techniques to use to green a hospital's environment. She founded the Environmental Center for Pediatric Oncology® at the

Hackensack University Medical Center in New Jersey. The mission is "to identify, control and ultimately prevent exposures to environmental factors that may cause adult, and especially pediatric cancer, as well as other health problems with our children."[7] In addition, there is a myriad of information relative to the "Greening the Cleaning Program and Products,"[8] a program designed to remove caustic and toxic cleaning products from the hospital environment.

Another effort that is occurring in healthcare facilities is recycling. The following questions can be asked about recycling efforts:

- Do we have one?
- What are we recycling?
- What are we not recycling that we could be (eyeglasses, cell phones, waiting room magazines)?
- Is the recycling effort we have "easy to use," convenient?
- We have sensitive data that needs to be shredded. Is that shredded material being recycled? Do we use it as packing material when we send samples out to labs?

Your Team

While many of the facility questions can be asked of your team, some additional questions to consider in the team environment to minimize environmental impact are as follows:

- Are they turning off their computers when they leave work?
- Are they turning off equipment and lighting when not needed?
- Did I consider people's schedule when I put my team together to minimize overtime or have people come in when they aren't scheduled to save energy and resources?
- Do we have some small incentives available to reward green efforts?
- Do I provide suggested Web sites, books, or articles to help my team members understand and appreciate green efforts?

Your Project

Projects can be a great source for mining green efforts. Suggestions include the following:

- Just-in-time equipment and supplies to save inventory resources. Of course, critical items must be stocked.
- Look to books like *Green Project Management*[9] for information, tools, tips, and techniques for managing projects.
- When deciding on projects or how to pursue a project, consider the environmental impact.
- Work toward instituting green thinking in brainstorming sessions, project suggestions, and all project communications.

Yourself

There are many things that you can do for your own green efforts, some of which I am sure you already do.

- Bring your lunch in reusable containers.
- Use old printouts as notepaper. Run it through a paper cutter for convenience.
- Use reusable mugs for coffee and take them with you to your favorite store or café and have them filled rather than using single-use items.
- Encourage children to take part in green efforts. The Web site www.greenallowance.org offers a unique way to involve children in the effort.

There are a variety of things that you can do for your organization, facility, team, and yourself to participate in and encourage green efforts. It is not only good for the bottom line, but it is good for the environment, and as stated in the assertions at www.earthpm.com, "A project run with green intent is the right thing to do, but it also helps the project team do the right thing."[10]

ENDNOTES

1. U.S. Environmental Protection Agency, *Sustainability: Basic Information*, http://www.epa.gov/sustainability/basicinfo.htm
2. Willis, Brett, *The Business Case for Environmental Sustainability*, Rev A02 Jan-05-09, http://www.leanandgreensummit.com/LGBC.pdf, pp. 1–5.

3. Greenality is defined as the "the degree to which an organization has considered environmental (green) factors that affect its projects during the entire project life cycle and beyond," Maltzman, Richard, and Shirley, David, *Green Project Management*, CRC Press, New York, 2010, p. xxiii.
4. The Natural Step, *The Four System Conditions*, http://www.naturalstep.org/the-system-conditions
5. U.S. News and World Report, *U.S. News Best Hospitals 2010–11*, http://health.usnews.com/best-hospitals/rankings
6. Rose, Kevin, *Lean Healthcare Can Mean Green Healthcare*, GreenNurtureBlog, http://blog.greennurture.com/2010/08/lean-healthcare-can-mean-green-healthcare/
7. The Dierdre Imus Environmental Center, *The Dierdre Imus Environmental Health Center*, http://www.dienviro.com/
8. The Dierdre Imus Environmental Center, *Greening the Cleaning Program and Products*, http://www.dienviro.com/index.aspx?lobid=958
9. Maltzman, Richard, and Shirley, David, *Green Project Management*, CRC Press, New York, 2010.
10. *EarthPM's™ 5 Assertions of Green Project Management*, http://www.earthpm.com/mission/

Appendix A

A NEW WAY TO THINK ABOUT PLANNING—SET THE STAGE

Planning is one of the most important processes that a project manager can undertake. It sets the stage for everything that comes next. In Chapter 1 we discussed the project life cycle: planning, organizing, and controlling a project. The change in thinking about planning centers on a shift in the traditional method of planning. By nature, project managers are "control freaks." That is not a slam, but rather a statement of fact. The job of the project manager is to have control of the entire life cycle of the project. Many times the project manager isn't in the project loop until the project becomes reality, thus the discussion of the "accidental project manager" in the Introduction to this book. Whether you are brought in from the beginning or inherited the project, you will still have some planning to do. Because of that opportunity, you can provide some guidance. As Sir Francis Bacon said, "He that will not apply new remedies must expect new evils; for time is the greatest innovator."[1]

We've all been there. The typical planning session can be unfocused, devoid of leadership, and sometimes just a waste of time. Nothing seems to get done until individuals take on the effort. But there is a way to "lead" the session, and that requires getting away from "groupthink," a term coined by social psychologist Irving Janis (1972), which occurs when a group makes faulty decisions because group pressures lead to a deterioration of "mental efficiency, reality testing, and moral judgment" (p. 9). "Groups affected by groupthink ignore alternatives and tend to take irrational actions that dehumanize other groups. A group is especially vulnerable to groupthink when its members have similar backgrounds, when the group is insulated from outside opinions, and when there are no clear rules for decision making."[2] Janis also defined eight symptoms of groupthink that are detrimental to good planning.

1. Illusion of invulnerability – Creates excessive optimism that encourages taking extreme risks.
2. Collective rationalization – Members discount warnings and do not reconsider their assumptions.
3. Belief in inherent morality – Members believe in the rightness of their cause and therefore ignore the ethical or moral consequences of their decisions.
4. Stereotyped views of out-groups – Negative views of "enemy" make effective responses to conflict seem unnecessary.
5. Direct pressure on dissenters – Members are under pressure not to express arguments against any of the group's views.
6. Self-censorship – Doubts and deviations from the perceived group consensus are not expressed.
7. Illusion of unanimity – The majority view and judgments are assumed to be unanimous.
8. Self-appointed "mindguards" – Members protect the group and the leader from information that is problematic or contradictory to the group's cohesiveness, view, and/or decisions.[3]

While the new method removes groupthink from the process because of the above stated reasons, it doesn't remove team from the equation. Rather, it increases team power while reducing individual power. It moves the project manager from *authoritarian to cofacilitator*, sharing the duties with an individual focused primarily on reducing risks (as outlined in Chapter 9).

Prerequisites and Assumptions

- Team members need a thorough understanding of the project's goal and objectives. (See Chapter 3 for more information on goals and objectives.)
- Team members become stakeholders.
- It is a team-focused environment (see Chapter 11).
- The project manager, while being the team leader, needs to listen more than direct.
- Focus more on the work breakdown structure and all of the tasks to complete the project.
- Team dynamics will play an important part in the success of this environment (see Chapter 11).

The Planning Session

The planning session now includes two leaders: the project manager and an individual who focuses on the sole purpose of meeting the goal and objectives of the project, while the project manager concentrates on the global view of the project and the team dynamics. That second individual may be someone who is not associated with the project, but rather is an objective outsider.

The second key to a successful planning environment is to have all of the key players available as the planning team. Those key players' functions are directly associated with the project. One thing to remember, however, is that the more key players there are, and the more diversity there is within the team, the greater the chance that more focus on team dynamics will be needed. Additionally, with an increase in outsiders, like customers and suppliers, again, more focus on team dynamics will be needed. I have found that the more homogeneous the group is, the less focus on team dynamics is needed, and vice versa. Clearly defined roles for those individuals from more diverse backgrounds may help (see Chapter 7, Planning for the Team).

Advantages of Co-facilitation Environment

- Coaching/mentoring – The ability of the project management to focus on the team dynamics allows them to more easily identify those individuals who may need coaching or mentoring. Everyone can use some coaching and mentoring from time to time; this allows the project manager more freedom to work with individuals.
- Because the key stakeholders are available to the team, there is a better chance that the work breakdown structure (WBS) will be more accurate. Also the two views by the co-facilitators, the global and the focused, will help ensure that each task is as complete as possible.
- Because so much of the project's success is based on the WBS (see Chapter 3 for information on the WBS), the above focus and effort will allow a more accurate time as well as budget estimate.

Role of Co-facilitators

- Focusing on the specifics, the global view, and the ability to mentor and coach will allow for more informed and therefore better decision making.

- Providing the team with better information about decision-making processes (see Chapter 2).
- Clarifying expectations.
- Conflict management during idea generation.
- Team building.
- Enthusiasm, especially during idea generation.
- Feedback providers.

Advantages to the Project

- More focused approach, leading to a project plan in less time.
- Varied points of view for better decisions, risk identification, and problem resolution.
- More commitment from stakeholders by being part of the process.
- By having the people who actually do the work help define the project, the resulting WBS will be more accurate and even may reduce budgets and time because of any duplication of effort uncovered by the stakeholder review and input.
- With direct involvement, issues will be quickly captured, action plans accepted, and lessons learned easier to document.
- Other resources (capital purchases, for example) can be quickly verified by having the team members available, perhaps, again, saving project resources.
- Once jointly defined and agreed to by the team, the scope of the project will be more accurate because of the diverse and timely team inputs, and it will be more easily executable because of the inherent buy-in by the members.
- Part of the process will be agreement on change control, escalation, and jeopardy (see Chapter 8).

Disadvantages of Co-facilitation Environment

- There are two schools of thought: project management is a portable discipline. Once learned it can be transferred to any industry as long as the project manager learns the technology. The second philosophy is that you must learn the technology first, and then become a project manager. I'm not going to get into the debate, but the common thread in each philosophy is learning the technology. When a project manager does not understand the technology involved with the project, the team can get discouraged. The co-facilitator is outside of the project and therefore is no help here.

- Along with the philosophies of technology is the issue of organizational culture. If the project manager does not understand the organization's culture, team members can become easily frustrated. The real disadvantage could come in the improper handling of conflict resolution and the way team members may anticipate resolution methods. Even though the co-facilitator is outside the project, the project manager must ensure that the co-facilitator understands the organizational culture to be as sensitive as possible.
- Without the proper skills of conflict management, leading, motivation, team building, and communication, the project manager and the co-facilitator will be at a disadvantage (see Chapters 7 and 10). It is not necessary to be an expert in all of these skills, but a level of proficiency is needed.
- In order to be truly effective, the planning process as described is accomplished in a relatively short time frame. Team members and co-facilitators therefore have to dedicate time to the effort. It cannot be "whenever I get a chance." While it is being co-facilitated, the effort still involves people, and because of the compressed timeframe, miscommunications could cause people to divide jobs and rush to get them done. Additionally, errors in judgment in both time estimation and cost estimation can occur in the rush to get the job done.
- Related to the previous item is the fact that in most cases, the team is not "hand selected" but rather inherited. In this case there will be different levels of expertise to properly estimate time and costs.
- If some of the steps required of the co-facilitators and the process, specifically the goal and objectives, are not well defined, issues can arise, tasks can be missed, and therefore the WBS will not be accurate.

Planning for Planning

To get the benefit of the advantages and minimize the impact of the disadvantages, careful planning of your session is required. The more effort invested in the upfront planning, the greater the likelihood of a successful session and the greater chance for project success. After all, there is no guarantee of project success; we can only do what we can to give it the best chance to succeed.

Step 1

- Focus on identifying all of the key stakeholders (resources) required and desired. This may result in two completely different lists, depending on the number of resources available to you.
- Identify a contingency plan in case required resources in the previous item are not available.
- Identify session goal and objectives.
- Prepare a session agenda.
- Include a clear purpose for the planning session: what is being requested to be accomplished?
- Identify topics.
- Identify the order of importance for discussion.
- Allow time for conflict management and discussion.
- Identify the co-facilitator.
- Prepare a letter of commitment and obtain signatures for team members.
- Understand the technology.*
- Understand the project management discipline.*
- Review skill sets required to properly facilitate the session.*
- Clearly identify the roles of the co-facilitators.
- Prepare an "ice breaker" for the purpose of introducing each other.

*If any of these are in doubt, the session and the project will be in serious jeopardy.

Step 2

- Identify the dates of the session with sufficient notice for all involved.
- Determine the location of the session. Sometimes when very intense planning needs to occur, it is better to move the meeting to an off-site location that is easier to control. Participants will not as easily be able to return to their desks during downtime; therefore, they may be more available.
- Ensure that the session has all the necessary tools: paper, pens, Post-It notes, and string for "cards-on-the-wall" exercises (see Chapter 3).
- Ensure that there are snacks and meals available. If these are provided, there is a chance that the participants will have a "working lunch or dinner," thereby devoting more time to the task at hand.

- Prepare and send notices to participants.

Step 4

- Ensure that there are snacks and meals available. If these are provided, there is a chance that the participants will have a "working lunch or dinner," thereby devoting more time to the task at hand.
- Prepare and send notices to participants.

Step 5

- Ensure that there are snacks and meals available. If these are provided, there is a chance that the participants will have a "working lunch or dinner," thereby devoting more time to the task at hand.
- Prepare and send notices to participants.

Implementing the Planning

What Needs to Be Available?

- Agenda – formulated in the previous stage (see Figure A.1)
- WBS
- Project Organizational Structure – to determine what communications and resource request channels are available (see Chapter 2)
- List of all team members, contact information, and their functions
- The Project Charter (see Chapter 3)
- Project Goals and Objectives (see Chapter 3)
- Signed Commitment from team members
- Preliminary Budget (may be identified in Project Charter)

- Introduction of participants and ice breaker exercise
- Discussion of the session goals and objectives
- Explanation of roles and responsibilities
- Discussion of how the planning sessions will work
- Group work if appropriate
- Return to full group if group work
- Questions, issues, and action register discussion

FIGURE A.1
Sample agenda for planning session.

- Draft or "first pass" requirements including contractual obligations, if any
- Other draft documents that may be available (i.e., design)
- Other information that may be available (i.e., prototypes or mock-ups)

How Do I Capture the Information Once the Planning Session Starts?

- Identify scribe for tasks like:
    - Cards-on-the-wall transfer to a spreadsheet or project management tool (i.e., Microsoft Project).
    - Action Item List – for items that cannot be resolved in session. Includes issue, who is charged with resolution, and timeframe for resolution.
    - Meeting minutes.
    - Video/audio equipment for recording sessions.

SUMMARY

It is critical to the planning process that you set your own stage. Whether you utilize the model proposed in this appendix or have one of your own, a planning process will greatly enhance the possibility of a successful project. It ensures that key areas of the process are included: clear objectives, explicit roles and responsibilities, and necessary project artifacts, for example. As I said before, nothing guarantees project success. We can only do everything possible to aid in that endeavor.

ENDNOTES

1. Bacon, Sir Francis (1561–1626), English philosopher.
2. Janis, Irving L., *Groupthink: Psychological Studies of Policy Decisions and Fiascoes*, 2nd edition, Houghton Mifflin, New York, 1982.
3. Janis, I. L., and Mann, L., *Decision Making: A Psychological Analysis of Conflict, Choice, and Commitment*, Free Press, New York, 1977.

Appendix B

REPORTS REPORT

This is the title of a memorandum I issued in 2000 when I thought that my boss at the time had me writing more reports than I wanted to write. I thought a lot of them were frivolous and unnecessary. I was right; there were many redundant reports that wasted my time and the time of people who had written them. There is, however, a minimum set of reports that project managers should embrace to provide a record, keeping stakeholders informed of project progress. Stakeholders have differing needs and therefore differing requirements for communications. It can be just as detrimental to project success to not inform the right stakeholder with required information as it is to miss a major milestone. (See Chapter 11 for more information on project reporting.)

Informational Reports

The Project Report

This is a report that contains information about the project's scope and objectives, as well as costs and time targets. It is written in a more conversational style and is less detailed than either the Project Charter or the Scope Statement. The purpose of this report is have a high-level summary of the project available to those stakeholders who may want to know about the project, but who may not need the detail of other reports. Additionally, once the Project Report is built, it can be customized for particular stakeholders' needs. Suzanne Robinson[1] points out that there are many stakeholders who are not "producers," or who "decide the details of precisely what the product will be and then work together to build it so it satisfies the requirements." Those producers need a different level of reporting. The Project Report should also include a summary of significant milestones and their scheduled completion dates.

There will also be information on the project financials separated into year-to-date, estimate to completion (see Chapter 5), expected revenues versus expenses, and contingency allowances (see Chapter 5), if any. The business goals will also be included in this report as a baseline to compare whether or not the business objectives are being met during a gate process (see Chapter 12), for instance.

Executive Summary

An important consideration in the Project Report is the executive summary. The intended audience is obvious, although executive can be defined loosely, from your immediate supervisor to the CEO. It should also be in narrative form. It describes the overall status of the project and provides the summary of any issues that have occurred. It should highlight schedule, escalation, jeopardy, missed milestones, any upscope,[2] financial issues, customer relations issues, personnel issues, technical issues, engineering status, construction status, and installation status, if those processes are part of your project. Also consider any other area of concern. Remember, projects should be run in an open-communication environment. This report is intended to be a true picture of the project, good or bad.

Supplemental Reports

There are some reports that you should consider as very important, not just nice to have. They include the following:

- High-Level Schedule Summary – a graphical (Gantt) representation of project activities. As the project progresses, the actual versus planned can be compared.
- Detailed Schedule – again, a graphical report, but with the day-to-day schedule management in mind. This is the "working" schedule from which you will be managing the project. It will contain percent complete and actual versus planned, so that a quick glance of the report will reveal if there is a potential problem in the schedule. For large projects with thousands of tasks, a scheduler should be assigned to manage the schedule.
- Jeopardy Report – In Chapter 12 we talked about the jeopardy process. This is a living document that will be updated as jeopardies are added or cleared.
- Escalation Report – Again, in Chapter 12 we talked about the escalation process. As with the Jeopardy Report, this is a living document.

- Earned Value Report – In Chapter 13 we detailed earned value management. This is a report that summarizes a snapshot in time of earned value. You may want to have specific times to do this, either a timeframe, weekly, monthly, or triggered by an event, like a major milestone. The importance of this report is that it is a view of the present status of tasks: the work expected compared against the expected time and expected costs of those tasks. More importantly, it allows you to calculate the cost performance index and the schedule performance index from the information. That information is then presented in the Earned Value Report.
- Business Case Report – A living document that monitors the status of the business case. Granted, there are many reasons for projects to be undertaken other than financial gain, but the Business Case Report will at least capture the effort against the plan. It is necessary for the gate process anyway.
- Risk Report – Another one of those living documents that will be updated continually throughout the project. Risks captured early in the project become resolved, and new risks occur. Some of these risks include risks to quality, safety, schedule, costs, and configuration, among others. It keeps significant risks visible to the team, as well as any actions affecting the project that are being taken and any resolution. (See Chapter 13 for more information about risk.)
- Contract Report – If the project involves a contract, then this report would track the project deliverables against the contract deliverables to insure compliance with the contract. It would also consider any contract issue escalations or jeopardies and monitor compliance not just to the body of the contract, but also to any contract clauses attached. It is better to have an ongoing report than to have any surprises at close-out. (See Chapter 9 for more information about contracts.)
- Change Control Report – Whether there is a change control committee, as is sometimes the case in large projects, or a committee of one, the project manager, with smaller projects, a summary of the changes to the project is necessary. These changes can include scope changes, including upscope, schedule change, cost change, or quality change. Scope changes can also include project configuration changes. For instance, if a project encounters an obstacle that it cannot overcome, like obsolescence, the project may need to change

direction, be reconfigured, or even be abandoned. (See Chapter 12 for more information on change control.)

- Products or Services Status Report – In some instances, your project may include externally provided products or services. A good way to monitor those items required for your project is to have this type of status report available. At a glance it can give you the status of delivery or production of those products and services. While most of the larger items required for a project are visible to the project team, some of the smaller items may not be. This report will keep all of the products and services required visible. Information in the report should include what the deliverable is, the party responsible for delivery, the team member(s) responsible for accepting delivery, when the delivery is planned, the actual view of the delivery date, the actual delivery when made, and the effect on the project if delivery is not made, i.e., impact of shortages.

Other reports that you may want to consider are as follows:

- Project Personnel Reports – show how effectively you are using project and extended team resources, both administrative and technical resources
- Inventory, Accounting Reports – If you are responsible for accounts receivable or payables or inventory

These reports may look overwhelming enough for you to write a memo about "reports report," but a structured approach to your report making can make your project management more effective. Everyone is overly busy. It has become standard operating procedure to "do more with less." If these reports are visible to you, you don't have to worry about missing something in this busy world. There are plenty of project management tools to help, from a simple spreadsheet to sophisticated project management software. There are a variety of Web sites that supply free templates to help the report process. All you have to do is search the Web for them. Once you decide on the best templates and they are populated, for consistency, they can be reused for every project. The advantage of standardizing your reports is that whoever needs to see them begins to become familiar with the reports and knows exactly where to look for information, saving you countless calls and e-mails.

Project managers are required to access and report on the progress of their projects. Projects need to be managed. Reports are more than just reporting out to the stakeholders; they are effective tools to help manage projects. The easier we can make them to use and read, the better for effectively managing our projects.

ENDNOTES

1. Robinson, Suzanne, *Project Sociology: Identifying and Involving the Stakeholders*, The Atlantic Systems Guild Ltd., 2000, p. 2. www.systemsguild.com
2. Upscope—anything identified by the project team that could positively affect the customer deliverable, but also needs to go through the change control process because it can adversely affect the schedule, quality, or costs.

Appendix C

THE IMPORTANCE OF COMMUNICATION AND RISK MANAGEMENT

One of the keys to a successful project is being able to engage anyone and everyone who is impacted by your project as early in the process as practical. Be a sponge. Take input from wherever you can get it, again, as early in the process as possible. One of the key areas of engagement is during decision making. As Will Rogers once said, "Even if you are on the right track, you will get run over if you just sit there." Be proactive in seeking input, especially in the pre-planning stage of a project. The more information you can gather about a project, the better your decision making will be.

Keeping your stakeholders informed as to the progress (or lack of it) is, from a credibility standpoint, crucial. It has to be timely, too. One of the worst situations you can have is to sit on negative project information. Because when it comes out, the first question that will be asked is, "How long have you known about the situation?" I like to say, if you feel you've communicated enough, communicate more! You know as well as I do that once is not enough. Information needs to be repeated to fully understand a situation. The more critical the issue, the more it needs to be understood, the more it needs to be communicated, and perhaps, the wider the distribution. Deciding the frequency of communicating using the various methods of communication is difficult, and the core team may have some ideas.

Methods of Communicating

The three representational systems we talked about in Chapter 11 are visual, kinesthetic, and auditory. Your communications need to take into consideration that we all are not in the same representational system when it comes to communicating. Some people, the visuals, do better with written communications, including e-mail, while others, the auditory, need the story to be told to them. Web-hosted conference calls, phone, and in-person are the best ways to connect with people in that representational system. The kinesthetic people respond to movement and color. So adding color to your written communications and perhaps a visual element, like video conferencing, to your Web-hosted conferences can help ensure that the message is getting across. Here are some specific ideas to help with your message for those in the different representational systems.

Visuals

- Newsletters
- Executive summaries
- Road shows
- Web site posting
- Video teleconferencing
- Person-to-person

Auditory

- Phone calls
- Person-to-person
- Teleconferencing
- Webinars

Kinesthetic

- Person-to-person (you must move about)
- Video teleconferencing (you must move about)
- Road shows
- Color brochures
- Web sites with motion

Successfully implementing an effective communications plan greatly reduces risk on projects. Risk mitigation is probably the number one reason for developing an effective communications plan. The reason behind this statement is that projects are all about change. By human nature, change is unpopular.

Selling a Change and Reducing Project Risk

Projects fail because people don't want to change. It is the job of communications to convince stakeholders that they want to change and that change is good. Remember, the change could be a change in the way projects are planned, organized, and controlled. The stakeholders in this case could be the project team. Although a "directive" from the top is "nice to have," it is not very motivating for stakeholders. It may, in fact, be a demotivator, increasing the risk of project failure. A better way to communicate is to provide information that changes the mindset from being unwilling to change to desiring to change.

- Why the change is important to you.
- Why the change is important to the organization.

The communications must be convincing so that the stakeholders believe the change's importance to themselves and to the organization. Even though I said that the top-down directive approach to change may be demotivating, top-down support of change is a must that has to be communicated.

Targeted communications are the most effective form of communications to reduce project risk. They accomplish two things: (1) focusing on the issues of select stakeholders, and (2) making those select stakeholders feel that they are getting special treatment.

Some of the concerns that have to be addressed to specific stakeholders using targeted communications are as follows:

- What is my job situation if this change occurs? (employees)
- How does this change affect the organization's future? (employees, stockholders)
- How will this change affect the way I use the product/process/procedure? (employees, end users [patients, community])
- What kind of transition support will I have? (employees, end users [patients, community])

Another way to reduce risk by communicating change is to use focus groups and sub-teams involving targeted stakeholders. With groups in place, the project manager can design communications with the information relevant to those groups and deliver targeted information to the targeted groups. A major advantage of this strategy is that there is also targeted feedback that will be very helpful to the project team going forward.

SUMMARY

Project managers tend to err on the technical side of things. We focus on conveying technical information about how we are meeting requirements and specifications. That mitigates one risk, but sometimes we forget about the human side of communications. There are stakeholders who are more concerned with the personal issues of change: "How will this affect me?" In order to use, we need to focus on select groups of stakeholders, satisfy their needs, and consider the human side and the different representational systems they manifest.

Index

D

H

I

J

N

S

U

V

W